Life and how to live it

Volume Two:
Near Wild Heaven

by:
Chaz Holesworth

ISBN: 979-8-9942411-0-3

Prologue

Welcome to volume two of Life and How to Live It. The beginning of the crazy, whacky Chaz years. A mesh of Forrest Gump, Jack Kerouac, and whatever it takes to survive. The story picks up after my first emotional breakdown at the end of volume one, after getting kicked out of the born-again Christian schools that ruined me.

I was thrown into the big, bad secular world to fend for myself. Numb, uneducated, and believing the world and God were out to get me made navigating life difficult. The only thing I had was my love of music, friends I held close to my heart, love from girls, and that steady, optimistic hope that drove me even when it didn't make sense.

I needed these things to counter the negative thoughts and people that crossed my path and tried to make me feel worse. Those out for themselves who attacked anyone alive or looking for more. Betrayals, blackmail, and manipulation had to be countered with my love of everything beautiful and the positive souls I was fortunate to have in my life. All the ugliness I saw from the worst people was balanced with the beautiful ones I met and will always hold dear to my heart. They are the real heroes of this book.

It was hard to write about this period. The first part was gumdrops and rainbows compared to the aftermath of my breakdown. It is filled with insane, irrational thoughts and embarrassing points of weakness. The tribulations and darkest moments lingered for years. Somehow, I got through it. But I took the long way to adulthood. At least I have some crazy stories to tell. And away we go . . .

Chapter 1:
Locked Out, Numb,
Not up to Speed

I lay on the uncomfortable couch full of bed sheets and wrong-sized pillows in my parents' apartment, trying to get a grip on my feelings and thoughts. It was the first time I wasn't in a born-again Christian school. I got tossed into the cruel world to make it on my own. What was a fellow to do?

I left my parents' apartment emotionally hungover. I went to Ray's for the rest of the afternoon until I could return to my grandma's and eventually my fast-food shit job. That first day of feeling numb and shell-shocked didn't concern me yet. I thought I would wake up the next day feeling like myself. But that didn't happen. I still felt like a truck ran over my feelings. I felt like I wasn't experiencing life at all. I had some feelings, but not nearly as strong as before, and I lost my confidence and the belief that things would work out. I was in total survival and defensive mode.

The emotions I had after that day in March were dragged through another loop when Laura called me two days later, breaking the news, I had expected for weeks. I decided not to tell her about getting kicked out of CIBA, so she wouldn't have to lie or keep it from her parents. I intended to regroup and get my head straight, then form a plan and tell Laura about it. It didn't matter. Her parents said we couldn't see or talk to each other anymore.

They found tapes I made for her containing "ungodly" music and anti-Christianity poems. They said I was too much of a bad influence. I thought, "Of course, this is happening." Maybe this was goodbye forever.

Boom. Another blow to my psyche. I didn't give up on her, though. I figured she couldn't talk to me freely with her parents around. I hoped she would sneak a call to me over the weekend. She did not. So, I took matters into my hands and took three buses to her school to meet her when she finished class. It was a lot easier to just walk into a school in 1995, so I waited for her at her locker.

After her last class, she walked up to me and wouldn't even make eye contact. She was cold and short. She said she had to go and couldn't see me anymore (though I saw some love in her eyes). Then she turned and walked away, leaving me standing alone like a fool. I fell to my knees and cursed God, feeling more alone and lost.

Everything I built over the last six months was taken away. It was the only time I was happy and thought I could live a meaningful life. The only time I let myself think past the rut of being a poor Kenzo. The only time I led myself away from the safety net of mediocrity and thought I could avoid my fate of being another bum from the neighborhood.

If my school and church weren't so strict and run by lunatics, I would have graduated from school, gone to college, dated Laura, and sung and written away my sorrows. I would have grown up and dealt with my demons healthily and creatively. Instead, I was thrown into the world at age 17, confused without an education, without my love, and without feelings.

Chapter 2:
Uncomfortably Numb

Once I started to see I wasn't myself and couldn't sleep off this muck or numbness, I was terrified that it was my fault. I wasn't happy or sad. I was depressed and overwhelmed with doubts that plagued me before my fall. Without my feelings turned up high to keep them at bay, I jumped to every conclusion that entered my brain.

My lack of confidence and intuition got replaced by feelings of being a nobody. I felt like a clueless little boy who couldn't take the heat. I thought I would be stuck this way forever, and I deserved it for not dealing with the situation and letting it overcome me. I felt like I was in an emotional coma, my thoughts hindered and fuzzy. I knew what I loved and wanted, but it was a continuous struggle to feel worthy of these things. I constantly tried to keep my hopes up from these dreaded thoughts that haunted me with doubts.

If I knew then what I know now, I would have told myself to see a shrink and get drunk to relax. But I had no idea how to see a shrink since I didn't have health insurance. I also didn't know how to explain what was going on with me, whether it was just temporary, or one day I would wake and be in tune with myself and my feelings again.

I also thought a shrink would only give me meds to make me fake happy. I didn't want that. I wanted to feel better on my own, and I knew this was not a chemical imbalance in my brain. I was a kid with normal thoughts and feelings reacting to horrible situations. I knew pills wouldn't help me. Maybe therapy would help since my mental problems were caused by trauma, but I didn't have anywhere to go for it. I also didn't trust anyone with my thoughts and mental issues.

Over the next few months, I talked to anyone I trusted who would listen. Most people gave me the same answer: feelings change when you grow up. But I knew that was bullshit. Granted, it was mainly teenagers with zero knowledge of the human condition and teenage trauma. However, friends and peers are the ones who really guide some in such circumstances.

This wasn't a normal growing-up thing for me. I had a breakdown and was stuck in my head, fighting off compulsive thoughts that popped up every waking hour. They were thoughts and feelings I collected over the years from those who made me feel small and foolish, including my sister and dad. I thought I did what all the other born-againers did when they left the church to be worldly, and now I must return like them and be another "Yes" man for Jesus.

I thought I was being punished by fate or God for having too much fun with my friends and being the center of attention while my life was in ruins, and I didn't deal with it. This thought made me become a hermit. I decided I didn't want to be the center of attention, pretending I was happy in front of big groups at the mall. I started to think this was why I was so numb and unconfident.

I was smart enough to know this wasn't a good thing. I could easily fall into a rut at this place, surrounded by kids who liked me and gave me the attention I always craved. I decided to stop going to the mall and cut off anyone I met there or spent time with. This separation included Eddie and Johnny H., which I regret more than anything I did then. I didn't know what was wrong with me, and I had a pressing feeling that if I didn't fix it soon, I wouldn't be able to.

It was hard and borderline insane to cut off my best friend. But I was desperate and paranoid, and Eddie reminded me of what I thought was my downfall. I was mad at myself for having fun with people my age and thought I was neglecting my lot in life. I had intense regret and remorse. I had to run away from anyone involved in my mistakes. Eddie would call me to see if I wanted to hang out, and I pretended I was busy. I thought I was cheating on my feelings, or I wasn't strong enough to have the balance of being a party animal and a poet, so I had to cut one persona out of my life. I chose to put the party animal to rest for a bit.

I was starting to jump to outrageous conclusions and paranoia. I thought I was wasting too much energy entertaining people, causing me to feel numb and out of touch. I believed I had to focus on my problems to get back to myself and my dreams. I thought I was losing myself and the strength I gained from enduring pain and suffering by being a clown in front of strangers. I thought I was going to lose everything I loved, or the feelings of love, because of my weakness.

I thought there was a pattern or structure of negative and positive energy at play, and I was neglecting the negative things for the easier positives that lacked the stamina compared to the negatives that always surfaced. Meanwhile, I was ignoring Laura (and the hand dealt to me) for a bunch of cheap thrills I got from being a ball of energy for a bunch of kids I barely knew that didn't know the real me. The real me was the poet/thinker who wanted to know the ins and outs of the universe, and if this god character was based on Moses' father or just a lack of imagination. These thoughts were ridiculous, especially for a kid, but this was the true me. So, I cut ties with every one of them and focused on the ones who were not a part of that short-lived moment for me, mainly Uriah and Ray.

Chapter 3:
What They Did to Me

Irelived that day in March a zillion times. I wonder what I could have done differently, why it happened that way, and if it was predetermined or just bound to happen. When I finally broke down, I thought God was fucking with me by placing my dad, a guy I loved and hated simultaneously, into a scene he was clueless about.

My first (juvenile) thought was that this was the last straw or the icing on the cake from this vengeful god for doubting him. He set this course of events to kick the shit out of me emotionally. It seemed so well orchestrated, like everyone played their part in the play of my fall.

I had the gall to start thinking for myself and the crazy notion that I was like those people I was meeting outside of the church, who could say what they wanted and listen to music they liked without repercussions. I was a fragile 17-year-old kid who was raised in a cult that made me think the creator of everything was out to get me if I thought about a girl sexually or romantically, or thought beyond the boundaries set by this mystical white guy in the sky who chose them to be the end-all of the life experience in a limitless universe. Like it's all only for one race of apes, on one planet, in one galaxy that has existed for a blink of an eye compared to the infinite capacity of everything!

Not only was I trying my darndest to figure out what the fuck was going on with me internally, but I was also back to harming myself. I went back to cutting myself, attempting to feel something other than a lack of confidence. I thought it would wake up my feelings and make me feel alive again. And since Laura was out of the picture, there was no reason not to hurt myself. This, of course, didn't fix me either.

I was better when I was around people or distracted. But I was still stuck in my head, going through a series of panic-stricken thoughts that would make me jump to conclusions during a conversation or put me on the verge of another breakdown. It's what I feared the most, whatever diluted feelings I had left.

I had feelings that got muffled by powerful doubts that I self-consciously used to hurt myself every waking hour. I would combat these racing thoughts and doubts the only way I knew. I would chant or think of things that I considered good or beautiful. I relied on my upbringing of prayer without religion or saying prayers to any dogmatic figure. It was the old way of thinking that I got myself out of before the breakdown, where I would have to constantly cleanse my "soul" before praying to God.

Back then, I needed to be pure before I had a conversation with god or else he wouldn't hear me. I did my best to push away thoughts of sinning, then I prayed. If sinful thoughts entered my brain during the prayer, I would have to start all over until I got through the prayer with a pure mind. Maybe God would hear me and save me from my hell of a life. This is what they taught me in those schools.

It became a game I played with myself. I wasn't satisfied with my prayers and asking God for help unless I earned the prayer by fighting off negative thoughts. It was a race or competition to get through a prayer before sinful thoughts rushed into my head. When I tried to prevent these thoughts from coming in, they became harder to ignore, like saying to yourself not to think of something, and all you can do is think about it. I know, it sounds fucking loony to me too. I was younger and believed God was listening, and that prayers meant something to him. I always ended my purified prayers with, "In the name of Jesus Christ, I plead the blood, amen." It comforted me from the eternal judgment of God for a few moments until I felt guilty or thought it was time to do it again. I wasn't that bad at overdoing it since my anxiety level wasn't as high as it was after March 2nd, 1995.

On my own emotionally, I was back to the same routines and rituals. I tried to drive away bad thoughts (the doubts and crushing force of others' opinions) by chanting the things I loved, in place of God or Jesus' blood, since I didn't believe in them. It was more about thinking and feeling the words rather than chanting them. I usually only did that when I was having trouble concentrating on the exact order and feelings of love for the things. I had to think so I could feel secure. I was stuck in a state of confusion and went back to a defense mechanism. I thought about people I loved. I needed to push away the doubts and those that had been ugly to me. I didn't want to be like them. I said things in my mind like, "Tori Amos, R.E.M., Uriah, Laura, Sue," felt the love and strength from them, and ended the insane ritual with the word "Forever."

I didn't realize it, but it was the same feeling of absolution I got when I prayed to God and pleaded for the blood of Jesus to protect me from bad things. I was throwing what I loved in the God category, and the devil's slot got filled by those who caused me pain. Saying "forever" was my way to curb my anxious thoughts about external forces (God) trying to get me. It calmed my racing mind until something made me feel bad or worried again.

My anxiety would be in the form of an interaction with someone, a song, a memory, or a thought that cut me down to size again. I had thoughts that I believed were mainly external that would rush into my head. I couldn't control them. These negative thoughts tormented me throughout my day. Sleep was the only time I felt relief. The anxiety I felt from this trauma became enhanced by my consistent reminder of how I was on a time limit in life.

I knew that the way I was wasn't normal. I hoped daily I would wake up and be my old self again. But the fact that I was so obsessed with that made it impossible to heal right or to move on to a clear thought pattern that would let me be less anxious. I had a million thoughts and conclusions about what was happening to me, and I didn't know which was right, so I tried to work it all out on my own. If I didn't do something to change this, it would become my routine way of life. I didn't know if this was another hurdle I would conquer and get back on track. Part of me was tired of living and wanted nothing to do with pain or feelings that led to more pain. I was terrified of the next blow or bad thing God or life would hand me, so my rituals from my childhood mixed with the things I loved helped coast the storm in my head.

I wish I could tell myself this obviously stemmed from my hellish childhood and those who influenced me. I had two completely opposite parents who implanted their ways of dealing with life in me. I had an ultra-sensitive mother who believed in a faith that commanded one to turn off the logical parts of the brain to believe it. And I had a logical, realistic father who was barely there. The only emotions he showed were usually anger or belittlement. I attempted to be my own person (even if it was a Michael Stipe wannabe), but it was a lot harder than before, breaking down and losing the confidence and knowledge that I knew I was right over these things.

Chapter 4:
We Walk

I didn't tell my grandma I got kicked out of CIBA or what was happening in my head. Mainly because I didn't know what to do next. I was a bit of a coward who couldn't face reality. I figured I was bound to come back and have my wits about me any day. Until then, I went day by day, waiting for something to change in me.

I had to pretend I was still in school. I woke every day at 7 am and got ready like I was still going to CIBA. I would have to find something to do from 8 am until my grandparents went to their night jobs around 3 pm. Then I went to my job at fast-food hell around 5 pm.

I had to kill some hours and didn't have many options. My job didn't have any morning shifts for me, and I didn't think I could get another job since I could barely do the shit job I already had. Some days I hung out in a coffee shop or at Ray's house. For the most part, I just walked places. I would get up at 7 am and start walking in any given direction until I couldn't walk anymore or it was time to go to work.

One day, I walked north along Frankford Avenue (in the Mayfair neighborhood), which turned into Rt. 13. It took me to various small towns in the Bucks County suburbs. I walked for miles and miles. I would listen to music on my Walkman and think about everything. Sometimes I walked down to South Street, many miles from Mayfair.

I walked to Laura's school once, hoping to catch her to see if she still had feelings for me. But I got to the school too late, and she was gone (or her friend, Layla, said that to get rid of me).

All this walking happened from March to May and didn't do much for my mental health. I was alone for the most part and overthought every situation. I would replay the morning of March 2nd repeatedly, trying to make sense of it and see where I went wrong, so I could perhaps fix it. I would replay everything that happened to me over the past few months and try to figure out what I could have done better and what it meant for my path of discovery.

I pondered my dreams, thinking my chance to be with the girl I thought was my soulmate was jeopardized due to my lack of feelings. I was too weak to deal with my shit. These thoughts came rushing in and delivered a sharp pain to my stomach. I was scared that bringing them into existence was enough to make them real, and this might be my fate now, like God was reading my thoughts. This is what they did to me.

I overcompensated for these fears by being overly positive that Laura and I were meant to be. I just needed to be true to her and what I wanted. It was all struggles that I must go through to be happy. I must go through hell to get to heaven. I based my life on this for way too long. It was meant to be; I only had to want it hard enough.

At the same time, I was coming up with theories that would consume me, like I can't be positive or think good things will happen to me, or the opposite would happen. If I thought the most negative outcome, it would keep that thing from happening.

I tried to keep myself from being too positive about a situation. If I got excited, I would quickly try to find something negative about it. All to stop me from getting hurt by getting my hopes up and thinking God would make whatever I wanted not happen, since it made me happy. I would then think of the most pessimistic outcomes or scenarios to cover my bases and feel safe that bad things wouldn't happen from God or life. This is what they did to me.

It was a vicious cycle. I get now that this was all me, and it was nothing external. I get it was me either defending myself or torturing myself as a sacrifice so that God would leave me alone or help me. I was utterly alone and confused as to what to do.

I went through this every day, countless times, and only had limited moments to myself to think clearly and be productive or do things I enjoyed that were anxiety and stress-free. These thoughts and compulsions wasted so much of my time over too many years. I got used to them. They became second nature while having negative thoughts. I didn't notice it most of the time.

Before this time, I had some grasp of reality. My tight grip on my feelings kept me sane. Now I needed to feel absolution again (feelings they made me addicted to). The Christians said that nothing was as fulfilling as Jesus, and you will try, but not even love can do what Jesus can do for you. I was panicking that everything I loved wasn't good enough. I had to make sure I loved things almost every waking moment, or I wouldn't deserve them or would give it all up, taking in the absolution of Jesus and his love. This, my friends, is what they did to me.

One theory I came up with during my long walks around Bucks County was that these crushing doubts that were torturing me all the time were implanted by the Xians to get me to come back. I thought that was how they hooked you for life. I couldn't have that, so I did more of my rituals to push those thoughts away.

I realize now that I was in a state of traumatic shock, and these thoughts came from my anxieties and feelings of despair. But, in 1995, I thought it was up to me to battle these demons with rituals, listening to music, and writing poems.

Despite my disbelief in the Christian God, I still believed in a higher power and thought there was a destiny for me. I wanted to be important and matter to people like me. I aimed to help others see past their roadblocks and make the world better.

These dreams (or delusions of grandeur) were a double-edged sword. They gave me hope and made me feel that all the terribleness that happened to me would have a purpose, and I would make everything good for myself. I just wanted something of merit to come out of all this suffering. I was letting my mind drift toward a bigger scope where things happened to me for a reason.

I was trying to calm myself down and not give up on my dreams. Walking alone wasn't the best for my mental health, but it seemed my only choice. At least I burned a lot of calories.

Chapter 5:
I Am Tired of Second-Guessing

Irrational thoughts aside, I had some sensible ideas about what happened to me on March 2nd. I thought about what could have happened differently. If Holden waited ten minutes or so to tell me I was out of the school for good, or if he waited until the next day, or if I chose to take one more day off from school, would my dad be at that exact time and space to push me over the edge?

I went even further back. In 1994, when I ran away from home, my sister left shortly after. Then my grandma put the house we lived in up for sale. My parents had to find a cheap place to move to, and the only one they found on such short notice was on Paul Street, spitting distance from CIBA. My actions in leaving home led to my dad being within walking distance of my mom and me standing outside after Holden threw me out.

I concluded that every action has a reaction. In one way, this was partly my fault for my actions the year prior. If I hadn't hit my boiling point and left home, I wouldn't have been placed in this exact moment, and my dad wouldn't have been there. I placed my dad at that exact moment since it was I who forced them to move to Paul Street.

I based everything on this belief. I pushed family and friends away, along with school and social causes, thinking, "Once I am me again, I will make it all better." I was functioning like my hair was on fire 24/7, waiting and trying everything I could to get back to myself. I was too obsessed with it.

The truth was, I was just a kid. I was jumping to conclusions that I would be numb forever and have to give up what I loved because it's what happens when you get older. This wasn't true. This was just one of many unfounded negative thoughts. I automatically would think of myself as an idiot kid who didn't know shit, and everyone was smarter and more powerful than me. I was still a kid who hadn't developed his inner strength and was easy to push around, even by those who weren't around me.

Part of me wanted to stay down and not feel or live. That part wanted these thoughts to consume me so I would stop hurting. I was more afraid of future hurtful situations. Every time something painful happens, I revisit the day I snapped. A feeling of "not again" rushes over me. It was a constant balancing act. I went from trying to focus on my worries, panicking, pushing the thoughts away with overly positive reassurance, then getting scared that would lead to negative reactions from fate or God. It was as exhausting as it sounds and wasn't great for the old healing process.

Chapter 6:
Time and Time Again

The one thing that helped me was the constant of my entire life: music. Walking for hours, I spent most of the time listening (and absorbing) my favorite songs. I could only listen to music that didn't conjure too many memories of my fall, which I thought was my fault.

I listened to music that reminded me of things I held dear to my heart, such as Laura. My favorite artists and songs made me feel like I wasn't alone in this sudden mental battleground.

Any songs I thought were hitting home over my emotional demise made my list. It wasn't a long list of albums. Tori Amos' *Under the Pink* remained a constant. NIN's *Broken* EP also made the cut. "Last," "Gave Up," and "Wish" got played the most. I listened to music I was listening to a lot the year prior, hoping it would get me back in a structured mood.

I gave a lot of spins to Duran Duran's self-titled album, Depeche Mode's *Songs of Faith and Devotion,* and The Smashing Pumpkins' *Siamese Dream.* "Mayonnaise" played on a loop during my walks through Bucks County.

Other albums, such as Peter Gabriel's *So* and U2's *Achtung Baby* and *Zooropa,* provided moments of clarity during daily suffering. And, of course, I relied (as always) on R.E.M.'s catalog. The songs provided my only comfort. They helped me ignore my demons. It was the only time I felt things freely.

Counting Crows' *August and Everything After* was perfect for this time. I liked it before, but losing Laura and reaching my emotional limits made me love it.

I would listen to it and think about what happened to me. I thought of the last time I saw Laura at her school after she told me we couldn't see each other again. I saw her at her locker, and she just walked away from me. The song "Time and Time Again" fit perfectly for what I was going through, not just then but during my entire young life of disappointments. It was just another letdown in a long line of letdowns, time and time again. I wanted her to walk away from without feeling she was leaving me alone.

The best songs on *August and Everything After* are the ones that weren't overplayed radio singles. Each is full of emotion and lyrics that painted a colorful spectrum of feelings I related to. It was the closest thing to therapy I could try.

It was just enough mix of wisdom and sorrow to distract me and let me feel something. I worked out some of my frustrations. Songs like "Perfect Blue Buildings", "Raining in Baltimore," and "Murder of One" all came in handy that year.

Listening to this album helped simmer my doubts so I could hear myself clearly. The feelings I got from the songs washed over me.

The last line on the album was a good wake-up call: "You don't want to waste your life." It motivated me to keep fighting my inner demons and not miss out on life. Just keep going, Chaz.

Chapter 7:
Don't Give Up

Peter Gabriel's *So* album had many songs I loved, especially "In Your Eyes." It made me think of Laura (and Lloyd Dobler). "Red Rain" is a beauty, too. But it was Peter's duet with Kate Bush on "Don't Give Up" that provided comfort when I felt I had already given up and was hanging by a thread. Peter sang about how frustrated he was after giving it his all, with Kate Bush's unique voice singing about hope and not giving up on who you are. It was a beautiful song that brought tears to my eyes, even when I was too afraid to shed them. It was full of beautiful lines but the basic message that Kate was trying to get to the listener was do not give up, you have something to live for.

To this day, I listen to that song and get teary-eyed. It makes me want to keep going through this unfair life. Especially the line, "You know it's never been easy." I thought, "Why the fuck did you think, Chaz, it was going to be easy from now on? Why did you think things would suddenly work out for you? This is just how it is for you, and you must keep going." Of course, not giving up is why the cliché "easier said than done" was created.

Chapter 8:
R.E.M. is God

R.E.M., like many times before and after, was the rock I leaned on the most. They were my constant. It's a good thing I discovered them and gravitated to their music. There is a R.E.M. song for every situation. If I felt it, they had a song about it. I fit their songs into my life, looking for insight and strength to push through the mess I was dealing with.

"World Leader Pretend" from their album *Green* took on a new meaning during confusion and inside battles. It was my theme song about the conflict inside me. I was waging war on myself and needed to block out the naysayers and those trying to hurt me or bring me back to the fold. I created mental walls to defend and protect myself. These lyrics hit close to home:

"I sit at my table and wage war on myself, it seems like it's all, it's all for nothing."

"This is my mistake, let me make it good, I raised the wall, and I will be the one to knock it down."

"This is my life and this is my time, I have been given the freedom to do as I see fit, it's high time I've raised the walls that I've constructed."

I also had *Automatic for the People* for emotional support with songs like "Everybody Hurts" and "Find the River." There was the romantic side of R.E.M. that I listened to a lot, including "Country Feedback" with lines like, "I had control, I lost my head, I need this, I need this," and "It's crazy what you could have had, I need this."

"Losing My Religion" was once again my anchor. With bands like NIN and Nirvana, I listened to them based on my raw feelings and pain. With R.E.M., it was never about that. They were a comfort and a source of knowledge. They showed me who I wanted to be and how I wanted to act. Even though sometimes my pain and anger may lead me away from their core message and wisdom beyond their years, I would always come back to them, catch my breath, and keep going. It will always be me in the corner and in the spotlight. I will always be choosing my confessions, and losing everything, trying to keep up.

I will always have to be reminded that everybody hurts, and I am not alone, even when my hurt drives me to madness. I will always speak up when I see something wrong because silence means approval. I will always have to be reminded to get up, even when life is hard. And that if I hold out, I can find the river, and things might come my way. These are some things I have learned from my favorite band in the world.

Chapter 9:
I Took Your Name

Monster was the newest R.E.M. album, so I played that a lot, too. I cozied up to it after it not being my favorite initially. I thought of the songs as R.E.M. showing all these alt-rock bands that they inspired that they could rock as much as anyone. I thought Michael Stipe was writing in characters rather than the songs being from his point of view or experiences.

Michael was cooler than ever in appearance and attitude. Every interview on TV had him looking sexy and marvelous with his freshly shaved head and his stand-out-in-a-crowd rock star clothes and moves. He was wearing nail polish and eyeliner and came off as extremely confident. His charisma was shouting out of him, and his eyes showed the soul of a poet and the wisest man in the room (if not the planet).

His beauty leaked out of him and was evident in how he carried himself and interacted with those around him. He was a beautiful man (and, in my opinion, the most beautiful person in the world). In every music video, interview, and live footage Michael appeared in, I was in awe of how great he was. He was my hero, and I wanted to be like him more than ever.

Some kids grow their hair like their idols, Eddie Vedder and Kurt Cobain. I decided to idolize my hero by shaving my head for the first of many times. I loved how it looked. I was 145 pounds, bald, and looked like I could be Stipe's clone.

I shaved it in his honor, but I also needed a change. I had a mop of hair that looked like I didn't know how to brush it (because I didn't), and I hid it under a hat all the time. I had already painted my fingernails, but now I would wear eyeliner whenever possible because I wanted to be as beautiful and great as Michael Stipe.

R.E.M., especially Stipe, gave me the foundation to keep going and some stability in my tormented life. Thank Jebus for them and their "life in constant motion" songs.

Chapter 10:
Feeling Supersonic?

E ven as a shell of myself, I still tried to be a functioning kid. I was a mess inside, but hid it the best I could. Only I knew about my conflict. I still hung out with friends like Ray, Christine, and Uriah. I would interact with them, but spent time in my head and wouldn't always be fully there in spirit.

I mostly hung out with Ray, usually at his house, South Street, or at concerts. Ray wanted to see as many shows as possible. Even if they were bands that he only knew one song by, or knew I liked them but didn't give a shit about them. I think he just wanted to do something besides sitting around, and he wanted to meet girls.

The first show we saw after my emotional breakdown was in March 1995 at the TLA. I liked Oasis a lot. I had their first album and wanted to see them the year prior, but they played a club in Philly called J.C. Dobbs that had a 21 and up entry.

The British pop scene was getting ready to break in the U.S., and Oasis was the first group I saw live. I had looked forward to this show for months, but thanks to my mental state, I didn't feel as excited when it was here. I danced to some songs and tried to get lost in the moment (my favorite thing to do at shows), but I was too out of it to let loose.

Liam Gallagher, the lead singer, seemed like a real dick and acted like he was the biggest rock star of all time. I understood he played in arenas and stadiums in Europe, but most Americans didn't know who he was. They had to play in front of 800 people instead. I saw them a few more times later in life, with a clearer head, and enjoyed them thoroughly. Bush also played the TLA the same week, but I chose (wisely) to see Oasis instead, as they were the better band.

Ray and I saw Letters to Cleo at the Troc on 4/7/95. They covered Nirvana's "School" as a tribute to the first anniversary of Cobain's death. I jumped on stage and staged-dived for the first time. I thought it was awesome, and it couldn't have been that bad for the people I jumped on because I only weighed 145 lbs.

We saw the 10,000 Maniacs (without Natalie Merchant), Luscious Jackson, Velvet Crush, and a few more at the TLA. These bands were fun and got me out of my head for a bit, but I thought what would make everything okay (at least for a while) would be if R.E.M. came to Philly. Then they announced three Philly dates!

The dates were going to be in October at the Spectrum in South Philly. Tickets would go on sale in May and be cheap for possibly the biggest band in the world - $35 a ticket. This was well-earned and good news for me. It gave me something to look forward to. My favorite band and my hero in life were coming to Philly for the first time since I fell in love with their music. I couldn't wait (but had to since it was five months away).

Chapter 11:
Teenagers Scare the Living Shit Out of Me

When I first moved in with my grandparents, I was a sad kid, but I could function at home and be involved for the most part with my family when they were around. My grandma's house was the hub for all my other relatives. My cousin lived there for his entire life, and his mom and my other aunt and uncles were always there when my grandparents weren't at work.

My dad's brothers and sisters were usually around on weekends. My aunt Mary lived about a block and a half away, and I would visit her whenever she was bored or I wanted a change of scenery. We would watch movies or just talk about life. She was a nice woman who had a lot of love in her heart for everyone she knew. My uncles Mike and Tommy would come over and check on their parents as good sons do, and my aunt Margie was also around to give a hand. My uncle Joe lived in Florida, so he wasn't around as much, similar to my aunt Theresa, who lived in Virginia with her Navy husband and their growing family.

I was 16 and hanging out with my relatives much more than when I lived in Kensington. Previously, I would only see them at weddings, funerals, and Christmas when my immediate family made an appearance. Now, I would see them every week or more. Someone was always popping in.

The first few months were a blast. I would sneak some drinks with them (some cool aunts and uncles let me drink), and we would have fun talking about life, music, family, etc. One day, we had a family event for my cousin's catholic rituals.

We had a great time at the party held at a banquet hall. I was dancing (somehow, without having any rhythm, I was a good dancer, like Elvis meets Michael Jackson). I was drinking the cheap beer that was available and was quite drunk. I asked the DJ to play R.E.M. and Pearl Jam, and I got "The One I Love" and "Daughter." That made Drunk Me happy.

At the end of the night, we returned to my grandma's house and continued the party. While we were there, sitting at the kitchen table, my grandma was talking about how much she loved Billy, my cousin, in front of me. The only people there were Billy, Aunt Mary, Margie, and maybe Uncle Joe was nearby.

Aunt Mary saw on my drunk face that I was hurt by grandma saying she loved Billy so much, but said nothing about me. Mary, in her loving, helping way, said, "Mom, you love

Chaz too, right?" My grandma, who was also pretty tipsy, replied, "I don't know him. How can I love him if I don't know him?" Ouch, that stung.

Mary quietly said to me, "She loves you. She's just joking." I nodded in agreement, but didn't know what to make of it. I thought about it for a while, and it was awake up moment. I assumed, before that moment, that your relatives loved you no matter what.

I know she cared and loved me, but I took for granted the idea that relatives and those who you have known your whole life love you for you and not because of obligations to having the same bloodlines.

It wasn't my fault. I didn't know I wasn't close to my relatives. I assumed our relationship was normal since this was how it had been my whole life. I knew that my immediate family was the black sheep. I didn't see my extended family much due to my parents and our crappy neighborhood. It was always my parents who initiated contact.

I was used to only seeing them a few times a year at best. Now that I was living with them, I saw them a lot more, and I enjoyed their company since they were not born-againers and were nice people. They were structured and fun to be around. I was taken aback by my grandma's comment. Now, I know she only said she didn't know me well because I wasn't around much. But at the time, I felt like I didn't belong and shouldn't have left home.

I tried to function with my family throughout my time there until after my breakdown. After March 2nd, I was so confused about how to act or who to trust. I spent most of my time in my room. I was a gloomy teenager who probably seemed sad, going through the motions of growing up. But my mental health was in jeopardy, and I didn't know what to do about it. Avoiding people was the best way to handle it.

I had a lot going on in my head. On the outside, it must have looked bizarre. I wore the same outfit daily because I lacked the motivation to wear anything besides my army green pants, a flannel, and a band t-shirt. I hardly talked to anyone. I only ate when no one was around to avoid contact. I wasn't eating much, anyway.

My Aunt Mary would invite me over and try to get me to open up to her. I would tell her and her boyfriend what was going on. I was fond of him because he loved rock music and wanted to know about bands like Nirvana and R.E.M. They told me I should loosen up, relax, enjoy myself, and things will work out.

It was great advice if one wasn't raised as a born-again Christian and had everything ripped from them. Once, they encouraged me to have some alcoholic drinks with them to relax. I didn't want to because I thought that would show weakness, and that weakness got me into this situation. I thought God or fate would punish me for relying on alcohol to live. Also, I didn't want to start depending on alcohol to feel and function (I wish I had this motivation later on). But I wanted to feel better and thought drinking vodka would do the trick.

I had a few drinks with them and loosened up. Suddenly, I wasn't the constantly stressed-out, fragile kid I was 24/7. I liked the feeling I got from drinking, which scared me since I didn't want to depend on a substance like my father and his father, so I cut it off almost as fast as I picked it back up. I might have drunk 4-5 times that week before I got a grip and swore it off for good (meaning a few months, since I am my father's son).

Even my aunt's generosity and empathy didn't help shake my cloudy mind and confusion. I didn't communicate well with my grandma since I felt this wasn't something she would understand. I just kept going, which led to some turmoil.

In April of 1995, I was drinking at my aunt's house when she went out for something, and I was by myself. I had MTV on since they still played music videos and didn't let generations down by becoming a reality TV channel. A video came on from a band that would become very important to me.

Radiohead got written off as a one-hit wonder in America after their song "Creep" got a lot of play. I loved it like most alt-rock fans in 1993. Two years later, Radiohead had a new album and a beautiful new single, "Fake Plastic Trees." And boy, they would show the world how they grew as artists and musicians.

I wasn't listening to anything new besides *Monster* since my crippling depression made me lose interest in new music. But this song struck a chord with me. It caught my attention and brought some emotions into my troubled heart. The singer seemed vulnerable and earnest. You could feel his pain and feel that he meant every line and note he sang.

The lyrics to me came from a guy who has been through it all and scraped by something terrible like I was. The emotional build-up at the end leads to a faster tempo as the singer gets louder and more passionate, so you understand what he has gone through.

I heard it a few more times in the spring and summer and listened to it at the local music store. They had *The Bends* set up to sample through headphones before buying it. I mainly listened to "Fake Plastic Trees" and played the title track and a couple of others. But I wasn't in the mindset to buy new music, so I didn't get the album until a couple of months later.

Radiohead soon became second to R.E.M. (and maybe Tori). I met the band a few times and flew to Europe to see them perform. I even got a tattoo of artwork from *Ok Computer*.. Little did I know, watching this colorful video with a blonde Thom Yorke getting pushed around in a shopping cart, that this band would help keep me intact too many times to count.

Chapter 12:
Fuck and Run

My depressed antics didn't sit well with my grandma. I understand how it looked on the outside with me. I get that it looked like I was miserable living there, but it wasn't that at all. I liked living with my grandma. It was a lot nicer than Kensington. I liked not having roaches and mice everywhere. I liked walking around without the fear of getting killed. It was great having hot water and being able to take a shower. I enjoyed being around my relatives because they were fun, and I cared about them. But I was out of my mind for the first time.

My Uncle Tommy, whom I liked a lot, tried to get me to open up to him once. I think my grandma asked him to find out what was happening to me. He asked me if my problems stemmed from my dad and his addiction. I said, "No," and he questioned how it couldn't bother me. I said, "It doesn't bother me." (Even though it did). But I was more concerned with my mental and emotional state. I did not bring this up. I just wanted this conversation to end so I could resume racking my brain with rituals, overthinking, and trying to feel again. But the conversation continued.

He brought up talking to someone. Not a doctor, but a group meeting like AA or NA, for kids who have gone through rough childhoods. I didn't know if they could help, but I didn't show interest. I was still on the borderline that this was temporary, or God/fate would stop punishing me and make it all okay.

He tried to help, but I was beyond the normal teenage blues phase. It was the beginning of a forever problem, and I had no idea how to fix it. I was having trouble trusting anyone since they didn't know what I went through. I was scared that they would tell me what I was afraid to hear: this was normal, and how I feel is how it is when you "grow up." I had too many thoughts and muffled emotions running through my head to make sense of anything, and I wasn't getting better.

Easter was coming, and family from out of state was coming to stay with us at grandmas. Since no one was getting through to me on behalf of my grandma, she took it upon herself to talk to me. She asked me if I was happy there, and I replied," Yes," but I recall being scared to say it out loud for fear of God taking something else from me.

She said I looked miserable and that maybe I should find somewhere to live where I would be happy. I was never happy, but was content living there over my other options. How could I be delighted with my life? How could I smile and think everything was okay when it wasn't? I wanted to be happy, or at least feel again. But I didn't want to smile and fake it. I hardly wanted to get out of bed, let alone act like I was on the bright side of life.

My grandma wanted me out of the house for Easter week so the out-of-town family could have more room and wouldn't have to be around this moody sod of a lunatic that I was. I understand and don't hold any grudges. It wasn't my fault, but I was a mental mess. My grandma wasn't used to a person with deep emotional and traumatic experiences.

One of my relatives asked me if I was on drugs, and I told them the truth, that I was trying my best to stay away from drugs so they wouldn't take over my life. My grandma could have handled drugs if that were my problem. That was more normal for a teenager growing up in a working-class family in Philly during those years.

My problems were internal and wouldn't go away with a drink or a shrink. I guess she also thought that maybe I missed my parents, and they could deal with me and my mood better than anyone there could have. The last thing I wanted was to go to my parents' apartment.

I didn't make a fuss or say I would work on myself to stay at the house. I just took it as another blow. I got my things together, put them in my trusty black school bag, and left.

I was half numb, half a bundle of confusion, wandering around Mayfair on a chilly April night. I had a few options and decided to go somewhere I could sit and think. I returned to the old familiar ways of sitting in a Dunkin' Donuts for the night, sipping tea for hours. The only difference was that this Dunkin' was in the Northeast and had a working bathroom.

I was in the same situation as the previous year. Somewhat homeless, sitting in a fast-food chain, drinking tea, and thinking about my next move. The one good thing: I had my Walkman and my favorite tapes. I sat there for hours listening to Tori Amos, R.E.M., and others, staring desperately out a rain-covered window on Frankford Avenue. Where do I go now?

I decided to pull a page from Kurt Cobain's book and sleep under a bridge. He would run away from home as a teenager and sleep under a bridge until he decided to go home. I went to Pennypack (the woods that covered most of Northeast Philly) and found this bridge over the creek. It had a spot on the top of the foundation deep enough for shelter and long enough for me to lie in.

I brought a sheet with me when I left my grandma's, thinking that sleeping outside would be one of my options. I lay there for a while, unable to sleep due to my fear of bugs. I slept an hour or two before sunrise, then got up and walked around the park like I did when I pretended to be at school.

I was hiking and came across an area a lot lower than the trail I was on. It was about 20 feet down, and everything was covered with trash. I decided to see what was happening down there. I made my way down, and it looked like a war zone. There was trash, plastic bags, and clothes all over the ground and trees. It went on for 100s of feet. Then I heard a noise. I looked up and saw 10-15 deer looking down at me.

They surrounded the trail, almost in a circle. There seemed to be deer everywhere. They looked at me like I was intruding on their land. They didn't do anything but wouldn't take their eyes off me. It was clear they wanted me to leave their home.

I went up the hill behind me, where there weren't any deer, walking backward so I could keep my eyes on them. I was worried they would charge me. I wouldn't know what to do except run as fast as possible.

When I reached the top of the hill, I was only a few feet away from a major road, Roosevelt Blvd. I hopped over the metal barrier and never went back to that area. I always think about that spot when I drive on the boulevard since it's such an urban and fast-paced area, and right there, just a few feet away, was a deer living space.

The next night, I planned on repeating my sleeping situation from the night before. During the day, I hung out with Ray at his house, went to work, and then went to Pennypack to get ready for another uncomfortable bug-filled sleep.

I tried sleeping, but couldn't. I was too freaked out by all the bugs and spiders I kept seeing. I couldn't take it anymore. Around 3 am, I got up and went to the payphone near the entrance to the park. I used Ray's idea and called one of the crisis center helplines to see if they could help me find a shelter for the night.

I told the woman on the line that I was on my own, looking for a place to sleep for the night. I told them I didn't want to go to a friend's house because I didn't want to bother anyone. And the last place I wanted to go was my parents' apartment. I told her about getting kicked out of school, losing Laura, feeling confused and numb, and getting kicked out of my grandma's house. She asked if I was depressed, and I didn't lie. I told her I had always been depressed.

She asked me if I had any weapons on me. I admitted I did. I thought nothing of it. I had the knife I used to cut myself with for protection. I didn't put two and two together that she thought I was going to kill myself. We then talked about finding me a place to stay when I heard a car pull up behind me. It was a cop car with flashing lights to stimulate my eyes and mind, letting me know this was real.

The woman told me to stay where I was. I hung up, thinking, "I thought these calls were supposed to be confidential." Two male cops came out of the car, one in his late 50s (the good cop) and the other in his 30s (the bad cop).

They asked me the usual questions: my age, why I was out there in the middle of the night, and where I lived. They also asked where the knife I had was. I told them I didn't have one (it was in my front right pocket). They searched my school bag and patted me down. To my astonishment, they didn't find the six-inch knife in my pocket.

The good cop searched me while the bad cop removed my possessions from my bookbag and laid them out on the hood of their car. It was extremely embarrassing, especially when the bad cop made cynical comments about my music taste ("Nirvana *Insecticide,* no wonder you want to kill yourself."). He was disappointed that a weapon wasn't found.

I told them I made it up and was wandering around before work. I said I had to work at the fast-food hellhole at 5 (which wasn't a lie; I worked at 5 pm, I just made them think I meant 5 am). They let me go and said they would see me soon when they come into McShit for breakfast (like hell you will). I swore I would never call a crisis line again and kept that promise.

The next night, I stayed at Christine's house in Kensington, but I knew I couldn't stay there more than a night, especially with Easter approaching. I bit the bullet and asked my mom if I could spend a couple of nights at the shithole apartment on Paul Street. Of course, she said yes.

It was the first time I saw my dad since I freaked out on him and called him a drug addict. It didn't come up. We just buried it down and ignored it as we did with everything. Like father, like son. I spent a few nights on the cat-piss-stained couch in their tiny living room. My dad and I didn't say much to each other, and I didn't do much besides sleep or watch TV at night.

Thankfully, I got to see R.E.M.'s video for "Strange Currencies," the song that Laura showed her affection for me via a letter. I (also like my dad) needed to fall asleep with a TV on. As I lay my head on the pillowcase stained from decades of use, I heard the familiar opening notes that reminded me of my Laura. I got up and reached for my glasses to see the black-and-white video. Michael looked beautiful as always, staring out the window of the car the band was driving. Seeing the video was a little spark of joy amidst my newest darkest moment.

Chapter 13:
I Love it When a Plan Comes Together

With everything that had come undone for me, the last thing I wanted was to go far off track by moving back in with my parents in absolute poverty. I would do anything to avoid this predicament. Ray and I talked about our options to get out of our situations, even if only temporary. He was fed up with his abusive dad and the "same old, same old" home life of not having, and most likely never having anything. It was the common outlook in Kensington. I was trying my best to get away from it.

I told Ray about my summers in Wildwood and how kids had their own affordable places. He was on board, and soon found us a place to stay. A $100-a-week shared room in the middle of Wildwood.

I called my old manager from Burger King and secured jobs for Ray and I. We couldn't move in for another month. I didn't want to stay with my parents that long, but I was trying to get through the week.

I asked my grandma if I could stay at her place in Mayfair for six weeks. She said it was fine. I bided my time there until Ray and I could move. Wildwood would let me rest my head and take it easy, like so many times before. Except this wasn't like any other time.

Chapter 14:
This Is How We Do It?

I usually stayed in Wildwood with my Grandma Holesworth (my dad's stepmom), but I didn't ask since Ray was coming. I also didn't know how to approach or talk to her after my breakdown and lack of an education plan.

Grandma Holesworth believed in a proper education and a plan for one's future. I was constantly stressed out and avoided discussing my education with her for years. She told me in the '80s that computers would take over the world, and every school should be using them and teaching kids about them. I was in a poor Baptist school that didn't even have teachers. .I felt dumb and worried about at the tender age of 10 but blew it off because I thought God was in control.

She was quite proud of her nephews and nieces and their "normal" (Catholic) education, safe and sound lives, and chances for a successful life after school. I heard about how well my cousins did in school with sports or their grades. My one cousin was a kiss-ass brown noser who was always the center of my grandma and her sister's attention.

When I was 15, it became clear that my future wouldn't be so bright thanks to my born-again, Lifepac education. I felt inadequate compared to my cousins. My grandma thought (rightfully) that the born-again religion wasn't the way to go, and the education was nothing compared to the Catholic ones.

I felt I had to defend my mom and our faith when my education got brought up and subtly compared to the superior Catholic education. I had to hide how inferior it was.

I already felt lousy about myself for being poor as fuck and having a drug addict for a dad, while these kids grew up in the exquisite (in comparison to Kensington) Northeast Philly. I wasn't just jealous of them but all the kids who had it better than me growing up. I had the "I wish I had that life" syndrome, and usually tried to change the subject when my grandma questioned me about my future.

I didn't know what I wanted to do, and God knows my parents didn't know or seem to care. I panicked whenever it came up. When she raved about how wonderful my cousins were at school, I would let her talk, grinned and bared it.

The summer before, in 1994, I was enrolled in what I thought was my shot at a future with Bensalem Baptist. It was the first time I was excited about talking about school with my grandma. I thought I would get taught by actual teachers, get graded, and have something to tell her when I was done like I got an "A" in English or I'm graduating and going to college.

I had some of those experiences during my four months at Bensalem Baptist, but after they kicked me out, I was scared to tell my grandma. It felt like I was in the same boat as when I was 15, with no future. After my breakdown, I didn't know how to face her with the news.

While attending CIBA, I could at least hide how bad the education was until our conversation ended. She had no idea, like most people, how bad these Baptist schools were and how they were not prepared to educate kids. But now I was out of school, and instead of gradually being prepared for the world through senior year and graduation, I was thrown into it without confidence or control of my fears and feelings.

I didn't want to talk to any adults besides my mom. However, I don't know why since she stayed at CIBA after they kicked me out. She did so much for that piece of shit place. I really didn't want to talk to Grandma Holesworth with half my senses, thinking that God or fate was out to get me. There was no way I could face that pressure. I would rather run away and figure everything out on my own.

I knew she would say this was bound to happen; I should have done something different years ago (like attend a Catholic school). Unfortunately, I was poor as fuck in a house and neighborhood that society forgot. I went along with what my parents provided since I didn't know any fucking better. We couldn't afford to go to a better school, like those precious Catholic Schools, so I had to go to a public school and probably drop out for safety as Eddie did.

When I finally saw a way out of my "It's too late for me" outlook, I got kicked out for liking R.E.M. and not having enough money. No one helped us. No one would take me to a better school that cost more.

Facing my grandma was out of the question. I would postpone that meeting and conversation about my future until I got myself together and regained my feelings and confidence. I assumed once I came back from this thing I was going through, I would make things better with my grandma. It went on the back burner with many other regrets. I'm sure it looked like I didn't care about my grandma, or I didn't want to see her, but the weight of my problems was too much for me to even think about dealing with judgment. I had to figure everything out on my own.

Chapter 15:
Shiny Happy Chaz

The news I had been waiting four years for came. R.E.M. tickets were going on sale soon. They announced two dates, then added a third a few weeks later after the first two quickly sold out.

I needed to go to all the shows and get good seats. This could not get fucked up for me. I would do something I heard others had done for tickets - camp out for them at the local West Coast Video store that had a Ticketmaster booth inside.

Before online sales, the only way you could get tickets was by phone (repeatedly calling while getting busy signals) or by going to the box office or licensed Ticketmaster broker on the day of the sale. To guarantee good seats, your best bet was to be first in line when tickets went on sale (usually 10 am on a Saturday).

I was already down with sleeping under bridges crawling with bugs, so pavement in a strip mall in Northeast Philly was a breeze. I got to the store the night before. As I walked up, I had a rush of fear that there would already be too many people in line. Luckily, there were only two or three people ahead of me, so I got a place next to them and started my first (of several) ticket-camping adventures. Ray showed up a few hours later, and we were set to buy tickets for us and Uriah, who couldn't make it.

The main goal was to score good seats to the show, but you also got to hang out and sometimes party with people with similar musical tastes. I have so many fond memories from camping out for tickets. I met tons of like-minded souls (some I even dated) in these lines.

Camping out had an honor system. As you waited all night for tickets, many people would show up and get behind the last person. It was a very laid-back process, often organized by the first person in line. That person would start a list you signed to keep your place in line if you had to go to the bathroom or get something to eat or drink.

This show was going to be a big one. R.E.M. hadn't toured in six years and was huge. As crowds showed up, I was thrilled to be around R.E.M. fans. It was the first time I was surrounded by so many fans in one spot. I was having a ball. I forgot all about my mental illness for the night, getting lost in the excitement of being around like-minded people and the idea of seeing my favorite band soon. I was closer to being in the same room as my boys from Athens.

We met two girls around the same age as us from northeast Philly named Kathleen and Donna. They were huge alt-rock fans. Kathleen was a giant Pearl Jam nut, and Donna loved Kurt Cobain and NIN like no other (even more than me). We hit it off right off the bat and spent the entire night entertaining each other and talking about all the bands we loved with all our teenage hearts.

Usually, when I camped out for tickets, I would stay up for most of the night and catch a couple hours of sleep. This time I was so excited I couldn't sleep a wink. I was awake when it was time for the moment. I would accomplish one of my dreams.

Around 9:30 am, store employees lined us up to buy tickets. I waited patiently, constantly looking at the clock in the store to see if it was time to purchase tickets.

Finally, around 10:05 am, it happened. After the two people ahead of me got their good seats, it was my time to shine. I got up to the booth and quickly said, "Three best available tickets for both shows." She punched in the info and told me the price for both shows. I gave her the money, and just like that, I had tickets to R.E.M. for two shows! The first show would be on October 12th. Our seats were only seven rows from the stage!!! For the second show, October 13th (one of the greatest days of my life), we got tickets about 13 rows away.

I was ecstatic! I felt like I was on top of the world. Nothing else mattered. Not my mental problems or anything else. I was on a high that I rightly deserved.

Later that month, they added a third show in Philly on October 14th. When they went on sale, I was at West Coast Video again, this time alone, with fewer campers than before. I was first in line, and when tickets went on sale, I got 2nd-row seats in the center to see my gods! I got tickets for me and Uriah. Ray thought two shows to see a band he only sort of liked was enough. It was only right for us to be this close since it was our favorite band.

It was going to be the peak of my life. I could die right after this show and be okay with it. I had something to look forward to, something I waited years for. It was the underlining of the summer and all the events that came with it. It was the thing that kept me calm through the rough moments. No matter how terrible and insane my thinking got, I had three R.E.M. shows to look forward to.

The possibilities surrounding these shows were endless for me. R.E.M. was my identity and my passion. To be around thousands of fans who loved the band I loved sounded like heaven. But R.E.M. coming to my city wasn't the only great news around May 1995. The other thing I wanted more than life itself happened. Laura made contact.

Chapter 16:
With Love Comes
Strange Currencies

Laura made contact the only way she knew how; she had our mutual friend Michelle give me a message. Michelle told me that Laura wanted to see me. Laura wanted me to meet her at her school soon. And she missed me.

For the past two months, I was a mess. But I stayed true to Laura. I hoped we would get back together, or she still felt something for me. Could this be the start of us getting what we wanted? I was weary due to my OCD. Plus, the last time I saw her, she acted cold. She walked away, giving me the sensation she was leaving me alone.

I went to her school the next chance I got like she wanted. When I saw her, she ran over and gave me a huge hug and a kiss on my mouth. It was the opposite of the last interaction we had. She was gleaming with genuine happiness to see me. And her glow and beauty shining through made me feel the same way. She didn't have much time to talk. Her parents wanted her home right after school. But she had to see me and make things right.

She told me the day she turned away from me was terrible for her (for you? You have no idea, sunshine). She said she only did it because her parents were on a rampage, and couldn't do anything about it until now.

Her parents still forbid us to be together, nothing changed there, but she wanted me to know that one day she would break free (hinting at her 18th birthday a year away) and that everything we wanted could still happen. She still felt the way I felt.

This was music to my ears (almost as good as R.E.M.'s music). For a moment, I felt good again. If I could capture the good moments and display them in my memory bank to cleanse the bad stuff, this one would be a keeper. It's up there with getting R.E.M. tickets and the day Laura first told me she loved me.

Laura was excited for me about my R.E.M. shows and glad I was going to Wildwood for the summer. She had high hopes for me and still thought I could be something great, or close to it, with my words and how I saw the world. She told me I was her "Charles" and how she was almost like my cult member. She just wanted to listen to everything I had to say about God, life, and religion.

It gave me the hope I needed. Laura made me think things would get better, we were meant to meet, and our love was real. I told her what I had gone through the last few months. I didn't detail my panic attacks and the rituals I had to conduct to get to the next moment. I just told her how it was harder to feel and to care about things that used to come naturally.

I told her I cut off ties with people I felt only wanted one side of me (the party animal full of energy). That wasn't the true me who was full of misery and uncertainty. I told her I didn't want anyone but her.

But Laura needed me to understand that it would take a while before we could see each other like we wanted. She wanted me to live my life, meet people, and experience things the Christians were trying to keep us from.

She didn't want to stop me from meeting girls I might have feelings for. I told her I didn't want anyone else, and I meant it, I swear to Stipe. But she insisted I wouldn't let her keep me from forming relationships during the time it took for her to be free.

I took it, like everything, two ways. I believed her because she was unlike anyone I'd encountered (honesty and pure heart). It gave me hope that she meant every word. But my negative thoughts crept in too. Maybe it was just her letting me down easily. She told me to go find someone else so I would leave her alone, and she could find someone with a better future. I had to push those thoughts away with the over-the-top make-believe optimism I created to keep me afloat. But it will always be lingering nearby.

Laura then handed me a note and told me to read it when I was alone. My curiosity was at the max. We looked at each other and embraced for the last time in five months. She kissed me with her soft pink lips and told me to take care of myself.

She returned to her suburban home, and I went my way which consisted of three bus rides home. I left this brief encounter with higher hopes for our future. It felt like she took a burden off of me. She wanted me to live life to the fullest and not worry about her. She would be with me when she could. I watched her walking away without the sensation she was leaving me alone.

Chapter 17:
Letter Never Sent

Before all the shuttering demons of despair and doubt came flooding in, I felt I was on the right track, the one I was supposed to be on. Laura just gave me the right to have fun and live my life full of music and people like me. She wanted me to experience it all so I could write about it and tell tales to her when we were reunited.

I read the letter soon after I was alone. It was full of things about how wonderful I was. How I should never doubt myself and keep up with my dreams. She said the last day we saw each other (when she walked away from me), she burst into tears and wanted to turn around and tell me she still loved me. That part made me cry even with my numb heart.

I held the letter close to me for quite some time before losing it somewhere in my travels and nonsense-filled life. I read it whenever I wanted to feel connected to my Laura. It was a symbol of everything I had to remember. Of all the things I lost, I miss that letter the most. What I would do to read it once more.

Chapter 18:
Chaz Holesworth Will Have His Revenge on Bensalem Baptist

I had R.E.M. tickets, a place to stay in Wildwood, and Laura still loved me. What else would life throw my way to try to make things right (well as right as possible)? How about a little revenge on those well-off born-againers who started me down this downward spiral?

Uriah was still on his way to graduating. The graduation was coming up in the last week of May, and he wanted me, his oldest friend, to come to see it. After seeing Laura, I had some new life in me. I was starting to branch out again with people and wanted to experience new things with my fellow teenage humans. Ray and I were hanging out with the girls we met camping out for R.E.M. tickets, Donna and Kathleen, almost daily.

We hung out at the Roosevelt Mall, Donna's house, or just talked on the phone for hours about how much we loved our alt-rock heroes. Somehow during the conversations between us four, Bensalem Baptist (BB) came up, and how they wronged me.

I told them how BB kicked me out over money, which led to me losing the love of my life, and how I had a breakdown and was never the same. They were sympathetic and pretty much anti-organized religion themselves.

I told them about the graduation I should have been a part of and how I had to go watch my best friend graduate but hated the school for what they did to me. Then Ray came up with the idea for all four of us to go and get revenge on BB.

The girls were on board, and we decided to stand out during the ceremony. I liked the idea of making a splash and disrupting their pretend following of Jesus' ways. We told the girls to wear the most outrageous things they could find. Kathleen wore her "Citizen Dick" T-shirt (a prop from the movie *Singles*). Donna wore all black (a skirt, ripped-up fishnet stockings, and a NIN shirt). I, the only one who knew the lion's den we were walking into, wore a dress shirt and a tie with a floral design. But I also painted my nails, put eyeliner on, and on my freshly shaved head wrote "666" on one side and on the other "R.E.M." with black eyeliner.

Ray wore his usual rapper-wannabe jeans (baggie and falling off his butt), some name-brand sneakers, one of my Kurt Cobain shirts, and a baseball cap. The cap is the key item that ruined their happy gathering.

A day or two before graduation night, Ray and I decided to visit Bensalem Baptist during school hours. While hanging out with Uriah, Ray met his sister, Mary, and they became more than friends. I vaguely remember them having sex at someone's house and using a sandwich bag as a condom due to the lack of a real condom.

Mary invited Ray to the school, and since the school had the policy to let students invite other kids, how could they turn us down? Ray was the perfect instigator you could ever want. He was a true punk without the look. He only wanted to disrupt and get his.

Ray knew about my upbringing via my tales. He didn't get it, but he knew it was fucked up and easy to disrupt. Where I was still the nice guy, who didn't want to hurt anymore or make anyone feel uncomfortable, including those who did me wrong, Ray was the type to walk in a place (like BB) and burn it to the ground, laughing while it burned.

Ray went to public schools his entire life and was surrounded by thousands of kids who didn't give a fuck about religion and did what they wanted. So, a small-ass church that was supposed to be a school made him laugh and see it for what it really was: pathetic.

We took a couple buses up from our shitty poor neighborhoods in the inner city to the suburban *"Little House on the Prairie"* size of a building for education. We somehow made it through the doors without being stopped. There weren't metal detectors or a guard at the door, but I was surprised no adult figure noticed us and kicked us out on the spot.

Mary was the friend who "invited" us and was responsible for taking us from class to class. I thought I would be the red flag and caught instantly for trying to step foot in their precious building. I was obviously there to poison the god-fearing children with the devil's music.

I was on my best behavior and just wanted to see the kids I got to know over those precious months when I felt like a normal kid. I was happy to see Michele, Julie, Benjamin, and all the kids I would have had a great experience with if I got handed a different card in life.

If my mom became a born-again Xian while living in a middle-class neighborhood instead of joining their cult in the slums of the city, then I might have grown up with these types.

Cathy Holesworth fell for the typical born-again nonsense about how Christ accepts everyone and that we are one family. However, it's okay for Christians in the suburbs to have a better life and education than those in the fucking poor neighborhoods that are only miles away. Where is your Messiah now?

They sold my mom a lifestyle of oneness that almost made sense to those who want humanity to be one, but it had what every other aspect of society has, class wars. BB had more money since it was in the suburbs, and those people had money to send their kids there. CIBA is a broke-as-shit school and must give their kids borderline coloring books to learn how to write and figure out math.

They say it's all the same faith, that we're all born-again Christians. In my mind, and my mind was influenced by my mom's mind, if being born-again is not just a movement but a network of others who believe the same way and how it's the absolute truth that we are all in this together, then why don't these larger churches give to the lesser ones struggling in poorer areas?

The schools that preached the message needed help, but kids got turned away. It was supposed to be a hippie-like brotherhood that bonded people together to be better people. My mom fell for it and gave everything she had towards it, believing it was a system that would comfort her and take care of her and her children. She thought and convinced me no matter where I went within the boundaries of the faith, we were all born-again Christians and would accept each other no matter what. We are supposed to look out for each other because the ugly, secular world is full of monsters.

Their message that hooked my mom in 1982 about how God loves her, and we are all one under him, and we are all one brother and sisterhood, went to shit when they kicked out her son, who was the product of born-again teaching. If everyone under God is the same, those fuckers should have let me graduate and get something out of my devotion to their primitive belief system that only works if you give up logical thought.

But that's not what happened. So, instead, I sicked Ray on them. We got through most of the morning without being noticed. I have no idea how. Most of the kids I was friends with were happy to see me. My favorite teacher, who seemed to like me and would have been the teacher to "get me" if we were in a normal school, was pleased to see me and asked how I was doing.

Our presence caused a commotion during the lunch break. Ray hung out with Mary and her friends at one table while I sat with Uriah, Mike Harmata, and my friends from BB. Ray loved the attention he was getting from the girls. He got so loud talking to them that an adult figure caught wind that we were there, and all hell broke loose.

The ones that called the shots saw that a worldly kid was in their building, and he was with the return of the closest thing to the anti-Christ these people had known in 1995 (me). They quickly asked who brought us in that day, and Mary, with her Kenzo courage, said she did and thought it was okay since other people had brought kids in for visits before. But the other kids didn't bring in someone who was kicked out and considered a bad influence on kids with his music taste.

Pastor Love and the other school authority figures were trying to get us out, and it was making a scene. Ray loved making scenes and running his mouth during conflicts. The adults were slowly but surely getting us to leave the building. We were in the basement area near the classrooms, and the only way out was upstairs through the front doors. As they kicked us out (me for the second time), Ray was having a fit. He wanted to stay for the day and didn't think we did anything wrong.

Ray was cursing up a storm, making fun of their God and beliefs, making sure everyone heard him. I was on the calmer side and didn't want to be ugly about being there. I didn't want them to say how right they were about me and how no good I was. As we left through the main doors, Ray was fighting with Mrs. Skogen about God. She tried to throw some bible verses at him to show who was boss. Ray did not like it and did something I don't condone, but it happened anyway. While Mrs. Skogen was pushing us out the door, Ray spit on her face.

I was talking to Mrs. Skogen nicely as we were leaving and wasn't trying to be disrespectful. When Ray spat on her, I was appalled. I knew he had gone too far. I didn't even know why he did it. It wasn't like he was wronged by them like I was. He barely knew them.

If Ray was mad at Mrs. Skogen because she was the last face he saw as we got kicked out, that's fine. But it shouldn't have made him so mad to spit on another human being.

After that insulting gesture, we made our way to the main street as fast as possible. I was afraid they would call the cops on us over what Ray did, but they didn't.

Ray, Donna, Kathy, and I prepared for the Bensalem bible thumper event of the year, graduation. None of us drove, so we took buses up to the school. Donna used her eyeliner to write "R.E.M." and "666" on my shaved head. We got there right before it started. The place was packed with Xians from the school and their families. There were over a hundred people in attendance.

Michele Kelly met us at the door. She thought I should show up to see Uriah graduate. I don't know if she knew of my plan to make a scene and get a little revenge for myself. But she didn't seem to care when we all walked up, the girls looking like they were going to a gothic dance club and me with makeup and 666 written on my head.

There were no seats open in the packed room except in the front. Being up front for R.E.M. sounds great, but being up front for a sermon from people who think everything I am was a sin and will judge me nonstop is another thing. We all held hands, including Michele, and walked up to the 3rd pew in the church. We sat down and let the murmuring cease about how odd we looked in a room full of people in their Sunday best.

Almost every time there is a large gathering of people, the born-againers see an opportunity to preach their sales pitch about Jesus and how being saved is the only way to heaven. It may be a funeral, a wedding, or a graduation. They will preach their gospel and try to convert as many folks to their belief system as possible. This night was no different. The preacher talked about living for Jesus and not the world and hinted that he was talking about us. Ray didn't like this.

Ray was not helping the situation. He would laugh at parts of the sermon he thought were total bullshit. I was fine silently protesting and making a scene without much backlash besides making the Xians a little uncomfortable. Ray was out for total disturbance.

Mrs. Skogen knew she couldn't kick us out since it was a public event, and we were invited. She saw Ray, the kid who spit on her a day or two earlier, wearing his hat in church. That was a no-no in God's house. I don't know where it says, "Thou shalt not wear a cloth covering over thy head" in the bible, but this was one of the rules I was raised on. Ray was never a fan of authority, and when Mrs. Skogen asked him to remove his hat, he loudly refused. This led to a back-and-forth between Mrs. Skogen and Ray. I was scared he would spit on her again in front of everyone.

Uriah's mom got involved and tried to get Ray to remove the hat. She yelled at him and told us we were ruining Uriah's graduation. I disagreed with that. I knew Uriah like no one else, and I think he thought I made his graduation more interesting. While the arguing continued, someone (probably Pastor Love) called the cops on us. I wish I could have heard that 911 call. Calling the cops because four teenagers were dressed worldly, and one wouldn't take his hat off. Since we were in the suburbs and not much else was going on, two cops showed up. The four of us were told we had to leave. If we didn't, we would get escorted out. We caved.

We got up and walked to the front, where there was a huge window. We could see everything happening in the church, and the church could see everything happening in the lobby. All the Xians were staring at us with disgust and judging eyes. I wanted to give them all the middle finger and tell them how much their faith ruined me for life. Instead, we walked back to the lobby to talk to the cops about staying.

The cops seemed to think it wasn't a big deal and not worth a phone call. They were talking to Pastor Love, almost out the door, while the preacher kept preaching to the choir about how they're the only ones who have it right.

I told Uriah's mom I wanted to see my best friend graduate, and they made a big deal out of nothing. Ray finally agreed to take his hat off, and they allowed us to watch the rest of the graduation from the back. Meanwhile, churchgoers were peaking back at us through the window, most likely hoping we would be led out in handcuffs for wearing a hat indoors. But since everything seemed to calm down, the cops left without anyone getting arrested.

I watched the rest of the graduation with the satisfaction that I made their special night (which was also supposed to be my special night) a little less special. It was a small victory, but I took what I could get.

Afterward, I expected Uriah's mom to be mad at me and Ray, but she wasn't. She made sure we got pictures together with Uriah in the parking lot. Uriah and I were still close friends. I was glad to see that BB accomplished something good in our lives. They kicked me to the curb, but at least they let Uriah and Mary graduate from a somewhat decent school after those bleak years at CIBA and Maranatha.

After graduation, most people got in their cars and drove home. Me and Ray, as usual, waited for what seemed like hours for the bus to take us from BB in suburbia back to our homes and the reality of being poor and useless. It was the last time I ever stepped foot in BB. I drove by it with friends through the years and always gave it the middle finger. My small revenge that night of Uriah's graduation was the best I could do since I was so limited.

Future events made me think, "Maybe there is a God and maybe God is on my side." Later that year, Mr. Birdwhislte (or however you spell his name) died. He was an older man, so it wasn't that strange, but he died right after kicking me out of school and ruining me.

Then I found out that the principal of BB, Pastor Love's daughter Tonya's heart finally went, and she died young at 16. She was the girl at BB that I was sort of close to in my time there and she was born with a bad heart that the doctors all said she wouldn't live a full life. And they were right. I was sad since I cared about Tonya, and we bonded during my time at BB. But I also thought, "Pastor Love, where is your messiah now?"

Then society gave Bensalem Baptist the big middle finger. BB stood on Richlieu Rd., about a half mile from Street Rd. (I know, who names a road "Street?"). Between the church and Street Rd. is a huge open area, home to the evils of gambling at a horse racing track. It didn't really bother those at BB since it was low-key, and the races weren't 24/7. This changed in 2009 when someone opened Parx Casino in the open space for 24/7 gambling. Then, they expanded with a second building for more continuous gambling and a concert center to play good old rock music in BB's backyard. All that sinning is right in their view. That's some good old karma at work (if I believed in such a thing).

Chapter 19:
Frustrated Incorporated

Ray and I moved to Wildwood for the summer on Memorial Day weekend. I was looking forward to going to my beloved shore town, hoping for many cool experiences with other kids looking for the same.

It would be my first time in Wildwood without adult supervision and the longest I ever stayed there. Our place was in the middle of town, half a mile from the boardwalk and beach. The room we stayed in was the size of a bedroom, and it only had two twin beds, a sink, a closet, and a bureau. We had to share the showers and bathroom with the other tenants on our floor. I guess I would have called it a hostel if I knew what that was in 1995.

We were close to the area of the town that was party central if you like dancing and going to clubs. People who were single looking for other singles by buying watered-down drinks and listening to crappy techno music. I'd walk around and hear all the bad music coming from cars and clubs, thinking I was in the wrong place. I was starting to hate certain (shallow) people.

Ray and I went right to work at Burger King and were getting settled in a new place. We hung out on the boardwalk, meeting new people and having fun. We also ran into people from previous summers and picked up where we left off. One of those people was Tara (Glitter). Glitter and I "dated" (made out) a lot the summer prior but didn't talk much during the off-season. I met with her and her friend, a Dolores O'Riordan (The Cranberries) super fan. Like me with Stipe, she tried to look like her idol as much as possible. She had short hair like Dolores and dyed it to whatever color she had in the latest Cranberries video. She was a cute girl who liked to be called Dolores for fun.

One night, Ray was somewhere else, and I went to see who I could find on the boardwalk. I ran into Tara and her friend. The girls were roughly my age (maybe a year younger), and a taller guy, about 19-20, seemed to be bothering them.

He was trying to hit on Tara's friend, and she wasn't having any of it. She whispered to me, asking for help with the guy. Jokingly I said, in my best George McFly (*Back to the Future*) impression, "Hey you, get your damn hands off of her!" I don't know if he knew what I was referring to or if he knew I was kidding, but either way, he got flustered and walked off, never to be seen again.

I hung out with the girls all night and made out with "Dolores." She was the first girl I kissed since Laura. My first stumble back to kissing girls and putting my love for Laura on the shelf. Not too high on the shelf, but on the shelf, nonetheless.

A day or two later, Tara gave me a letter telling me how much it hurt her that I kissed her friend and how much she liked me. I was not ready for a relationship. I was okay meeting new people and connecting with them, but I was still a mental and emotional headcase and knew I only loved one girl. As the summer went on, and even further, I would tell girls that I went out with how I loved Laura, and one day we would be together again.

I don't know how the girls put up with me when I told them this, but they did. I guess in the mid-'90s, having low self-esteem was in style, so the girls didn't mind being with a guy who loved another girl. When I showed the letter from Tara to Ray, he pretended to eat it and said it was bullshit. I wasn't even thinking about jumping into a relationship that quickly, especially that soon into the summer. But I knew what Ray was getting at. I shouldn't get caught up with any girl that summer. Don't let any of them reel me in with sappy talk.

Tara was a part-time Wildwood girl. She would come down for a week or two, then leave for a while to be back later. If we had a relationship, it wouldn't last. So, we hung out that night on the beach (her Cranberries friend already went home) and made out. She tried to talk about her letter, and I changed the subject. I told her I liked her too but wasn't ready for a relationship. She came in and out of my life through the years, but that was the end of our semi-romance.

When we were on the beach, she tried to get me to look at the bright side of life. She pointed at the Ferris wheel and said it looked beautiful. I argued, "That's not beautiful. That's a bunch of nuts and bolts put together by men to sell cheap thrills." I pointed at the moon over the night ocean, its glow reflecting on top of the water, and said, "Now, that's beautiful." I missed Laura very much at that moment.

Chapter 20:
Fake Plastic Trees

The first month of the summer was slow until schools let out and families came down on vacation. Ray and I just worked and walked around, trying to keep occupied. Weekends in June were lively, but the weekdays were boring. People were down, but not as many as peak summer would bring.

I drifted apart from the local kids I had known for years. I was in a different crowd now that liked my type of music and enjoyed things more than sports. One girl I used to know saw my fingernails painted and told other kids we knew I smashed my fingertips with a hammer. It was a blueish-black color, so I guess she assumed that's what I did.

I wasn't the same person I was in '93/94. I was stuck in my head, trying to keep myself up and fighting off demons. I wasn't sure who I was supposed to be around people I hadn't seen in a year, and if I acted a certain way, it would be considered fake. I never wanted to be fake. I thought that being "fake" got me into this numbing mess.

I mistakenly thought some people around me were fake. I was confusing fake with shallowness or not wanting to think outside one's comfort zone. I thought the Christians were phony, but they were just shallow and too afraid to live to get past their beliefs. It was religion that was fake.

I was obsessed with being real and feeling real. I was extra self-conscious about my interactions with people. This caused me to steer from acting happy if I wasn't since that would be fake. I didn't know if I wanted to have conversations with people unless it was about music or theories on life or religion since these were the things that were important to me. If I talked about something else, I would be faking it or avoiding what was bothering me, as I did with the mall kids.

Most of these past friends of mine knew something was off with me, including the woman who worked at my favorite Wildwood store, Cookie's Fun Shop. She was an adult I trusted and could talk to. She knew something was wrong when I first came in to say hi at the beginning of the summer. I did not go into detail about my mental state but told her about BB and getting kicked out and how I lost Laura. I would talk to this woman via phone during the off-season. I mentioned how I met Laura and how happy I was. She knew the loss was tragic for me, and I told her I felt numb, and my feelings were muffled. She gave me some advice and told me I needed to take care of myself. If only it was that easy.

Chapter 21:
We're the Kids in America

As the summer picked up, more and more kids were coming down. The kids I knew from previous summers were coming down more, and I introduced them to Ray, including my cousin Mike. They quickly became friends. Since I always introduced Mike as "Cousin Mike," Ray called him that too.

I introduced Ray to my friend Robyn and her boyfriend, Ryan. Robyn's family had a house on the outskirts of Wildwood, and she was down for pretty much the entire summer. With Robyn came her cute friend Stacey. We ran into them one night on the boardwalk, and before I knew it, we were hanging out most of the time at Robyn's family home, which had a microwave and a TV. Robyn's mom was such a cool mom that we all called her "mom." She let us hang out and sleep over throughout the summer.

We listened to our CDs and the alternative rock music station and watched MTV, which always pumped out alt-rock videos. Mom always had soda and snacks and made me my first veggie burger. Robyn was also a vegetarian and made sure we had something to eat at the house. She was a hippie, full of love and kindness. She loved all sorts of rock music, but like all of us, she craved modern rock the most.

Robyn and Stacey were both skinny girls with long, straight blonde hair. They were from the same town and school in New Jersey. Thanks to their similar taste in music and closeness in age, we hit it off. Things went well for everyone except for poor Ryan.

Ray set his eyes on Robyn. He liked her and wanted to be in a relationship with her. Ray didn't care that Robyn had a boyfriend. He wanted her, and he was going to get her. It brought out a side of Ray I had not seen before. It changed our relationship and ruined my chance of a calm, healing summer in my beloved vacation spot.

Chapter 22:
Alone and an Easy Target

In 1995, alternative music was at its peak in popularity. Almost every kid I met was into an alt-rock band. It dominated the rock part of popular music. Ray didn't care about rock music or anything that came with it. He was a rap fan and wasn't interested in anything that might trigger negative emotions or thinking beyond what was in front of him.

It didn't bother me because he was my friend and made me laugh. He was there for me when I needed him and had more backbone than I did. I felt safe when he was around since he had my back and was such a strong personality. Unfortunately, this changed over the summer.

Ray liked some rock songs but was never crazy about deep music. I don't even think he owned any albums besides Snoop Doggy Dogg. He always wanted thrills, mainly sexual ones, and didn't think deeper than that. He started to like other stuff besides rap in the spring and wanted to see Letters to Cleo. But he didn't own an album by them; he just liked the one video they had out and had a crush on the girl singer. So, when he suddenly changed into an alt-rock king overnight, it was a bit strange.

I am not one to judge anyone. I was the king of "whatever makes you happy." So be it if Ray wanted to listen to alt-rock to broaden his horizons. Maybe music would do for him what it did for me. My favorite musical artist influenced me so much that it changed my life and thought patterns.

Unfortunately, Ray didn't want to listen to bands and get into them naturally. Instead, he pretended to be into them since day one and just to show how different and deep he was. He was the definition of a poser. But it was more than him pretending to be cool or like the other kids who liked popular rock music. He was trying to fool them into thinking he was something he wasn't by manipulation and being what I hated the most: fake.

I noticed his personality change after we met more and more alt-rock girls. I am not the most underground guy. I didn't own Nirvana's *Bleach* until after Cobain died because I didn't know it existed. I wasn't there for R.E.M. in 1983. But I will be the first to admit they were huge. Even if no one I knew liked them, they were still popular and mainstream.

Ray acted like he was the king of alt-rock since the dawn of time. He bought albums and pretended to be a lifelong fan. All the CDs in our place were mine, but Ray acted like they were his. He bought clothes more in line with being into alt-rock, including a bunch of Nirvana and NIN shirts. He was trying to be something without the merit behind it.

On one occasion, Ray and Robyn were roaming the boardwalk one night when they came across some of the kids who were staples to the Wildwood kids with no hope scene, kids that were a bit older than us and were seemed to be jobless and on some sort of drug. One of the people was this guy who always wore black, had dyed bleached blonde hair to his shoulders and often wore dark makeup on his eyes. He was known to be a wild guy and a big off his rocker. He had Charles Manson vibe to him and sense of danger when he was near.

On this night, Robyn, who talked to everyone and wanted to visit all those she considered to be her friends, dragged Ray to where this guy was hanging at. He was with his friends and was most likely on something. He took out a razor blade and started to cut his arm up and then his tongue, letting his mouth get full of blood. Ray made a comment about how fucked up that was, and this guy said to Ray while he was wearing a NIN shirt, "I bet you're a real Nine Inch Nails fan too?" Ray told me this story after it happened that night and he told me he felt embarrassed and after that is when Ray really put his act in full swing. He was trying to out crazy the crazies.

Soon, Ray started to say he was a bigger NIN fan than me. He knew not to mess with R.E.M. but went after the other ones I loved. I was mentally vulnerable and easy for the picking. Ray was showing his true colors. He was a sociopath and a manipulator. He was a conman and was starting to adapt to my personality and identity.

My theory is he saw that everyone we hung out with was into alt-rock for quite some time. He saw the writing on the wall and realized he had to adapt and see where it would take him. He didn't own an album by NIN in June, but by July, he was wearing their shirts and pretending to be the biggest fan. I didn't have a problem with him buying the shirt. It was the pretending and bullying that bothered me.

He would meet kids wearing NIN shirts and ask them what their favorite album was. When they said they only had one album by them, Ray would call them a poser and say they weren't real fans. It was the definition of the pot calling the kettle black.

It was uncanny. He was calling people out for precisely what he did a month earlier. He didn't care. It wasn't about the music or being the biggest fan. It was about manipulating sensitive kids who were drawn to this sort of music.

He was a diabolical genius with his manipulation of people. I would have called him out or put him in his place if I wasn't out of my mind. I lacked the courage to say something. I just went with the flow. He used this for his own gain.

If I had a bad day of anxiety or compulsive thoughts, he would tell me I was making it all up and that I wasn't depressed. When I tried to explain my mindset, he would laugh at me and tell me I was faking it, making me feel worse.

He would follow this up by complimenting me or bringing up how much I loved Laura and how real that love was. It was like beating a dog for an hour and then giving it a treat to make it love you.

Ray's conman way was to stop the only person who could tell the truth about him and his fake façade, so he could get into alt-rock girls (ripped-up) pants. He saw my weakness and used it against me. He made me doubt myself so much that I went along with what he was doing.

Part of me hoped I was jumping to conclusions, and he was actually finding himself. But it wasn't just about his alt-rock image con. He was trying to con people into changing their relationships and playing with people's minds.

It all happened during the summer, but it took until the fall to cut ties with Ray. I needed to escape from my problems, and Wildwood was my usual haven for a breather. Living in a room with a conman ruined that for me. Wildwood that year was anything but a break from my problems and a place to get my thoughts and feelings together. Instead, I was a prisoner in my head and in my room. It left me far worse than I was before the summer.

Chapter 23:
It's a Shame About Ray

Ray started to use his conman ways to manipulate the two young lovers, Robyn and Ryan, out of love. Robyn accepted everyone for who they were and took people at their word. She was too trusting (she and I shared these personality traits). Ryan had a "couldn't hurt a fly" personality. He was a down-to-earth fellow who would have a beer with just about anyone and always had a smile on his face.

The previous summer, the two were just friends. However, romance blossomed during the off-season in their New Jersey suburban hometown. They were back this summer as a couple. Ray had his work cut out for him. I guess he sensed a mutual attraction with Robyn and felt they should be together, and damn the feelings of nice guy Ryan. He had to convince Robyn (and me) how bad of a guy Ryan was and how he didn't deserve Robyn.

The problem was Ryan was a good guy and never did anything wrong to Robyn. I think Ray saw him as a bit of a jock/frat kid, and now that Ray was parading around like the alt-rock king, he thought Robyn wanted a guy like him. Well, a guy that he was pretending to be like.

Ray knew the right trigger words and buttons to push to get me on board with his scheme. He would say how "fake" Ryan was and how Robyn was only with him because she didn't think she could do better due to her low self-esteem. He said she was a beautiful person that he was falling in love with. It pulled at my heartstrings and made me go along with what Ray wanted. He found ways to make Ryan look dumb or not really into alt-rock, claiming he only acted like he was into it because it was the trend.

Ray was like Donald Trump before 2016 Donald Trump. He would accuse someone of what he did without a second thought, using his faults against people. He didn't care about being a hypocrite; he only cared about what he wanted. Ray was constantly making fun of Ryan behind his back to Robyn, and sometimes right in front of him, without Ryan knowing.

Ryan didn't see what was happening. He thought Ray was just another kid out for a good time with kids his age. Poor Ryan never stood a chance against Ray's diabolical mind. Ray was extremely clever and knew how to play people. I don't know if he was always this way or if it was a personality trait he acquired throughout the last few months. But it consumed him.

Ray was developing a huge ego. He thought he was the greatest thing to happen to everyone he met. He thought he was the smartest guy in every room he entered and thought everyone else was inferior to him. This sudden rush of him thinking he was an alt-rock god/genius happened quick. I can't even pinpoint when it occurred.

Even with my mental fog, I had a sense of what was happening with Ray. I knew he was putting on a new identity to fit in. I was okay with this and thought it was just a part of his journey to be a better person. In reality, he saw a bunch of kids (mostly girls) who were easily manipulated and successfully entered this alt-rock world of 50-100 kids in Wildwood. It went to his head. He used his false feelings to feed off their real emotions.

His ego got worse when he finally got what he wanted. He thought he was a mental giant after successfully breaking up a couple of teenagers. It took a week or so of implanting thoughts in Robyn's head about how wonderful and genuine Ray was and how Ryan was a loser who didn't treat her how she should be treated. Only the troubled soul of Ray could do that. She fell for it, and they hooked up one day when Ryan wasn't around.

When Ryan found out about it, he went on a rampage. It was his breaking point, and he decided to confront Ray about him stealing his girlfriend. Ryan (with Robyn close behind) stormed over to our place, and a shouting match occurred. It was Ryan's last shot with Robyn, and Ray used it to his advantage.

Ryan was angry (rightfully so) and looking for a fight. His demeanor didn't gel with a laidback, pacifist like Robyn and her hippy way of life. Ryan played right into Ray's hands. Robyn saw how angry Ryan got. Ray acted like he didn't want to fight Ryan but egged him on, making him look like a fool. When Ray ended the confrontation, he painted Ryan as the dumb, yelling bad guy and himself as the edgy, rebel-like cool kid with all the excitement a teenage girl would want.

Ray told Ryan he did this to himself. He said he was coming at him like he wanted to fuck him, then boldly pulled out his penis and said, "Here, Ryan, you want to suck my dick?" It made me do a double-take. Ryan didn't stand a chance and left with his tail between his legs.

They broke up soon after, and Ryan went home instead of spending the summer with his girlfriend and enjoying his teenage life. Ray did this. He ruined this kid's plans for the summer and opened a world of hurt because he wanted something he couldn't have. He created a problem in Ryan and Robyn's relationship that wasn't there. And I went along with it, like a putz, like the broken human I was.

Chapter 24:
State of Love and Trust

Now that Ray and Robyn were a couple, Ray and I spent much time with Robyn and Stacey at Robyn's summer home. We watched MTV as much as we wanted and ate food that wasn't from the boardwalk (which was mainly carnival food). We could eat something with nutrition and substance since Robyn and her mom were vegetarians.

Since Ray and Robyn were a thing, it was only a matter of time before Stacey and I became a couple. I thought Stacey was cute and fun to hang out with. I didn't know if I liked her more than that, but I went with the flow. She would be the first girl since Laura that I had some commitment to.

Stacey was a spunky, skinny blonde who went to high school with Robyn. She was a bit dramatic and once told me that her friend who died in a car accident was her guardian angel now and always around her. Then the wind blew (since we were sitting on the beach facing the ocean), and she said it was her friend proving he was there. I knew this was nonsense, but I let her think it anyway.

I dated her for a month or so. Most of the time, I was barely there emotionally. I was just going through the motions of being in a relationship that I knew wouldn't last since Laura and I would be together again soon. I even told her that. She was more vibrant than I was. She was eager to make out and go further physically. I had some fun, but my heart was never in it.

She was also the first girl I met who called rock stars "hot." She thought the guys in Bush were really hot. It seemed a bit shallow to me, and I figured that if it was 1985 instead of 1995, Stacey would have been a hair metal fan and would have said Mötley Crüe was hot.

The emergence of bands like Bush (who started getting huge) and Alanis Morissette was my first notion that this alt-rock thing wasn't as great as I thought. These were two acts that Stacey loved, and I thought they were okay but not nearly as good as R.E.M., Nirvana, and Tori Amos.

Don't get me wrong, at the time I was on board with any artist lumped in with alt-rock. However, I look back on that summer and realize it was the beginning of the cracks in it, and not everything considered "alt-rock" means it's artsy or had merit.

These acts weren't all bad. I liked some of their music (especially Alanis) but was catching on that bands like Bush were writing songs and lyrics that were mediocre but held up to the same limelight as bands like Nirvana. Stacey saying the singer from Bush was hot and how great she thought they were made me wise up. I was lucky enough to enter my love for music at the point when bands with merit were hitting the mainstream, and I thought it would last forever.

That summer was the beginning of what I later realized made Cobain so depressed. A bunch of good bands with merit were taking over the airwaves and influencing kids to think about important things, so the record industry machine pushed any band with long hair who knew power chords. They were selling themselves as angry and depressed. This wake-up call got even louder that summer when Silverchair, who was taking off in popularity, was considered to be in the same ballpark as Pearl Jam. "Industry plants" is the term that comes to mind in such situations.

There were a lot of copycats and wolves in sheep's clothing surfacing, and this alt-rock thing that I thought was based on wanting to change the world and be more thought-provoking was turning into a competition on who was the angriest and most disturbed. It led to the popularity of the worse type of music (in my opinion), the nu-metal bullshit that started that year with a shit band called Korn.

One night, Stacey wanted to be alone with me to have sex. I was not ready for it, but I went with the flow.

I didn't mind making out but going all the way brought on anxiety for me for quite some time.

Most 17-year-old kids would be excited that their girlfriends wanted to have sex with them. I probably would have if it was Laura and I was mentally sound. But I felt anxiety that I wouldn't be able to perform well enough for Stacey. I was worried about my penis being too small and Stacey telling people. I was concerned that I wouldn't last long without having an orgasm. I was worried about everything.

We went into the room Stacey and Robyn shared in the house they stayed at. We made out and started getting naked for sexual intercourse. It would be the second time I tried to have sex. The first time didn't last long due to my partner seeming bored. This time it was over quickly because I panicked and climaxed too fast. Perhaps a self-fulfilling prophecy. The exact opposite of what one wants to do in this situation.

I had an erection, so obviously, my body wanted to have sex, but the moment the act began, it felt like the weight of the world was on my shoulders. It felt like I was doing something wrong with someone I didn't have love or strong affection for. I tried to push these thoughts out and live in the moment, which led me to think I didn't know what I was doing and how to pleasure her. I thought I didn't have what it takes to be good at this and that I won't be able to keep up, and only an external force could help, and a good thing wasn't going to help since I was "sinning."

I thought I was just a little kid in over his head and would let Stacey down. I got too excited over how good it felt. I was also scared about not having control of the situation, so the experience only lasted a couple minutes.

I was glad to get it over with. It was like I had to do it, like a chore or a part of being an adult. After this embarrassing moment, we got up, and I felt self-pity. I knew the consequences of trying to be something I wasn't. Ray and others would talk about me and how bad I was, making me the laughingstock in our little group.

I started to think I could never have sex; another thing God or life would get me with. The only comfort I got at this moment was the song playing on the radio, "Immortality," from my beloved Pearl Jam.

I might have had a moment of sheer embarrassment, but I felt like my old self for a second and took comfort in Eddie Vedder's melodies.

I was already a mess mentally, but I now thought I was lousy at something that would be a part of my life in the future. I was once again thinking way too much and beating myself up for being a 17-year-old boy who was panicky about his second attempt at sex. I believed (like my feelings being gone forever) that this problem would be forever, and I deserved it. It was either how bad I was at everything in life ("I'm worse at what I do best") or because I was sinning and the Christians were right about everything. These were irrational thoughts, and I was again jumping to conclusions out of sheer panic and a negative outlook on life.

After this night, my damaged pride made me want to get away from Stacey as soon as possible. Then Robyn got into a fight with her, and she moved back to her house in New Jersey. I was glad to see her go; one last reminder of how I am worse at what I do best.

Chapter 25:
In That Great Street Carnival

By June, Ray had become a social butterfly with the Wildwood kids. It led to the one good thing he did for me that summer. My low self-esteem will always hold me back from things in life, and in 1995, I didn't think I could get another job in Wildwood besides at Burger King. Ray knew I hated it. I was a vegetarian touching dead meat all day. I did it because I needed a job. I was desperate.

Ray met someone who worked for a guy named Joe, who owned several games on one of the three amusement piers. He talked to Joe and got a job. He told me Joe would also hire me if I talked to him. I did this and was offered a job operating one of the carnival games.

I was scared I wouldn't be good at the job and was weary of quitting my secure job. But Ray talked me into it. He told me I could do it and how silly I was for thinking I couldn't do a simple job like working at a game. So, one day I didn't show up for my shift at Burger King and started working as a carnie instead. Ray was good for pushing me out of my comfort zone, even when it wasn't good for me, but this time it was the best move. He was right. The job wasn't hard at all.

As for seasonal Wildwood jobs, working at an amusement pier was a huge step up from fast food. For years I thought it impossible to get into that type of work. Yet here I was, operating games and being a part of the fun that people (who couldn't afford Disneyworld) did to feel like they were on vacation to take their minds off everyday life.

Instantly I knew I was not a good carnie. I didn't try to bring people over with a sales pitch and didn't care if people played the games. I was already of the mindset that money was bullshit. It was based on a manmade concept of worth from things that can't even back it up now. I understood that money and the economic system were to keep the hamster wheel running and to keep people fed and clothed without becoming a welfare state. However, I viewed things like boardwalk games as a waste of money and time.

Getting people to waste their money was how carnies made their living. I didn't want to be an obnoxious carnie type who calls people over to play the games I was running. I didn't want to be "that guy."

I thought the same thing about the rides at the park. I watched people stand in line for hours to ride a rollercoaster that would only give them a minute or two thrill. It didn't seem worth the wait. And it seemed people would wait that long because it was what you were supposed to do on vacation in Wildwood. It made the hours of waiting normal since everyone else was doing it.

I didn't want to waste my free time. I knew I had to work minimum wage jobs due to my stature in life. But I would rather listen to music, write (bad) poetry, or hang out with cool people I met that summer rather than do things I thought were distractions from our dull lives.

Out of the ten games (and a snack bar) that Joe owned on the pier, you think I would have been placed at the least popular rides with less traffic (like the duck pond game where you pay a buck to pick a rubber duck out of a pool of water to win a cheap prize). Everyone started working on the smaller games, but a few days later, you usually got put on a better game. The biggest money maker was the frog toss game in front of the pier. Joe, his wife, and the other adults who helped run the games mainly stayed there.

The other big money maker was the classic game of hitting stacked bottles off a table with small bean bags. It was located by two popular rides on their pier, the main rollercoaster on that side of the boardwalk and the Music Express, which was a ride where you sat in a booth and went really fast in a circle formation. I was placed at this game for most of my time working for Joe.

I guess it was a good fit. I drew a lot of business because of my game booth's location. I made tons of money for Joe, but not because of my carnie skills. I was at the right spot to do a half-ass job and still bring in cash. I mostly sat there writing poems on my notepad and talking to friends I made through the job who worked near me.

I befriended the guy who operated the Music Express. One of his duties was to keep the music playing loudly throughout the pier. He was a big alt-rock fan, so I brought 20 of my CDs for him to put on during his shift. We had two shifts for this job - 10-6 pm and 4pm - closing (usually at midnight or 1 am, depending on how many people were still consuming all the Wildwood fun).

I got to hear my favorite songs throughout my shift. However, during peak hours (8-11), the music had to be top 40 dance shit that was super popular. Songs like "Cotton Eye Joe" got played three times a night. It drove me nuts. Then groups like the Real McCoy and songs like "I'm the Scatman" would blast all night.

The guy who operated the ride knew how much I hated that sort of music and would throw me a bone with a Red Hot Chili Peppers or Beastie Boys song that was upbeat but had some merit. After long hours of listening to mindless dance pop, I knew it was all over for the night when I heard one of my CDs being played. I would hear a song from the Smashing Pumpkins or Live and feel relieved.

We got paid under the table (no taxes and more money in my pocket). It was $5 an hour and time and a half for anything over 40 hours. We would often work doubles to make more money. We were making a lot more money than before and hanging out with all kinds of new people from the pier.

I was even a little close with my bosses. Well, two of them. Joe's wife was very nice. She liked me since I wore my heart on my sleeve and was always talking about poetry and music.

She had the same passions. She would encourage me to write and to get my GED since I told her about my schooling situation.

She might have been right, but I wasn't ready to go down that path. I thought life or fate would set me right. I just had to stay on its path. Somehow it would work out for me. I had time, right?

Chapter 26:
Army of Me

Working at this job gave me a lot more time to think. Since I was in a better place financially, doing a job I didn't hate, my mental health improved. I watched and met people all day who came back and forth to see me and the game. Now that my confidence was getting a little better, so was my outlook on life. I had more time to ponder my favorite subject - life and the point of existence.

I theorized that life is just negative and positive energies at war, and we are pawns in this war. I thought perhaps that negative and positive energy was pulling at us in our minds and emotions and how each can't exist without the other.

I was working out the religious cobwebs in my head. Finding a compromise between what I was taught and what I thought made sense since what I was taught didn't make any sense. I didn't believe there could be a physical place like heaven or hell because if we had a soul, it wouldn't feel physical pain after death.

I thought they were metaphors for periods in one's life. If one stays with the positive or good parts of life and is focused on that side, it will lead to "heaven" (a good time period). I came up with patterns of people, including myself. With almost every theory or rabbit hole I go down, I use myself as the prime example. If one chooses to be positive or good, it will use the same energy amount as a negative mindset.

I also concluded that there was no progress or anything that came out of being negative. While being positive would only lead to progression and things that would bring one toward "heaven." I thought that in every situation, one has the choice to give in to negativity or to look at the positive. You can only choose one to get the feeling and adapt it to your life. I pondered these things sober, operating a game on a busy boardwalk during the peak of summer.

Every time something happened, I could go down the road of negativity and accomplish nothing for the greater good or focus on the positivity and get what I was supposed to from the situation. If a girl calls me ugly, I could start feeling ugly and sorry for myself, which wouldn't accomplish anything. The other option would be to listen to a song or write down how I felt and create something progressive and worth experiencing.

I was coming to terms with Christianity and trying to find a happy medium. It had tones of the new age religion I heard about from Ed in Virginia during Thanksgiving of '94. I was trying to find meaning in life and something positive that could come out of my struggles. Since I felt better, I wanted to live and figure things out. I wasn't committed to anything. Through all the years of trying to figure out life and God, I always keep my mind open to new ideas and thoughts that my brain processes from experiences.

My thought pattern was leaning toward bright, positive energy that I wanted to be a part of. I believed the more I thought about positive things, like music or Laura, in stressful times, the better I felt for staying positive and not wasting energy on negative thoughts.

The problem with this thinking was that my doubts and negative thoughts would use this against me. I thought these doubts and bad memories were connected to the negative energy that fed off me.

It wasn't that crazy. If my doubts made me feel bad, I would go down a hole of self-pity and an overwhelming sensation of not being good enough. If I listened to the part of me that I felt was the real me, I would be positive and want to do everything I want in life and be a ball of energy, a light helping others to be full of energy and life. But now that I tried to only think of positive things, my compulsive thoughts would rush in with the most negative thoughts due to my fears that if I don't think of it, these things would come true or if I was too positive, life would punish me with negativity.

Man, I was a crazy kid. Most 17-year-olds were trying to get laid or worrying about school. I was doing my best to understand God and the meaning of life (this is what they did to me). I thought maybe the Christians were on to something. Maybe the ones who made the religion got the concept of what I was thinking and made this belief system to help people stay positive and offset their negative feelings and thoughts.

Possibly the concept of God and the devil were to put positive and negative into categories or give them a name to help conceptualize them. And the point they had was to have a collective mindset that would stay positive by wanting to be good (God) and not evil (devil). Then our collective consciousness would help create more positivity in the world.

I wasn't totally on board with this yet I thought about it during my alone time. I think I was giving the makers of religion too much credit. They made the concepts to control and keep order and give one hope that there is an afterlife when they take their final breath.

I didn't always think this way. It was the rabbit hole I was in that summer. I was becoming a borderline hippie and didn't know if this was what I wanted to be. These thoughts didn't crack the big one I always had. Why did there have to be negative and positive, and what came first? One would hope positive energy was first, and somehow negative energy came around. But what if negative was first and always took the lead? What if negativity is the life force, and positivity is just our way of making sense of it? That didn't make sense because nothing productive could come out of the negative thought pattern unless it turned positive.

I eventually theorized that whatever it (God) is must be neutral, and the positive and negative forces or energies were an afterthought or what makes life happen. They are just feelings that stem from being human and being conscious. And maybe you can't have one without the other. Or you can, and I didn't know shit because I was a 17-year-old kid with major anxiety and mental problems, raised in a cult, and now was trying to get rid of the demons and anxiety the only way he knew how, by thinking it out.

Besides all these thoughts, I had other stuff that occupied my mind. I figured my ideas were a work in progress, and I had time to figure it all out. I also thought that the experiences that life threw at me were all part of my development and for me to figure out what I thought everyone figured out on this journey from birth to death.

(Haha, Chaz, Haha).

Chapter 27:
Let Me In

I wasn't always in deep thought and wonder of the universe. I was also meeting people and getting to know anyone who came across my path. Our apartment complex wasn't just for kids who stayed there for the summer. People would come down and rent a room for their week's vacation. One week, Uriah, Mary, Andre, and other people from Bensalem Baptist came down for the week and stayed in our building.

Ray and I went our own ways for days at a time. I would see him at work and our place, but I was running around with other people while he stayed with Robyn most times and of all people, my cousin Mike.

One week I palled around with Uriah and company, and it was a great time. We did more innocent things like swimming at the beach, acting like normal kids. However, I wouldn't remove my shirt since I had mini man boobs. I also didn't put sunblock on my freshly shaved head, and I got a bad sunburn on my scalp. It hurt so bad I couldn't shave it again until it healed. My hair was growing back in over the dead skin. It looked like a layer of skin sitting in my hair. I could take my hand and brush through my scalp, making it look like I had bad dandruff.

Uriah went to someone from Bensalem Baptist's party, and Laura was there. I was so jealous when he told me he saw her in person. But Uriah brought good news.

She told him to tell me if I called her, her mom might let us talk. She also told him she still cared about me and gave him a folded-up piece of paper to give me. It read "Let Me In," the title of the R.E.M. song they wrote in tribute to the late great Kurt Cobain.

It felt good to think of her and comforting to see the song title, knowing it came from her heart. I called her from a payphone on the boardwalk one day after Uriah relayed her message. She answered and asked her mom if we could talk. To my surprise, her mom said it was okay.

We talked about the concerts I went to so far that summer, what I was up to in Wildwood, my thoughts on life and God, and the new music we were listening to. She was really into the latest offering from Annie Lennox. I told her about the R.E.M. concerts I had coming up. She was so happy for me as if she was going too. We admitted how much we still loved and cared for each other. She called me her "Charles" and said to be patient and to wait for her. Like I was going to.

Talking to her, just hearing her voice again, made me feel whole again for a moment. My teenage soulmate was still in love with me. Time to take that one in and dwell on it for a bit, Chazzle Dazzle.

Chapter 28:
Ridiculous Thoughts

Concerts were a big part of my life that summer, even though I was in Wildwood. I would take the bus to see acts like The Cranberries. I went with Johnny M., Rich Torres, Jen (who replaced me in Bensalem Baptist when I got kicked out), Mary M., Uriah, Michelle Kelly, and The Harmatas.

It was odd going with Johnny and Rich to a rock concert after years of them bullying me. Now they embraced what I liked and seemed to respect me for who I was. I found my way and didn't care what they thought anymore. They were on my turf now - a rock show.

Ray stayed in Wildwood for this one, so it was just me and some childhood friends having a good time watching a band I liked a lot. It was comforting. I also showed them I wasn't doing too bad after getting kicked out of school and still had some life in me. Even if I was a bit of a mess inside.

I had a Zen moment when The Cranberries played "Ridiculous Thoughts." I had my own ridiculous thoughts, and it was nice to have a moment to let out a couple tears and vent while I danced my little heart out.

After the show, a drunk Mary kissed me when we hugged goodnight. It was out of nowhere, and I chalked it up to her being buzzed and left it at that. It was another in the heat of a concert moment sort of thing. I have been caught up in such things, like the moment at a show is the only thing that matters, and the good feelings from it made it seem like it would last forever. The type of thing that makes you want to keep this feeling going on forever, the feeling that anything can happen and that being this alive is the key. This happened at Lollapalooza in 1995.

Chapter 29:
Softer, Softest

Lollapalooza came to the Philly area in late July 1995. It was the place to be for the alternative crowd that year. The lineup had alt-rock legends Sonic Youth and every alt-rock girl's favorite band at the time, Hole. Hole was the one I also wanted to see the most. I played their album *Live Through This* a lot when I was getting kicked out of school and losing the love of my life.

We had a good time at the show. I danced up a storm, which I loved to do at shows. We had a good-sized crowd, including Uriah,, and kids we met from Wildwood. We also met more kids we had things in common with, including some girls from Morristown, a suburban town in South New Jersey.

The show was at the Blockbuster Entertainment Center, which we all called the E-Center for short. This was the year it opened, and through the decades, it would change its name numerous times after it exchanged ownership over and over again. But I will never stop calling it the E-Center, even though it was only called that for a few years.

We were on the general admission lawn area on a big hill behind all the good seats. They were considered the bad "seats," but it was where you wanted to be to have fun and party. Ray and I had better seats that we used for Hole, Elastica, and a few other bands. The rest of the time, we stayed with friends on the lawn.

Alternative rock concerts were a place to meet people you had things in common with and would want to see again. I made a bunch of concert buddies for a good part of ten years. You would run into them at different shows and catch up or get their numbers and hang out outside of the shows. It was a great place to network, creating bonds with diverse people over your love of music.

We were talking to three girls from Moorestown, NJ, and I was hitting it off with a cute girl named Megan. She was petite, with short, light brown hair, blue eyes, thick lips, and pale skin. Megan was something else. She was an old soul, and I instantly felt a connection. She wore a homemade Kurt Cobain shirt with a line written on it that her friend came up with, "I liked to wear my heart like a necklace, so I can take it off sometimes" or something like that.

Megan was more into the punky side of alt-rock, including Hole, Nirvana, and Sonic Youth. But she also loved R.E.M. and Tori Amos, so she had my full attention. With her were two other alt-rock girls, Katie and Janine. Bill, a guy we worked with on the Wildwood pier, was hitting it off with Janine. They hung out together for the rest of the show.

Megan was now in my arms as we sat through a band's set, I think Pavement or Beck, when we kissed for the first time. Suddenly someone began yelling at us with what sounded like a voice box, telling us to knock it off. It was Megan's dad sitting behind us. He was there to supervise her and make sure she didn't do anything too wild (like making out with a strange boy).

We stopped kissing and would only continue if her dad wasn't looking or if we went to another part of the venue. At the end of the show, we all exchanged phone numbers. Our number was the front desk's number at our apartment, and the landlord would come and get us if someone called. We had to keep the conversations short. But it did work to keep people in touch with us.

I was used to meeting people at concerts and only seeing them again at another show, so I figured it would be the same with Megan. But she called, and we talked on the phone a couple times. It seemed like she wanted to continue something between us.

During these calls, I learned she was three years younger than me. I thought that would be a problem. Even if I felt a strong connection to her, I didn't know if this was something I wanted to pursue. I thought she would be someone I liked and talked to occasionally, but that would be that. Plus, none of this mattered because I would get back with Laura when she was ready (or so I thought in my naïve mind).

What I didn't know was Ray was talking to Janine off and on, and a plan was hatched for her and her friend, Katie, to run away from home. They needed to escape from their controlling and "abusive" parents (according to Ray). They showed up at our apartment, looking for somewhere to stay a couple of weeks after we met them. Now Megan would be in my life a little longer.

Chapter 30:
Teen Age Riot

Ray and I were always going to be there for any runaway, and we took their word and reason to run at face value. They were on vacation with their parents in New Jersey when they took off and came to us.

Ray and Robyn were still a thing, but the end was near. Robyn was getting tired of Ray, and they were spending less time together. It gave Ray something to pretend to cry about and time to talk to Janine. During these talks, Janine told Ray how bad she had it and how she and Katie couldn't take it anymore. They had to escape their home life.

Ray knew that we couldn't keep them at our place, or we'd get in trouble for hiding runaways. Instead, we used our connections with other teenagers to move the girls from place to place until we could figure something out. Ray was the mastermind here. I just went with the flow again, following his lead. I also believed the girls since I thought most people who liked alt-rock came from broken homes or had similar problems as me.

After the first day or two, Megan called the front desk at my place and asked me if I knew where Katie and Janine were. I believed she was being told to make this call, so I played dumb and acted like I didn't know. Janine's parents knew about a bunch of boys from Wildwood their daughter had met. They had Megan call me to see if I would tell her what was happening.

Since I didn't reveal anything, after a couple days, Janine and Katie's parents went on a rampage looking for their daughters. For some fucking reason, they came after me instead of Ray.

I was working at my bottle game during the day when Janine's dad and mom showed up screaming at me. They swore I knew where they were and would be in trouble if I didn't tell them. I calmly said I didn't know where they were. Then Janine's mom started talking about her love for rock music and being a vegetarian too. Things she knew about me, trying to gain my trust, like she was playing the good cop.

I said, "I don't know what to believe. I hear you're abusing her." The dad then threatened me. It tipped me over my boiling point, and I yelled at him with all the frustrations that I had bottled inside. Months of mental issues from people telling me how terrible I was. I shouted, "You have no fucking idea how much pressure I am under, and I don't fucking know where your kid is!" It was true. The girls were at our friend Apple's (yes, Apple), but I had no idea where that was.

The commotion brought over one of the bosses that ran the entire pier. He came over when the parents started yelling at me. When I hollered back, he stepped in and told me to take a break. While the boss, who was in his 30s, talked to the parents about not yelling at staff members, a cop showed up. The other parents looking for their daughter had brought a cop over to my stand.

The cop told the pier boss I had to go to the police station with them. I was given the cop talk about how much trouble I was in while they asked me again where the girls were. My answers stayed the same.

I knew I couldn't be in that much trouble at age 17, and the cop knew this too. Instead, he came after my job. He asked, "Do you have your boardwalk work license?" I never heard of such a thing (and this was my third job on the boardwalk), so the answer was no. I knew where he was going. He was holding a loophole over my head. No one had a boardwalk work license. I still don't know if he was bluffing, but he was blackmailing me. He said, "Well if you can't turn these girls up, and I know you know where they are, you won't be able to work on the boardwalk anymore."

He turned and gave a nod to the guy running the pier. It was like I walked into some small town in the south and had to do what I was told, or I'd be fucked. I told the cop (in private), "I don't know where they are, but I'll see what I can do." He said, "You better," and I told him I would be in touch.

I returned to the pier and told my boss what was going on. Why he didn't fire me, I'll never know. He just told me to work it out as fast as I could. I went to where Ray was on the pier. He called Apple and told them we must have the girls go back home now that Chaz is losing his job over this. Apple told me to come over. After she gave me the address, I rode someone's bike (I have no idea who's) to the North section of Wildwood.

All the cops in Wildwood were looking for these girls. They had their pictures but couldn't find them. Being the biggest case they would probably have all year, I thought they would be more invested in finding the girls. Meanwhile, I, riding my bike with scratched-up glasses found Katie in 20 minutes, walking from a store back to Apple's friend's house. So much for the Wildwood Police Department.

I went with Katie back to the house, which was really a duplex. I told them what happened and how I lost my job. I asked what they wanted to do, and Katie said she wanted to go home and missed her parents. Katie was younger than Janine and was probably just going along with her friend.

Janine didn't want to go home. She hated her parents. She was having the time of her life, I thought. Hanging out with older teenagers who let her do what she wanted. She was staying on a couch with a cool girl (Apple), watching movies like *The Breakfast Club*, and listening to music. It must have been exciting compared to her boring, suburban life.

I wasn't sure what to do. One girl would go home, and the other wanted to stay on the runaway train. I talked to Ray about it, and we went with what the girls wanted. We set the plan in motion to return Katie to her parents. I told the cops I couldn't turn the girls over now, but I heard from the Wildwood teenager grapevine that they would be at my apartment around 9 pm. It was good enough for Wildwood's chief of police. They set up a sting operation outside of our place that night.

Two cops asked if they could see our place. Since the girls weren't there, we let them in. After realizing no one else was around, they told us we should wash more of our clothes. We didn't do much since we didn't own a washer and had to go to a laundromat. We were dirty kids, but it was the days when grunge was king, so it worked to our advantage.

By nightfall, a cop car was parked in the lot across the street from us, just out of view. A few more officers in street clothes were around the building. Ray and I were sitting on our porch. The plan was for Katie to show up and say that Janine returned home to her place in Morristown. It would get the cops and Janine's parents off my back. Instead, Katie got lost, and it took an hour to find her.

We gave her good directions, but she was young and didn't pay attention. She ended up a mile from us in a dangerous part of town. The cops got a call from another cop car that they found her wandering around the projects of Wildwood. The cops took off like it was a drug raid. They took Katie to her parents, who were waiting at the Wildwood police station, and she told everyone her friend was on her way home on her own. The cops bought it, and the next day I was back at work without a boardwalk working license.

We still had to figure out something with Janine. Ray and I were returning to Philly for a couple shows, and Donna and I were going to camp out for NIN and David Bowie tickets on sale that week for their E-Center show. The plan was to get Janine on a bus with us back to Philly, and then we could get her lost in the shuffle of our Philly friends until Janine wanted to go home.

I talked to Megan right after it all went down, and she told me Janine's parents thought Ray and I were a part of the teenage runaway sex trafficking thing they saw on *20/20*. I had to laugh. I thought that was insane talk, and made me think maybe Janine was getting abused.

A couple nights later, we went for the great escape. We dyed Janine's red hair blonde. We were too scared to walk the few miles to the bus stop, so Ray decided we should take a cab. I didn't like it from the start. I was already feeling nervous and anxious about the whole week, and when the cab came to pick us up, I had an unsettling feeling.

We all got in the back seat of the taxi, and I heard the cabbie radio to someone, "I got them." I looked at Ray and said, "Did you hear that?" He looked at me like I was hearing things, and I thought maybe I was. My heart was pounding, and I was on the edge, full of anxiety. Every car behind us with their headlights burning holes into my neck, I was scared was a cop. I was getting paranoid, but just like Cobain said, paranoia doesn't mean they're not after you.

We exited the cab at the bus stop and went into the lobby to buy bus tickets. The cops swarmed us. Five or six of them ran up to us with a picture of Janine, comparing it to her person, and they knew they had her. The jig was up. They beat us. The police took Janine to her parents and escorted Ray and me to the police station. I was a nervous wreck that week, barely eating and sleeping. Part of me was glad it was over, but what would the cops do now, make me forfeit my job?

The same chief of police I dealt with earlier was sitting in his office when the other cops brought us in. He had a smirk on his face like this was a big bust, like this was something he did on his own and not because Ray and I were sloppy.

I was humble, trying to keep myself composed after the traumatic event I just went through. However, Ray (knowing we were minors and that they couldn't do shit to us) was laughing at the cops while they gave me the riot act. The chief said he couldn't wait till I turned 18 and he gets to arrest me and put me in jail, and how they'll love me in there with my painted nails.

I took it all in, letting him say his speech that was supposed to set me straight. I told him that Janine said she was getting abused, that I ran away from home the year before, and that I wanted to help her. All he did was grill me more. He said next time, I should tell her to call someone if she was getting abused. I wanted to say I wasn't a criminal or a bad egg; I just wanted to help those who were down. But I kept quiet.

Ray kept laughing, which really got on the cop's nerves. They eventually kicked us out, and we took the bus to Philly with our tails between our legs. Janine went home with her parents to her suburban home, which was probably a mansion compared to where Ray and I grew up.

After these events, the girl's parents made a pact to ban Ray and me from their lives. This Included Megan. The rumor was if the cops in Morristown saw us, they would pick us up and take us to the town border. I don't know if this was true, but it would be the second girl whose parents forbade me to see them in only five months. Maybe I was the anti-Christ.

Chapter 31:
Big Me

I had a couple shows that week at the Troc. One was a little band called the Foo Fighters, which Ray accompanied me to. The other was Letters to Cleo (again), with Sponge and Ned's Atomic Dustbin. My cousin Mike went with me. It was an extremely mid-'90s sort of show.

At the Foo Fighters show, I met Pat Smear outside the venue. I also successfully stage-dived for the first time. Ray tried to do the same but got dropped by the crowd. I think it was because I was as skinny as a stick, and he was over six feet and husky. I also got to hug Dave Grohl when I jumped on stage, but I dropped my flannel and saw him kick it to the side when he left.

My Cousin Mike was really into Sponge, who I thought was okay but somewhat of an STP wannabe. We stood outback of the Troc to meet the lead singer. My cousin was shocked to talk to him, but I didn't care. It was fun to see him excited to meet one of his idols, though. I was sure if I met Stipe, I wouldn't even know what to say to him. I would be in awe.

Between these two shows, I camped out with Donna at the Blockbuster video rental store for NIN tickets (the most '90s thing you will ever hear) for two days. They would go on sale that Saturday, but we wanted to make sure we were first in line (we were by a whole day). At one point, I left Donna, went to see a show, and returned afterward to keep her company. We were still the only people in line. It paid off when we got three tickets (one for Ray) in the pit area at the E-Center. If we got to the show early enough, we could have a front row spot to see NIN!

Around this time, Kathy, the other girl we met camping out for R.E.M. tickets, got tickets for them in Hershey Park, PA. They were playing with a little band that I would grow to love, Radiohead. She was offering for Uriah and me to come with her. The show would be two weeks before the Philly shows, and I jumped at the chance to see my favorite band earlier than planned. The show was on September 30th, which was still a while away. But now, I would see NIN and R.E.M. within a week or so.

Chapter 32:
Welcome to Paradise

August, to me, was the Sunday of the summer. It is the last chance for excitement and fun before the fall, as Sunday is to Monday. During late August, there is a sense that the Wildwood summer fun is nearing its end. However, because we didn't have anywhere to go and didn't know what to do, Ray and I were stuck with the likes of Apple, working until the end of the season in October.

I was so tired of Ray's mind games and him making listening to my favorite bands a competition. We still got together with the late-night crew that worked the boardwalk, but I chose to hang out with other kids I met through work or chance encounters.

One particular group was three girls who worked at an arcade on our pier. Ray and I got along with them since they were from Philly (near Kensington) and were our age. One girl's favorite singer was Bryan Adams. I still had a place in my heart for pop music, especially Bryan Adams, so we had that in common. They lived with one girl's older sister and boyfriend. The boyfriend was my guitar teacher in Kensington the year prior, who taught me the opening parts of Nirvana songs. It was either a small world or us kensos flock to Wildwood like the seagulls flock to anyone eating boardwalk fries.

One day, Ray did something to piss them off. Ray was so full of himself and thought he was better than everyone that he would do whatever he wanted, not caring who he hurt. He was being a bully and making fun of the girlfriend and went too far in a sexual tone.

Ray might have thought he was just fooling around, but the guitar teacher was mad. He wanted to fight Ray (and me since I was friends with Ray). I calmed him down, but Ray was banned from their place, and they all tried to stay away from each other. I was relieved it wasn't just me who was getting tired of Ray's shit.

One of the gals wrote amateur poetry like me and was telling me how she was published in an anthology. She showed me the huge book of random poems from the same company that tried to get me to send them money so they could put me in this anthology after I entered a "poetry contest" the year before. It reeked like a scam, like they wouldn't put the poem in the book unless one agreed to buy a copy, so I didn't fall for it. She did, but at least it made her feel good.

Once, I brought a couple street punks to their place since they were looking for a place to crash for the night. I talked to anyone who was remotely nice or into the slightest similar music as me. I only knew punk rock music in the forms of bands that were local or on MTV (Green Day and the Offspring) or the local alt-rock station, WDOX. I was never crazy about that style of music. I will come to like the '70s/early '80s stuff that was considered punk (bands like the Talking Heads, Blondie, Patti Smith, and Television) but the fast, loud, angry-driven sounds of punk rock were never my thing. I respect it, but it was too aggressive to like or be obsessed with.

I met these three punks after my friends and I finished work around midnight. They were fans of Rancid, Total Chaos, Descendents, and Dead Kennedys. Not Green Day. Punk was their lifestyle. We usually got pizza from shops that wanted to unload slices they didn't sell that day. Instead of throwing them out, they would sell them to us cheaply. Then we would hang out until dawn, all wired from work, go home, wake up around noon, and start the day again.

One of the guys wore a bomber jacket and black plastic glasses that reminded me of Elvis Costello.

One donned a newsboy hat, *A Clockwork Orange* t-shirt, and plaid pants. The other guy was on the chubby side, had glasses and a spikey black leather jacket with bands I never heard of spray painted all over it.

They were all from the Northeast and Frankford sections of Philly. They seemed like nice guys and were eager to talk to me and my alt-rock friends. They were in their 20s but didn't mind talking to a bunch of teenagers.

I found out they were in town for a couple nights but didn't have a place to stay. They were trying to "Jack Kerouac it" and let the road and the mad ones find them a place to stay. The road gave them me, the maddest of the mad, and I told them I would try my best to help them find a place for the weekend. Hell, I just helped a couple girls hide from their parents and the cops. I was sure I could find three guys a spot to crash.

Ray wasn't part of this adventure. He was sleeping at Robyn's or someone else's place for those nights. Since he wasn't going to be home that night, I thought about having the guys crash with me, but I was afraid because my landlady didn't allow guests without a daily fee for each person. I told them that I would hang out with them all night, and if we couldn't find a spot for them, we would stay up all night and go to my place after dawn to crash a bit.

We went to the kenzo girl's place for the first night and stayed up until dawn. The punk rockers were happy to stay somewhere. They were having fun drinking and playing games. One of the guys tried to hook up with the poetry girl, but it didn't happen. Maybe if he read her poem, he would have had a better chance.

We went back to my place, I snuck them in, and they crashed until I went to work at 4 pm. The guys were nice to me. I'm not sure if it was because I was nice to them and helped them out, but when they came into my room and saw my alt-rock god posters all over my walls, they showed their punk rock elite snobby ways.

They made fun of all my posters, especially the one Laura got for my birthday (the sketches of R.E.M., Morrissey, Tori Amos, Bjork, Pearl Jam, Nirvana, U2, etc.). They made me feel insecure and ashamed for liking these acts. It was the first time I felt that way, aside from people making fun of R.E.M. for being "gay" or saying "they suck."

This was my first inclination that these artists I like can be mocked. Before this, I assumed everyone who enjoyed different music was on the same page and part of a community based on the love of music. I had some attributes of a born-again Christian, thinking we all had the same mindset, no matter what band or style of music we loved. We were all part of something bigger than us, and it was geared toward the greater good in life.

I thought everyone felt the way I did about their favorite bands. I thought they wanted to open their minds and be a light. I believed the creative side of rock was what brought us all together.

I wasn't and never will be in any music scene. I wore band shirts with my jeans and Converse and dressed like my hero, Michael Stipe, as much as I could. I didn't realize that punk rockers could be such judgmental bullies. They didn't go too far, probably because I was the only one being nice to them. They seemed like nice guys, but they made me doubt myself (just what I fucking needed, more doubts) and made me feel like my feelings didn't matter. I felt like a trendy idiot.

It was ridiculous. I loved my music and felt almost every song I loved. This side of alt-rock music was more like a cult and all about belonging to something that made you dress like you had a uniform to identify yourself as "punk rock." I later thought those punk rockers weren't even different. They weren't like Stipe and Cobain wearing makeup, making people think about gender identity. People weren't shocked when they saw them walking around since now they weren't labeled "freaks" anymore by how they dressed and wore their hair. Now they were labeled "punk rockers." It seemed more about style over substance and a love of creative music that was intertwined with feelings and progressive thoughts.

It wasn't the last time I saw cracks in the armor of my beloved rock music. I got kicked out of two schools and pretty much left everyone and everything I knew behind for my love of music. I think losing everything for R.E.M. and Tori Amos is way more punk rock than wearing a leather jacket with spikes and only liking bands because no one has ever heard of them.

Most of the punk rockers I will meet in my day will come from neighborhoods and backgrounds far better than mine, with the luxury to dress punk so they could fit in with their punk rock friends. I am a defensive person and always will be. If you make me feel this way, I will overthink the situation to death. I also hold grudges. However, my guests kept the mockery of everything I loved to a minimum, so I let them stay until they woke up and told them to not let the landlady see them.

The next night, we did the same thing until they left to get the bus back to Philly. I only saw them once or twice again. I saw the guy with the Elvis Costello glasses on a bus when I was going somewhere in Frankford. He thanked me again for helping them out, and it was the last time I saw him.

I never saw the guy with the *A Clockwork Orange* shirt again. I think he was the one would have beat the shit out of me for my music taste. He seemed like the typical punk rocker asshole (if you don't know what I mean, lucky you). The third guy opened up a store on South Street (I don't remember what kind) and was featured in a local newspaper. I saw him around South Street a little over the years but never talked to him. I thought he would just mock me again for liking Bjork, R.E.M., and Tori Amos. And you know what? Decades later, I still fucking like those bands.

I was still okay being into my favorite bands, holding on to everyone being into music, and being part of a community like the hippies of the 1960s. I didn't even express how I didn't care for bands like Everclear, Korn, and Silverchair, especially to those who liked those bands. I didn't want to judge anyone how I was for my musical taste. It won't be the case shortly when my defensive side takes over and I start to hate more bands than I like. But at this point, I just wanted everyone to get along in this music-loving world.

Chapter 33:
A Headbangers Ball

The punk rockers weren't the only ones who showed ugliness with their opinion of music and looked down on me. Ray was hanging out with local and seasonal kids who were into darker, heavier music. NIN was as far as I went down that rabbit hole of bands that seemed angry and depressed 24/7. I was an angry guy sometimes, but never listened to music to make me angrier.

I liked stuff that made me feel something better than what I was feeling or enhanced my life in a progressive, practical way. Ray, who started liking NIN in June, was now all about Marilyn Manson, and Korn (God, I hated that band).

I was also turned onto heavier bands by a kid named Rich, whom I worked with and took a shine to. Rich operated the test of strength game. We would go over to his house, and he would play guitar, and I would try to sing (not well) to Nirvana songs he knew.

He made me a tape of Tool's *Undertow,* which I loved, and Rage Against the Machine. The latter was something I liked, but mostly because I was all about their political message. I heard both bands on MTV, but this was the first time I gave them a full listen. They seemed to be in different leagues than the Korn and Mansons of the world. I liked the merit behind them.

I listened to Ray and others say Korn was great. I tried to like them and find something worthwhile in their music. The vocalist was singing about his pain and suffering, so I appreciated that, but it seemed so forced and gimmicky. The video for one of the songs had the band looking all scary and disturbed in it. I wondered how many takes it took to look that crazy. In one song, the lead vocalist was crying about his dad, and I wondered how many times it took to get the crying down in the studio. The music wasn't good to me at all. Similar to how everyone went apeshit for Bush and Alanis Morrisette, now it was Korn and Manson that were taking the youth of Wildwood by storm.

The more aggressive kids were saying these bands were better than Nirvana. It was ridiculous, and I needed to talk to a like-minded person with similar tastes. Someone who liked good, creative music and was in a similar boat as me. An ultra-sensitive person who came from a terrible background. Someone like Eddie Maurer.

Chapter 34:
This Is a Call

I pushed Eddie and John H away out of fear and a reminder of what I thought was the cause of my mental state. I tried to not think about Eddie, and of course, the way my mind works, I thought about him more, along with all the kids from the mall. I didn't want to see Eddie because he took me to the mall with kids who were drawn to my energetic personality. I thought it was why God took my feelings away and put me in a tortured mindset. I didn't know what caused my emotional numbness, but I cut out anything that might have helped my demise.

If I talked to him again, I would go down the same road and never be sane. My confidence and feelings would be ruined. I would give in to a side of me that was less feeling and more instinctual and out for fun.

In late August '95, I saw a 6-foot-tall skinny kid with an R.E.M. shirt walking down the boardwalk. It was Eddie. Eddie knew I was in Wildwood by word of mouth. He was happy to see me. He had no idea (since I never explained why I cut him off) that I wasn't exactly glad to see him. I felt panic. I wondered what it meant for my path in life. Was it a test? Was it supposed to happen? I wasn't sure if I should embrace him. I thought that would be going to the other side of my mind and giving up on myself and my soul.

I couldn't ignore him. He was right in front of me. So we talked, and I felt surprisingly better. He was his usual gentle, "nice guy" self. He was down the shore with our mutual acquaintance, Jay, and his mom for the week. He left Jay at the hotel because he wanted to stay in. Eddie wanted to see if he could find me on the boardwalk.

Eddie was a breath of fresh air compared to Ray's torturous mind games and out-of-control ego. I walked him back to his hotel, and we talked about the R.E.M. shows and everything we had done that summer. He was working at a sneaker store in Kensington, under the El, living partly with John and a home in Kensington. He told me how much he loved R.E.M. and how he must get concert tickets. He was willing to do whatever he could to get them.

We hung out the next few days, and I felt I could handle it. I didn't feel a sudden urge to not feel or think about things that mattered. I wasn't acting crazy, trying to entertain people like I did at the mall. I realized seeing Eddie would not push me into that behavior that I blamed for my muffled feelings. Not yet, at least.

We both still wanted to be singers, and I wanted to be a better person. Eddie brought up Freddie Mercury, who eventually became his favorite singer. He explained how modest and shy Mercury was performing in front of crowds (even small ones). He went off on how gentle and charitable Freddie was. It was so nice talking to Eddie about the bands and singers we loved. I liked talking to the one guy who always gets me and vice versa. He left a few days later, and I told him I would call him when I returned to Philly. I said we would get him in to see R.E.M., and that's exactly what we did.

Seeing Eddie reminded me of a part of myself I pushed away. I felt relieved seeing one of my best friends. I didn't feel numb or guilty for not dealing with my problems. It wasn't Eddie who did this to me. It was my own self-defense system that was preventing me from feeling. I made a mistake by pushing Eddie away and embracing Ray.

With Ray, I was always the calm adult in the room. I thought I was supposed to be around him to regain my balance. I was wrong. I felt more confident and thought I could cut Ray out. I didn't have to depend on him anymore to keep me from being a wild man. Eddie was my best friend, while Ray was becoming my worst enemy.

Chapter 35:
I Got a Girl

I didn't know what to do in the upcoming months. We had our place and jobs until the end of September, so by October, I had to find a job in Wildwood during the off-season (which is near impossible for a high school dropout kid) or go back to Philly without a promise of a home. I wasn't ready to cut off Ray, but the seeds were planted. He was becoming so fake and such a manipulative asshole that I was closer to setting myself free.

The weeks flew by, and summer was almost over. I started messing around with a girl from Israel who was in Wildwood for the summer. She was cute, but her name escapes me. She told me she had only seen one band live. The only band to play her part of Israel was Inner Circle, the reggae band that sang the "Bad Boys" theme song to the show *Cops*. When we first made out, I was sick and lost my voice. She didn't care about my illness, and we kissed anyway.

Most nights, we met random girls down for the week or weekend. Even with my mental state, I could get lost in the moment talking to people, especially new, interesting people. One night, a bunch of us were standing on the boardwalk when a bunch of girls our age (17-18) came up the ramp. One of our guys started talking to them. Usually, one of us would get the attention of a girl we liked in a group. We were young, and our courage to meet new people wasn't shattered yet.

One of the girls, who wore Citgo hat and was nicknamed Shitgo by her friends, seemed to like me. She was cute and dressed on the preppy side of life and liked bands like The Dave Matthews Band and Live. She was from a wealthy suburb of Philly, and I knew she liked me, but nothing came out of it due to my financial situation. After the summer I saw her at the band's Live show in the fall in Philly. She seemed happy to see me there and we got to talking about this and that.

Our conversation turned to nothing when two (taller than me) frat guys she knew came over to talk to her. They had tons more in common, in style and promises of higher education and a financially secure future. I took the hint after the guys purposely directed the conversations away from me. I left to never see Shitgo Girl again. It was for the best (at least for her). It was another indication that I wasn't good enough for an all-American life full of college dorm parties and listening to jam bands. It was another scene or situation I didn't feel I belonged in.

Chapter 36:
Don't Go Chasing Waterfalls

One night, I got weary of being around Ray at our place and took a walk. It was one of those times when my chaotic mind had a glimpse of clarity, and I wished I had come to Wildwood alone to regroup properly. I walked down the strip where all the clubs and bars were, a couple blocks from my place. I was minding my business, trying to get my thoughts in order, when I heard a man yelling.

I turned to see a huge, muscular man, probably in his 30s, screaming at the woman he was with. The man was shirtless and, in a rage, shouting at her so violently that I thought he might beat her. I watched, knowing that I could not stop such a brut of a man, but thinking if he saw someone looking at his aggressive display, maybe he would reel it in.

He did not stop. Instead, he walked over and screamed at me, just like he was screaming at the woman, "What the fuck are you looking at?" Then he punched me so hard that my head bounced off the brick wall behind me, and I fell to the ground. They walked down the strip, yelling at each other, hopefully going home so he could cool off.

I got up feeling dazed. It was the hardest I had ever been hit. I chalked it up to my life and kept walking. I had the same thoughts as usual whenever something like this happened. I was a robot stuck on one command, trying to figure out how to get back to where I was before March 2nd. I wasn't thinking, what the fuck just happened? I just accepted the assault as normal and was more concerned about my internal struggles. I went back to my place and never told Ray what happened.

Chapter 37:
Don't Stop Swaying

I realized in late August that I had feelings for Apple. She was a fixture in my summer that year, but it took to this point for me to realize I liked her, even though I knew she was trouble and heartbreak in the making.

Apple's real name was Jen. She was a bit of a hippie, charismatic, and adorable. She was a wild child and liked to dabble with some harmless drugs (like weed and acid) and perhaps others that weren't so harmless. She was 17 or 18 but was an old soul or "wise beyond her years," which I was attracted to. She was troubled as well. She hung out with the seedy youth of Wildwood.

A crew of teens and young adults hovered all over the boardwalk, especially the main pavilion. They were homeless or squatters (the cool, trendy word for "homeless"). Some were really dirty punks, some were goth, and then there was Apple, a melting pot of style and culture.

I think most of them were runaways or kids who left their suburban homes to come and live (on a wing and a prayer) in Wildwood for the summer. They would try to find money and places to stay, but if they couldn't, they would sleep under the boardwalk or crash at a friend's house. This crew reminded me of the vampires from *The Lost Boys*. They were fun to talk to, but I knew they weren't the ones you wanted to bring in your place or leave your wallet out around them.

Sometime during July, the squatter crew moved to another town to see what it would bring. It was like *On the Road,* but I think they just went to another shore town, so we will call their adventures *On the Jersey Turnpike.* Only Apple stayed. She got a job through one of our seasonal friends and got a place like ours for $75 a week. She was always around now and seemed more together since the other "lost boys" left.

One day she told us she needed 50 bucks to keep her place, or she would get booted. I was going to buy a R.E.M. live CD bootleg that I saw at Cookie's Fun shop (which I did buy eventually), but I gave the money to Apple instead. Ray laughed at me because he knew she would use it on drugs, which she did. It bothered me she lied to me, but I still had a crush on her.

Apple was a hot mess and all over the place emotionally (like me, but more vocal about it). I never told her that I had feelings for her. I informed Ray, and he encouraged me to do something about it. He thought I had a chance and we would be a good couple. He also thought she was a bit too much sometimes. He recalled when she said she wore safety pins because it made her feel safe. He thought she was silly for this, but it made me more intrigued by her.

The closest I ever got to doing anything was at her place. We were listening to music, and she was singing out loud. She wanted to be a singer in a band. We were getting to know each other better, and my crush on her was getting bigger.

Apple had an album by Sophie B. Hawkins called *Tongue and Tails*. I was the only other person I knew who had that record. As I said, she was an eclectic person (like me). She put her favorite song on, "Don't Stop Swaying," the last track on the album.

As the song played, we embraced and started slow dancing in her room. It was a romantic, spontaneous moment. We were so close that I felt her heart rapidly beating. I knew I could look down at her, kiss her, and see where it would take me. Yes, I wasn't sure I could trust her, and I didn't know if she liked me or was humoring me. But at this moment, I didn't care. I was about to make a move when I saw someone coming up the stairs. They stopped at Apple's door, looking in at us. They weren't trying to disturb us but didn't walk away either.

The door to her place was 1/3 open, so it wasn't like this guy was being a creep. He was a mutual friend. I stopped dancing with Apple and let him in. I believe he was a homosexual, so it wasn't his intention to break up our romantic moment, but he did. That was it. There would never be another chance to sway the larger-than-life, cute-as-a-button Apple again. She would be on another train of thought now, and who knows if we'd ever be alone again (we wouldn't).

Sophie B. Hawkins had a single out called "As I Lay Me Down." Near the end of the song, a backing vocal that said, "Ooh La Kah Koh" or something. The only thing was, and this is how adorable and unique Apple was, Apple thought Sophie said, "Good luck, Apple." After she told me that, to this day, that's all I hear at that part of the song.

I had one of my first encounters with Apple when she came with a friend to visit me at the game stand I worked at. That was another thing we did as boardwalk "rats." We visited each other at our places of work if we were bored. It was around closing time, and the Music Express operator had switched the loudspeaker music to the alt-rock CDs I had on me. He put on Hole's *Live Through This*, and Apple asked to hear the song "Jennifer's Body." She said it was about her because her name was Jennifer. That was how I learned her real name and the first time I was intrigued by her.

During the off-season, Apple hung out in South New Jersey near her town. Tara (Glitter) told me Apple was the queen of the mall, similar to how she was the queen of the boardwalk that summer. It reminded me of myself at the Franklin Mills Mall that winter. Apple and I seemed to be two peas in a pod or kindred spirits in many ways. I will never see her again, but I think of her every time I hear Sophie B. Hawkins sing, "Good Luck, Apple."

Chapter 38:
What the Fuck is the Internet?

We worked with another guy named Bill. He was from the suburbs and seemed like he came from a well-off family. Janine was talking to him before she was forbidden to see any of us after running away.

He was a really nice kid, probably a year younger than me. He was into all kinds of alt-rock, like the rest of us. He was the only "skater" kid we hung out with. He was relatively new to skateboarding and mainly used it to get around town. I liked Bill a lot. He was kind and easy to talk to. Ray made fun of him (behind his back) and called him a dork.

I didn't like to call anyone names. I thought one of the best things about alt-rock and whatever community it created was that people who got called dorks or nerds had a place to go without being judged and ridiculed. Maybe it was due to being raised in a cult-like Christian community that preached acceptance and brotherhood, but this is how I saw the entire alt-rock fanbase.

I felt bonded with these kids over our taste in music since it was my everything. I assumed it was everyone else's everything as well. I was almost like a hippy. We were all a bunch of misfits responding to bands that were more socially conscious and made it okay to be sensitive and want to be different than everyone else. It was a great time to be a music fan if you liked music that was more creative and deeper than the average radio songs.

Even though Bill was a bit naïve, he was good company. He was 5'5 and super skinny, with short brown hair. Bill looked like a boy then, and I believed he would always look like a boy, even in his 30s. He lived on the other side of town with his two sisters (who were lesbians and turned me on to the beauty of the Indigo Girls) and his friend.

Bill's friend had a shoe on his shelf that belonged to Courtney Love. Supposedly, she kicked it off at a show (maybe Lollapalooza) into the front row, and this guy got it. It was a lot smaller than I thought it would be. For some reason, I thought she would have bigger feet than me since I was the same height as Kurt, and she seemed taller than him. But her shoe wouldn't fit me (yes, I tried it on).

Bill's house was nice. It had many rooms. He also had a computer with a thing I only heard of until now, a new fad called the Internet. I would use his computer and go on these crazy things called AOL chatrooms and type-talk with other folk around the country about whatever. What a world we were living in. I wrote Laura a letter on that computer and never gave it to her since I didn't have her email or even know what email was. I printed it out there but lost it among my travels before I could give it to her.

I was having a heart-to-heart with Bill (most of my talks back then were honest conversations about everything going on with me). It seemed most people were right there with me, trying to figure out our lives. I explained that I was so down and that everything was wrong. I felt like I couldn't accomplish what I wanted. His comforting response was his way of identifying with me and showing me, he knew what I was talking about. He told me he tried to learn a skateboard trick and couldn't, no matter how many times he tried. It wasn't the same thing at all, but it sure was a break from Ray. And I always liked having those.

Chapter 39:
Single White Male

One day in the late summer, I found something strange in Ray's drawer that was left open. In the '90s, since I didn't have a cell phone, I kept the phone numbers of those I cared about in my little phone book. I also wrote their addresses down (if I had them).

I noticed a phone number I knew by heart written on a small piece of paper. My heart pounded with fear and a sense of betrayal when I saw Laura's number. What the fuck was he doing with her number? I remembered arguing with Ray about his persona, maybe about how I didn't want to go along with his mind games.

He said he would tell Laura about the girls I had been with romantically that summer while pretending to be in love with her. I didn't think he meant he would really tell her since he had no way of getting a hold of her. I said that Laura and I talked about this, and she wants me to live my life and have as many experiences as possible until we can be together again.

He rolled his eyes at me, and the subject never came up, but now I saw what was happening. He went into my phone book and wrote Laura and her friend Layla's phone number down, and he was going to blackmail me if I didn't go along with his con games. I took the phone numbers and threw them out. I never brought it up since I hated confrontation, and to the best of my knowledge, he never tried to call Laura or Layla. Even with this evidence of his evil intentions, I still wasn't ready to cut him off, mainly because we had another month of living together.

After Labor Day Weekend, it becomes a bit of a ghost town in Wildwood. Once the tourists go, so do the jobs and income. Ray and I still had our jobs on the boardwalk. Most kids went home for school. Being the ones with least promising future, we picked up most of the shifts. Carl and his crew were still around, but our hours were from the afternoon to about 10pm on weekdays. Weekends were still busy, and Wildwood was still the hotspot. So, we still had some summer fun left; it was just crammed into those last weekends of September.

During the week, the big crowds and the feeling like you were in the spot to be dwindled, and you were left with a two-thirds empty boardwalk and a depressing sense that the end of the season was upon you. The world you were in the middle of, the one you never wanted to end, moved on and left you wanting more. It was sobering (if I wasn't so sober already). The ones that stayed (for work or lack of options) didn't speak of the feeling of the fun world moving on and how we were the ones that had nothing much to leave there for.

Ray and Robyn had broken up. They had a rocky relationship at best, and when they broke up, it took a month or so of teenage (and Ray being a mind fuck) drama for it to be over for good. It started with Ray pretending he was in love with Robyn and how her breaking up with him caused his downward spiral. It sounded awfully familiar. Ray basically "Single White Femaled" me. He used the relationship's bitter end to fuel his narrative about how depressed and how much of a tortured soul he was.

Most of our friends had gone. Cousin Mike, Glitter, Robyn, the Music Express operator, my Israelite girl, and even Apple returned home for school or whatever they had going on. The fun and the pretending that life down the shore is forever was over, and what was left was those who knew the brutal truth the whole summer long but kept it down deep. When the summer is over, and the crowds are gone, reality sets in, and you are left with (soon-to-be faded) memories of the season.

We hung out with the local kids from time to time, but even they had to go to school. Ray and I were mostly left to our own devices. Which made it even more depressing to stay there.

Chapter 40:
R.E.M. Gets Theirs

That first week in September, we watched the MTV Video Music Awards at Rich's house, my friend from work. We usually only saw MTV at Robyn's shore house (which wasn't too often). This was the first time I would watch the award show without knowing much about who was performing or nominated for awards.

I did learn from Uriah that R.E.M. was getting the Michael Jackson Video Vanguard Award (MTV's equivalent of a lifetime achievement award).

R.E.M. was at the peak of their popularity. They were popular throughout the years, but that year R.E.M. wasn't just my favorite band or the band that college kids and older alt-rock people liked. Grunge and alt-rock kids also thought they were cool.

R.E.M. was in a rare spot where they were considered legends and influential to the hot new bands but also very relevant to the current era. They were touring for the first time since becoming a household name, which helped make them the biggest band on the planet. *Monster* was their third hit album, with numerous singles on MTV and radio stations all summer in Wildwood.

That year, alt-rock was king, and R.E.M. was sitting on the throne (and they deserved it). Many popular, relevant alt-rock bands that the kids liked were paying homage to R.E.M. in 1995. Bands like the Smashing Pumpkins, Pearl Jam, Nirvana, Hole, Live, Hootie & the Blowfish, Local H, Radiohead, etc. stated how influential R.E.M. had been in the past and how they are the model of what they all wanted to be; a band that didn't compromise and made it on their own terms. R.E.M. were sort of like the alt-rock version of the Beatles. It was cool to respect and acknowledge their legendary career.

On the awards show that night, they played a new song called "The Wake-Up Bomb." During that tour, after Bill Berry's aneurysm, Mike Mills came down with a stomach illness that put the tour on hold. Then Stipe had to get hernia surgery, and the tour stopped again. But by now, R.E.M. was going strong. Stipe was on painkillers since his hernia surgery was around this time, and he was so out of it that he showed his surgery scar (on the lower side of his torso) on national TV. He looked good, though, with his blue suit and eyeliner on while they played their new song that would be on their next album.

Michael looked like a rock god. His persona for the *Monster* tour was full of confidence. He owned the stage with his cool "know it all" glare. He had his rock star moves down pat, screaming he was on top of his game. Whatever self-doubt or shyness he had before this tour was out the window. Stipe was on fire with high esteem.

For some reason, Ray decided to tell me how fake Stipe was because he was lip-syncing the song. I didn't know how to respond to that. To me, it was obvious that Stipe was singing live on MTV. Ray was just being a dick. He liked to get into my head and put doubts in there. He did it all summer by making fun of Stipe and his lyrics on *Monster*, saying he had lost it. It was constant ball-busting and bully tactics.

I ignored Ray. This was the night for my favorite band. It was as if the entire rock world was on board with how great they were. Even Hootie & The Blowfish got into the act while playing their hit song that summer, "Only Wanna Be with You." In the middle of the song, they stopped playing, and the singer held up a cup and said something like, "This goes out to R.E.M. If it wasn't for them, we wouldn't be a band!"

R.E.M. was the toast of the town in music, and the best time of my life was on the horizon. I was a few weeks away from seeing my favorite band in the world in concert. Not even Ray could stop me from that.

Chapter 41:
Home, Where
the Cockroaches Roam

I t was clear that I couldn't find a job in Wildwood during the offseason. I tried going to numerous places open all year and got nothing. I tried Dunkin' Donuts, a Chinese restaurant, a dollar store, and others. As September ended and the last weekends of business were conducted, Ray and I were out of jobs and options. We had to move back home to Philly, and I had to swallow my pride and move in with my parents in a one-bedroom apartment in Frankford.

I took the bus from Wildwood to Philly, and my dad met me at the El stop close to the New Jersey Transit bus depot. He helped me bring in all my belongings, which included a yellow 1970s-style suitcase filled with concert shirts, two pairs of denim jeans, a lot of my poetry, my radio, and a cardboard box full of CDs and tapes.

It wasn't the most exciting time in my life, and the ride home was a bit awkward as I was still mad at my dad. My mental state was in a bit of remorse and a feeling that I was going backward again.

Moving back in with my folks was another blow to my self-esteem and mental health. I hoped for something to change so I would be my confident self again. I wished something would open up for me to keep moving forward instead of backward. I left my hell of a home in Kensington a year and a few months earlier to better my life. Now I was back home, but it was a lot smaller place, and I had to sleep on a disgusting couch.

I had to put all my stuff in the corner of the apartment in boxes and trash bags. I would never have privacy or my own room as long as I stayed with my parents. The place was a piece of shit. It smelled throughout the building of something dead and was probably last renovated ages ago.

The bathroom was in a separate room right outside the apartment. I had to leave the apartment to go to the bathroom like it was an outhouse. There was no working shower, just a bathtub to get clean with.

My parents had their own room where my dad spent most of his time. The only light in the apartment came from the TV, so it always had to be on. The cat we owned peed all over the place and was never neutered. The couch (my bed) reeked of cat urine. The cat also pissed all over my things, including my knitted hippy bag I carried around on my journeys. The place smelt so bad that it gave me daily headaches.

The roaches and the mice came along in the move from Kensington. They were seen frequently, but mainly in the kitchen that looked straight out of the 1960s, including its appliances.

The neighborhood wasn't as bad as the one I grew up in on Wishart Street, but it was still a rough lower-class area with drug dealers on the corner. The block was full of German Shepherds and Rottweilers that would escape their flimsy fences and wander the neighborhood. Coming home at night was always an adventure. Sometimes I would get off the El at Frankford Ave. and walk down Womrath Street, where CIBA is located (I had to pass it going home for years). I would see loose dogs from my block roaming around, and I would have to call the police or take the long way home.

I felt defeated, and my underlining depression was getting worse. Not only did I lose Laura and my only shot at a high school education, but I was now in a borderline condemned apartment in an awful neighborhood, the kind of place where you realize your place in the world.

I was still hopeful (in denial) that things would work out for me, and I still had a crazy notion that I was meant for better things. I thought I could be like my idols and make something of myself. It was mostly high hopes one has when they don't have much going on for them. Mentally, I was still not facing reality, hoping things would work out and make me whole again. I didn't believe in the born-againers' god, but I still thought a higher power, fate, or the universe was in control.

I was living in the moment and for the moment most days. I couldn't grasp (or didn't want to) anything in the future, even the near future (besides concerts). I was in a desperate place and was hoping for external help to get me through this period. But that's not how it works. It would take way too long to grasp that fully. "Just keep going" was the motto.

Chapter 42:
Let the Music Carry you Away

I had some concerts that I was looking forward to amid my comings and goings between Wildwood and Philly. Ray and I saw the band Live at the Spectrum in Philly on September 20th. I saw Jill (Shitgo) again and realized how out of my league she was. I also saw PJ Harvey open the show, and she really impressed me. Eventually, I got her entire music catalog, and she became one of my favorite singers/artists.

Two days later, Donna, Ray, and I went to the NIN show with David Bowie at the E-Center in Camden. We planned on getting there as early as possible since we had pit tickets and wanted to be up front.

I got there around 12 pm. Ray and Donna didn't show up until much later. I woke up around 6 am on my cat pee couch after a night of trying to sleep and failing. I was so excited to see NIN that sleep wasn't much of an option. So, I decided to get there as early as I could.

I was waiting around the bus area where bands usually come in, hoping to meet Trent Reznor (this never happens). While waiting, I met two guys also trying to meet Trent. They were around my age. One guy wore a Marilyn Manson T-shirt since Manson was now the cool industrial band to like. We chit-chatted a little about music and shared our excitement for the show.

After an hour, a roadie came over and said he had a backstage pass he would sell us for $100. It looked familiar, but I didn't trust it. One kid fell for the pitch and bought it off him.

He tried to go backstage through the bus area. Almost instantly, he got called out by a security guard and was taken back to where I was standing. The guard confiscated the pass and told him it wasn't for that night's show; it was an old pass. They were giving the guy a hard time, saying they could arrest him. I chimed in and said he got it from one of the roadies. They made me pick out who it was, then fired the guy for the day.

The roadie threatened me, and I told him he sold a fake pass to some dopey kid who didn't know better, and he almost got in trouble. The guy said he'd get even with me, but we never saw him again.

Ray, Donna, and I were first in line to get into the pit area. We stood there for hours, waiting desperately to be as close as possible to NIN. When the doors opened, we ran inside and got our place dead center in front of the stage. We had to wait a couple hours before NIN came out, but we weren't going anywhere. We were waiting to be a few feet away from Trent.

Finally, the moment one waits for at a show happened. The lights went out, the house speakers stopped playing music, and the anticipation began. A fog machine made the stage so white I couldn't make out anything until I saw Trent appear out of nowhere, and they went into "Terrible Lie." It was hands down the best time I had seen NIN. Being so close to him made my 17-year-old blood pump faster than ever.

Concerts were like my haven or my church. No matter how fucked up my mind or emotions were, at shows, everything was usually okay. I would forget my problems for the moment. I got lost in the feelings and energy of the crowd and the artist. It was liberating. I wouldn't have to do my rituals, and the doubts would quiet down since I was occupied with the one thing I loved the most. This was one of those nights when I let it all out. I danced and sang along with every song that NIN performed. Donna loved every moment as well. It was like a spiritual cleansing. I blew off a lot of steam and frustrations from the past seven months.

During NIN's set, David Bowie sang "Hurt" with them. After the set, Ray came up with some nonsense about Trent giving Bowie a dirty look, and it looked like Trent was annoyed by Bowie.

Ray decided to leave before Bowie started and said something about him being fake. I stayed for Bowie and I'm glad I did. Ray took the ferry from Camden to Philly, and I met up with some concert friends on the lawn area of the venue. We had the time of our lives. I didn't fully embrace and appreciate the genius of Bowie for a few years. It was mainly because of John A. and how much of an asshole he was to me. His Bowie fandom ruined the artist for a while for me. But I just wanted to have fun and enjoy myself.

It started pouring nonstop. Now a bunch of us were soaked to the bone, and we all decided to start mud sliding since the lawn was one sloping mud hill. There were hundreds of kids covered head to toe in mud, gliding down to the bottom of the hill. It was like our own Woodstock. I even made out with one of the girls I knew. We were both covered in mud like two hippies and lost in the moment. If only being young lasted longer.

It was one of the best nights of my life at a show. I let go of all the stress and had fun living in the moment. Nothing else mattered that night. I was 17 and let myself act like it for a change.

When I left, reality set in. I had to take the ferry to Philly, then the El to Frankford Terminal to go home, all covered in mud. I went into the Dunkin' Donuts in Frankford and asked for water in a cup, which usually cost a dime. The worker looked at me with pity and told me not to worry about the dime.

I went home and took a bath (we didn't have a shower, just a bathtub). We also didn't have a washer and dryer (of course), so I would have to wait until we got to a laundromat to wash my NIN shirt and jeans. But that wouldn't happen because the mud from the night prior made my clothes so fragile that they fell apart with one tug. It was like ripping a piece of paper. I had to throw them out.

Now I was down to one pair of jeans. I would have to borrow some of my dad's and wear a tie for a belt since he wore a bigger size than me. But it was worth it for that moment of pure joy. And that wasn't even the best show of the year for me. I still had the peak of my concert life around the corner (and the spotlight).

Chapter 43:
Radiohead Free Europe

A week after the NIN show was my first R.E.M. show. What a week for me! The morning of the show, September 30th, Kathy, Uriah, and I rode with Kathy's dad to Hershey, PA. The show was at Hershey Amusement Park's concert venue. We got there pretty early in hopes of getting a good spot since we had general admission tickets. I was hoping for the ultimate prize, to meet R.E.M. when they came through the tour bus area.

Much like the night before I saw NIN, I could hardly sleep the night before because of how excited I was to see my favorite band live. I was a bit tired the day of the show, but I was running on pure adrenaline (which will happen to me a lot through my concert-going years).

I was like a kid on Christmas. I was so wired with every approaching moment of the show I must have seemed like a kid with hyperactive problems (which was not far from the truth). While waiting at the gate of the back area where the tour buses came in, a life-changing moment happened to me. The three of us were standing around waiting for the tour bus to drive through when I looked over and saw a skinny guy with dyed red hair walking around the area.

I recognized him as Thom Yorke, the lead singer of the opening band, Radiohead. I liked Radiohead but wasn't the superfan I would become after this show. But I knew who Thom Yorke was from the album *Pablo Honey*. I liked the song "Fake Plastic Trees" and the recently released video and single in America, "Just."

Thom looked bored like he was trying to find something to do to kill time. I called him over to where we were since we couldn't go to the tour bus area. To my surprise, he walked right over to us. He wore a red shirt, a book bag, sunglasses, and jeans. He looked like another alt-rock kid hanging out, trying to meet R.E.M.

Thom was so down to earth and nice that he hung out with us for about an hour. I asked him to sign my jeans since I had tons of things written on them by people I met in my travels. He signed them and wrote, "Leg by Thom," and drew a person on the right leg of my jeans. I lost those jeans decades ago, like many things, but boy I wish I still had them.

We also took a picture with him, but I lost that too somewhere in my travels. I had not been around many people from England before Thom, so it was hard to understand his accent. Most of the time, I just said "Yes" and nodded in approval when he asked a question or said something to us.

I asked Thom what his favorite R.E.M. song was. I was glad to hear it was "South Central Rain (I'm Sorry)." Thom knew his R.E.M. I asked him again in 2003 when I saw Radiohead, and he gave me the same answer. Then, in 2020, I went to a taping in NYC of *The Late Show with Stephen Colbert*. Michael Stipe was a guest on the show, and Colbert asked him what Thom Yorke's favorite R.E.M. song is. I said to the guy sitting next to me (who I don't know), "South Central Rain," and Stipe replied, "South Central Rain." So, not only is Thom super nice, but he's also consistent.

Thom hung out with us for so long that there were times when no one was talking. We all just stood there. When other R.E.M. fans approached the tour bus area with the same mindset of hoping to meet the band, I started talking to them. I introduced us by saying, "I'm Chaz, this is Kathy, that's Uriah, and that's Thom Yorke from Radiohead." It was fucking awesome.

I wish I knew then how much I would love Radiohead in the coming months. I would have probably been more star-struck to see him, and maybe I wouldn't have wanted to disturb him from his boredom. But I will have plenty of chances to be star-struck by Thom over the years.

After waiting a while at the tour bus area, more people arrived, hoping to meet the band. Suddenly, a white van pulled up to the back gate. The van was right next to me, and I saw it was the members of R.E.M. I was in shock when I saw Michael Stipe through the window of the van next to me. I put my hand up on the window, moving only with instincts, and felt overwhelming excitement being this close to my four favorite people. That would be the closest I would get to the band that day. They didn't come out of the van. Oh well, there are still the Philly shows to try to meet my idols.

We decided to get in the GA line for a good spot to watch the show. With my shit luck, I was worried something would happen to cause me to miss the show. I thought this day would never come. I was going to see my favorite band play live. It was a dream come true.

Unfortunately, I was wrong about the location of the GA section. I thought it would be like the pit area at the E-Center, or how it was for Lollapalooza 1994 (the first person gets the best, closest spot near the stage). That wasn't the case at Hershey Park. It was more like the lawn area of the E-Center. It had at least 50 rows of seats in front of the stage, and the GA section was behind them. We were first in line to get to the GA section. However, my first time seeing my favorite band was from a great distance. I was dead center to see them, but unable to see them up close like I hoped.

Radiohead opened the show, and they blew me away. It was like when I saw PJ Harvey open for Live. I left the show a huge fan. A little bit later I bought *The Bends*, the album that made me fall in love with Radiohead.

Every album and song I want to hear now is a click away. But in the mid-'90s, I was poor and had to wait to buy the albums I wanted. It made music more sacred and appreciated. Music wasn't something I'd download or stream instantly. I would save up money to buy a CD or tape I liked. Little did I know what was in store for me with the genius of Radiohead. No matter how brilliant Thom Yorke becomes, I'll never forget how down-to-earth and approachable he was that afternoon in the fall of 1995. And I will always appreciate the fact that I saw my two favorites on the same night.

In 1995, I bought a Radiohead book about their career. It had a quote from Michael Stipe that read, "Radiohead is so good, it's scary." Man, my idol was right.

R.E.M. came on shortly after Radiohead left the stage. The moment I had been waiting for was here. I might have been half a world away from the stage, but I had a clear view since I was next to the metal post that separated GA from the seats. Being 5'7 was usually a problem at concerts, but no one was in front of my short ass now.

I knew I had way better seats for the Philly shows, so for this show, I just took it all in from a distance. I was seeing my heroes from Athens for the first time, and I had a view of everything they would do as a band on stage. Boy, they put on a great show.

I sang along with every song I knew (all of them except the new ones). I loved watching Michael do his thing on stage. He was so cool and magnificent that I loved him more than ever.

The lead singer of Live, Ed Kowalczyk, did a duet with Stipe on the voting-for-change anthem, "Begin the Begin." Ed was from York, PA, which probably explains why he was at the Hershey show. He recently shaved his head and was on the record saying how much of an R.E.M. and Stipe fan he was. It was probably a dream come true for him to sing a song he loved with one of his heroes. It was a special moment to watch these two freshly shaved bald men feeding off each other's energy through the uplifting song.

The night was magical and will always be dear to me since it was my first time seeing the greatest band in the world. And I got to hear the song that changed my life, "Losing My Religion." Uriah turned to me when they played it and said, "This is your moment." It definitely was. Hearing the song played so loud made it more powerful than ever.

Hearing each song that I loved so much for years was amazing. I wanted more after they finished their 25-song set with their anthem, "It's the End of the World as We Know It (And I Feel Fine)." That's what R.E.M. shows do; once they're over, I wanted more. I had to wait twelve days for their three shows in Philly. Until then, I had some things to do, like see Laura Lee Sesar again.

Chapter 44:
In Your Eyes

Over the years, I worked up the courage to call Laura at home. Sometimes, I would get a family member telling me she wasn't home, and sometimes they put her on the phone. My favorite times were when she answered, and I heard her sweet voice. After the slew of shows I went to, I was full of excitement and feelings that anything could happen. I called Laura and got her on the phone in early October. We planned to meet up.

We met at her school on October 5th. She had some excuse to not go home right away, so we hung out on the grounds of her high school for an hour or so. It was the first time I had seen her since May. Little did I know it would be the last time for a couple of years (an eternity for a teenager).

She looked as beautiful as ever. We talked about what happened in each other's lives during the summer. I told her about the string of shows I just went to, including NIN, my first time seeing R.E.M., and the ones I had coming up. She was so happy and excited for me. Laura was always the selfless type who found joy in other's happiness.

We talked about how much we still loved and cared about each other and what our future would be like. Laura repeated the same thing from May, saying it would be some time until we could have a life together and for me to live my life to the fullest. She still wanted me to go have adventures and not be held back. She said to not give up on my dreams or on her. We will be together again.

We ended our meeting with a kiss and an embrace. Laura told me to take care of myself, which gave our love story (the worst one told) a slight ray of sunshine, followed by my clinging to the hope that we would be together again soon. It was the crazy dreams of a 17-year-old kid. The kind that makes sense to you, and you feel you need so much that they must come true or else.

Chapter 45:
Oh, You're the Best Friend That I Ever Had

I spent the rest of the time prior to the shows with either Uriah or Eddie, now that we were talking again. I was escaping the madness of Ray. We were all excited about the upcoming R.E.M. shows in Philly. Eddie was going to go with John H, who got tickets for them, for the first show, and then he was going to "wing it" to get into the last show.

Eddie and I spent a lot of time together that week. I was glad he was back in my life. He was a true friend and a breath of fresh air after five months of hell with Ray. Our music taste was so similar that we could talk about R.E.M. and Radiohead for hours. It was good to be around sound and kind friends again.

One day, I met Eddie at his work on Kensington Ave. When he was done, we walked down Allegheny Ave. toward John's house in Port Richmond (a two-mile walk). I saw a group of six or seven teenagers coming down our path. They were all wearing the latest trendy clothes, including sports team shirts, proving they were the best at liking other people's athletic abilities. They were whispering to each other and looking like they would harass us for being outnumbered. Clearly, they were going to jump and rob us.

This was the usual for Eddie and me in Kensington, so I said, "Maybe we should cross the street or go into a store until they pass by." Eddie replied, laughing, "Look at you. You have bright pink sunglasses (Kurt Cobain style) with a bald head, except for your Elvis-sized sideburns. You're dressed in black and have nail polish on. Just act crazy, and they won't do shit." So, as they approached us, I cursed and mumbled like I had mental problems and started banging my head with a Snapple iced tea bottle, yelling, "Rock music! Rock music! Rock music!" The teenagers walked around us saying shit like, "What the fuck is wrong with that guy?" We survived another day.

Eddie and I talked about our constant struggles with roaming groups of kids in our shit neighborhoods. They were always looking for easy targets to show off their toxic masculinity. Eddie came up with a way of thinking that I adopted as a teenager. He said he didn't want to live in fear of every large group of boys who came his way. If they were going to approach him violently, the worst that could happen would be they'd kill him. He didn't want to live in a world with people like that and didn't want to live in fear for the rest of his life. I liked this theory.

Hanging out with Eddie made me remember so much about myself that I had pushed away over the several months after my mental snap. It was great talking to someone I knew liked good music and wasn't trying to be something they weren't. He also didn't try to manipulate people. Eddie was (and still is) a kind person with a beautiful (sometimes childlike) soul (if souls exist).

For a couple of kids from rotten neighborhoods with parents who shouldn't have had kids, Eddie and I were both ultra-sensitive and open-minded to new things. We didn't realize our stature in life or at least didn't think it would define us. We wanted more than the lives we were dealt, even though we had no idea how to get something better. For some reason, we were attracted to things that weren't run of the mill.

The area we grew up in demanded you get hardened and tougher than the guy trying to steal your wallet. Eddie and I knew this life was terrible and wanted to leave it behind. Neither of us had a high school diploma or any idea of what to do with our lives. We were in the same boat in many ways, though his education was stopped by a fear of getting killed by his fellow students. Mine was cut short because of money and my love for the devil's music. We were still thrown into this society to figure it out ourselves.

Ray was also in this spot but didn't have the ambition or want to become something more. His only concern was to live in the moment. Eddie and I were living in the moment as well (as much as I could with my mental problems), but we were also trying our best to be better than the kenzos we were raised around.

Eddie and I differed in that he was smart enough growing up to take things easier and not be a total lunatic. I was the opposite and wanted to figure everything out immediately, getting to where I wanted to be or at least on the right track.

Eddie's mindset kept us from seeing Nirvana in 1993 out of the rational fear of coming home too late in our dangerous neighborhood. But it also got him out of his parent's place and into John H's house most days, which was ten times nicer. It also kept Eddie from going down the hurt-filled, mentally ill path that I went down.

During these years of chaos in my head, Eddie was calmer and would become a rock or a constant throughout the craziness. He would also go down the lunatic path, but his won't be as severe as mine and won't leave him as damaged.

These upcoming years, where Eddie and I really find out who we are and how much we didn't know when we were young, will be the closest we ever will be. We both knew we wanted to be in a band. He wanted to be musician, and I wanted to be a singer. Not only did we want it more than anything, but we also thought it was the only way we could make something of ourselves.

We weren't alone in thinking our dreams of being music stars were our only way out of a shitty life. Plenty of kids are born poor and come from broken homes and think the only way they can make it in life is to be like their heroes. Maybe they dream of being a famous rapper or a singer in a punk band, and they probably deserve it (like me and Eddie). They would probably have a chance to be heard if life was fair and there was a god. Eddie and I were the same, except Michael Stipe and Freddy Mercury were our role models. It was unique for the area and circumstances we lived in.

We both loved R.E.M. and got shit from other people who only liked heavy music or classic rock. But we both knew how great R.E.M. was, and we were gearing up for the best week of our 17-year-old lives (probably the best week ever for me).

Chapter 46:
Your Finest Hour

R.E.M. took over my city for three days and was the toast of the town. They were the biggest band on the planet and at their peak in popularity. Every rock station was playing R.E.M. nonstop. I heard songs from them that weren't played on the radio before.

Philadelphia finally caught up with me and Eddie with R.E.M. mania. I was in my element all week. R.E.M. being everywhere took me out of the reality of my living situation. The problem of what to do with my life was set aside. It was my time to rise.

The week leading up to the shows, the top 40 alt-rock station, Y100, had a weeklong contest for front-row tickets and a backstage pass to meet the band. It occurred during their morning show. The show's host would ask a daily question about R.E.M., and at the end of the week, the person who was first to call in with the right answers won. I knew my R.E.M. info like the back of my hand and knew I had a shot to win.

The morning show was your typical Howard Stern wannabe style of programming. Four people (three guys and a woman) talked all morning about nonsense, and then they would fill it in with half-ass jokes and prank calls. The show was hosted by a guy named Paul Barsky, and the show was called Barsky in the Morning. It wasn't a terrible morning show; it was just like every other one after Stern. It was funny sometimes but usually not worth waking up for if you didn't have to. I was usually up all night and would try to sleep past the time any morning show was on.

I learned about the contest from Uriah. I wanted to get the backstage passes so much that I woke up every morning to hear the question that day.

I wrote down all the answers, which were easy to figure out if you were an R.E.M. fan. On Friday, I called the station after they prompted listeners, and I got through but was put on hold because someone called ahead of me. If they didn't get all the answers right, I would have my chance. I waited, half asleep, listening to the show, selfishly hoping the woman before me would fail.

I don't remember all the questions, but the first one was: What was R.E.M.'s first EP called? I knew right away - *Chronic Town*. The woman ahead of me got it wrong. She said "*Murmur*" instead of *Chronic Town*. My heart skipped a beat, thinking that I would get my chance. I knew I would get all the questions right.

But the bastard that Barsky was said to this woman, "No, that is their first LP. I asked what was their first EP called?" Then the woman, clearly reading off a paper or AOL (1995's internet), said, "Oh, Chronic, Chronic Town." Since Barsky decided to give this woman a second shot, she got all the questions right. She won front-row tickets and a backstage pass. I found out later that she called in for her kids (who were at school). I was furious.

After the person operating the phone lines told me they had a winner, I went off on them. I stated how unfair it was to give this person another chance at answering the question when the whole point of the contest was to have the right answers to all the questions. I think he was the show's producer or at least found my rants entertaining because he asked if I wanted to tell my point of view on the air. I agreed, thinking maybe they had an extra backstage pass or something I could have.

The radio contests I won in the past made me comfortable on the radio. I also didn't think about thousands of people listening to me talk about R.E.M. I usually did things around this time without thinking much about it.

Barsky said he heard I was upset about who won the contest. I told him exactly how I felt. I said, "The contest was to know all the questions from the week, and that woman got it wrong. You should have hung up on her and gone to the next caller, which was me. I would have won since I am the biggest R.E.M. fan around here and I knew all the answers."

Barsky was like every other DJ and morning show host. He saw an opportunity to make a bit out of my anger. He asked me my name, and I told him it was Chaz. He then asked me why I wanted the tickets so bad. I told him how much I love R.E.M., especially Michael Stipe. I said I saw Stipe as a role model and a hero. I told him how much they mean to me and how meeting them would be a dream come true.

Barsky asked what I would do if I got to meet him. I thought it was an indication that he had an extra backstage pass. I was a little hopeful now. I told him, "I would shake Stipe's hand and tell him I love him, and he means everything to me, and then I would give him the poem I wrote about him." The last line grabbed the opportunist Barsky's attention, and he said, "You wrote a poem about Stipe?" I told him that I did, and he asked me to read the poem over the air. And the foolish but fearless me read my poem about Michael Stipe to probably tens of thousands of people listening.

I do not remember what the poem said. It was a couple pages long, and all the lines rhymed. I am sure it was basic for a 17-year-old's attempt at paying tribute to his idol. It might not have been the best poem, but I read it anyway. While I did so, the morning team laughed at me and played *Friday the 13th* sound effects to make it sound like I was crazy like Jason Voorhees.

I knew they were making fun of me, and I was fine with that. If you can't laugh at yourself, what can you laugh at? I was also aware that they were using me (and my innocent love for my favorite singer) to fill up time on their mediocre morning show and to make a fool of me over something they couldn't or wouldn't want to understand. I did what I always did. I went with the flow of whatever came my way, and still thought this interaction would lead to something good. It did not. I read my poem for the three minutes it took to read, and then Barsky wished me good luck and made fun of me some more before hanging up on me.

I didn't win the front-row tickets or the backstage passes, even though I should have, but I will get my way to the front of the stage and meet R.E.M. without the help of Barsky.

Chapter 47:
Life and How to Live It

R.E.M. week was here in Philly, and I was never so excited. The whole city was buzzing with R.E.M. fever, and I loved every moment. In a day or two, I would see the band I wanted to see more than anyone.

I did whatever I could to occupy my time and mind leading up to the shows. Ray and I had tickets together for the first couple of shows, so I was still stuck with him. We met up with Janine from New Jersey, whom Ray was dating. I think she lied to her parents to come to Philly and hang out with the likes of us. I was in the middle of South St., making my best impressions of Stipe's stage persona from the show I saw. I sang into an invisible microphone, doing his rock star moves like a nut.

A few older kids were handing out free instant cups of soups. It was some promotion, and they gave us each one to try. I didn't want it since it was chicken flavor, but I put it in my hippy-style bookbag to be nice. I forgot about the soup after we left, and it broke open. The flavoring pack spilled all over my stuff, including my white wool sweater I bought at a thrift store. It was extra-long, full of holes, and reminded me of the one Stipe wore on the cover of one of R.E.M.'s VHS compilations from the '80s.

I woke up early in anticipation of the first show on Thursday, October 12th, 1995. I shaved my head completely (except for my trademark sideburns) and got ready for the show. I decided to go to the show as early as possible. I was up for anything and everything. I hoped to run into the band or at least see them enter the venue. I also wanted to be in the area where the show was as long as possible. I hoped I could meet other R.E.M. fans since this was the best place to do so.

I arrived at the Spectrum around 1 p.m. and looked for people to hang out with. Usually, I find something interesting going on by walking around so much.

A radio station had a display outside one entrance and was broadcasting live. I don't remember if it was Y100 or another station, but the DJ referred to me as a walking Stipe shrine (bald head, nail polish, eyeliner, skinny frame, and a resemblance to Stipe). He put me on the air, and I talked about the lead singer of Live singing with Stipe in Hershey Park. I said that Natalie Merchant was in town playing a show this weekend and maybe she would pop out and perform with R.E.M. (it didn't happen, and I led people on like a tease).

Eddie and John H. had seats further back and to the right of the stage. Ray and I were in the middle of the floor, closer to the stage. Somehow, Eddie convinced Ray to switch tickets so he could sit with me closer to the stage since he was a huge fan. I don't know why, but Ray agreed. Eddie and I were sitting next to each other (like it should be), and poor John H. had to sit with Ray.

We all went to our seats with Uriah and were only eight rows from the center of the stage. I was thrilled to be so close. I could see everything clearly and make out every member of the band.

I thought Michael was so sexy, cool, and beautiful. He commanded the stage like no other. He was at his highest self-esteem. They played for over two hours. The set wasn't much different from the one in Hershey. Their setlists didn't change much throughout the three dates they played that weekend. Some non-R.E.M. believers asked me, "Isn't it the same show every time? I don't get your fandom." And I would say, "I would go see R.E.M. if they played "Shiny Happy People" repeatedly for two hours." I will learn that haters are going to hate. They changed a song here and there. The second night, they played one of my favorites that they didn't play the night before, "Welcome to the Occupation." I just wanted to be in the same room as my favorite band, so fuck off, haters.

The boys from Georgia were so good I wanted more after the show ended. And more was on its way; this was just the first night. I watched the people in the front few rows and thought how that would be me and Uriah on the third night, and I wouldn't know what to do with myself being so close to the band.

After the show, I must have seemed to be on crack. I was so energetic and alive that I was jumping off walls. We all met at the usual spot, in front of the Rocky statue outside of the Spectrum. Eddie, Uriah, and I were all on cloud nine, talking about how wonderful the show was. Ray must have felt left out and decided to go home (good riddance).

The rest of us met some girls from the suburbs named Shannon and Anna. We talked for hours, and John H. and Uriah kept in contact with them for quite some time. I think Eddie dated or hooked up with Anna after the shows. After that interaction, Uriah went home, and Eddie, John, and I went back to John's Port Richmond area and hung out all night with Nick and Eddie's D&D dungeon master, Matt. We couldn't sleep, at least Eddie and I couldn't, and we stayed up all night, going from house to house until the sun came out. I finally went home to my shitty residence and passed out on my cat-pissed-stained bed/couch.

While I slept, our cat peed on my hippie bag (in her defense, she peed on anything she could get to) with my sweater and cup of soup flavoring inside. The smell from the chemical combination would make anyone gag, but I didn't know it happened until it was too late.

When I woke that afternoon, I was still on my R.E.M. buzz. I grabbed my trusty hippie school bag and rode the El to the Spectrum for the second show. I got there at the same time as the day before and wandered around aimlessly until I found out about a R.E.M. party being held in one of the rooms in the Spectrum. It was hosted by my favorite station, WDRE. See, walking around will eventually get one to the right spot at the right time.

The party was in one of the business rooms the Spectrum had underneath the main entrance. It held hundreds of people. I hit R.E.M. gold. There were so many R.E.M. fans I was in heaven. The radio station had the band's 1989 tour video on all the TVs, blaring out through the loudspeakers. I was dancing and doing my Stipe poses while watching him perform songs like "Begin the Begin" and "I Believe" from the VHS tape *Tourfilm*.

After the tape ended, they played non-stop R.E.M. songs while I was there. I was by myself since Eddie was working (I was unemployed, living off the few hundred bucks I had left from my Wildwood job). Ray sold his ticket to Eddie since he wasn't really an R.E.M. fan, and Eddie wanted a good seat to the show. I didn't have to deal with Ray again all weekend.

Our tickets were the furthest back for this show, in the 13th row. I was okay with it because of the better seats I had for the previous show. But Eddie and I never even sat in our row.

I met a lot of people at the R.E.M. party, including Marylin Russell, a DJ from WDRE who was a big fan. She was nice, and I would pop into her at shows for a few years down the road. I was 17, but the average person was in their 20s or 30s. I think most people appreciated my enthusiasm for R.E.M. I was full of energy and pure love for the band. This vibrated persona of mine during this week attracted people to me who were also huge R.E.M. fans.

Two girls, Cheryl and Denise, were huge fans as well. I told them about Barsky and the contest I should have won. They said they heard me on the radio and thought my poem was good (it probably wasn't) and how I was robbed. They became fixtures at almost every R.E.M. show I went to in Philly and sometimes beyond for decades.

We became long-standing friends, seeing R.E.M. in NYC and Atlanta, GA, a few times. They were 19 or 20 years, so they always referred to me as their little baby brother. They were also from Kensington and knew how bad it was. They let me crash on the sofa at their hotel when I was broke, traveling to see R.E.M. in other cities without charging me. They even bought me food at shows if I only had money for a ride or a T-shirt. They are good people, like most R.E.M. fans.

Another pair of nice women I met were from Northern New Jersey. They are very important to the rest of this weekend, which may be the peak of my life. Their names were Sandi and Nancy. They were both in their mid to late 20s. Sandi had been a fan of R.E.M. since she was 17 when she saw them play in 1984 for the *Reckoning* tour.

Sandi saw me dancing (by myself) to the R.E.M. tour video and started talking to me about my love for the band. She told me I reminded her of herself when she was 17 and a total R.E.M. nut. I took this as a compliment. We talked about our mutual favorite band for a while and discussed all the albums and info we acquired about the band over the years.

This pair of girls bought front-row (or close) tickets for all three Philly shows. They got them from a ticket agency and paid a bit for them. Sandi put them on a credit card and didn't think twice about it. I understood this way of thinking. I was pretty much broke, but I would give all the money in my pocket for another R.E.M. ticket.

Sandi showed me the lyric sheet she got from Stipe the night before. Lyric sheets, if you don't know, are like concert treasures for fans to collect. After the show, if you were close enough to the stage, you could ask a roadie for the lyric sheets the band used during the show. Sandi got the sheet for a new song called "Undertow," which eventually appeared on *New Adventures in Hi-Fi.* I liked the song after hearing it played live twice.

R.E.M. played five new songs throughout the shows I went to. "Binky, the Doormat," "Departure," "Revolution," "The Wake-Up Bomb" (which I knew from their MTV VMA performance), and "Undertow," my favorite of them all.

The only lyrics I could make out clearly were the ones from "Revolution," which I found to be Stipe's finest political song since the songs on *Document.* Some lines I thought were strong were, "Revolution never happened, Oliver North is running for Senate. Bomb the abortion clinics. Reagan's defense was the deficit. The virus was invented. Black men can't get acquitted of all the crimes that we committed. The future never happened." This song showed how things haven't changed much and how the battle for a better democracy and society is constant.

Now that I saw Sandi's lyric sheet, "Undertow" painted a scene of a person confronting death, possibly by drowning. Drowning was being used as an example of how everything is connected. We are just matter, and atoms are made of water, so when you die, you'll become one with the atoms that caused your death. There is no heaven. They're not turning into an angel, and it isn't their time to go.

They were heavy themes and just what the doctor ordered. Stipe again comforted me with lines like, "I don't need a heaven, I don't need religion, I am in the place where I should be." I took that as not just the person dying and realizing they don't go to heaven because the natural sequence in death is where they are supposed to be, but also, I took it as, in this life (especially my life), I don't need heaven or religion talk. I am in the mental and spiritual place where I should be.

I told Sandi and Nancy about my Y100/Barsky experience, and they also thought I got robbed. Sandi told me that she and Nancy had front-row tickets (which she paid a hefty price for) and that she would sneak me up to the front row. I told her I had my friends Eddie and Uriah sitting with me, and she said she could probably get all of us to the front. I was so excited, but at the same time, I didn't get my hopes up too high. You never know if something could happen to prevent it (like getting caught by security). But Sandi had a plan that I would adopt going forward at shows. It was a simple plan that worked for us that night, and every time I tried it since. I am giving away a big concert junkie secret here.

Sandi and Nancy each had a ticket for the front row. When they got to their seats, Sandi would take her and Nancy's ticket stubs and go up to the concession area, where Eddie, Uriah, and I would be waiting while Nancy stayed in her seat. She will then hand me Nancy's ticket stub, and I will go back down the stairs with Sandi to make our way to the front row. The usher would see I had a ticket for the front row and let me go through. Then, we would do the same with Eddie and Uriah.

We had to wait until R.E.M. was about to go on so we could get to the row when everyone was standing up and leaning on the gate that separated the rows from the stage. If we got there sooner, we would be the odd men out since there were three extra people with no seats to sit in.

I was worried it wouldn't work, but it all went according to plan. Sandi and Nancy came through like guardian angels. We were in the front row, stage right, between where Stipe and Buck usually stood (though Stipe didn't usually stay in one place). My heart was pounding with excitement as I was going to be within a few feet of R.E.M.!

I was still a little scared that we would be found out, but we stayed in the same spot, pressed up to the front by bodies that also jumped their seats to be closer to the stage for the next two and a half hours. When R.E.M. hit the stage, and I saw them clearly, without anything in my view, I was never so happy. Nothing mattered outside of that show and the energy I felt being so close to my favorite four people.

I danced and sang along with all the songs. I could even sing along with parts of the new ones by now. I loved every move that Stipe made. His presence on stage was powerful and demanded my attention. He came out in a suit with an orange T-shirt underneath. He had sunglasses on for the first few songs, then tossed them off to show his blue eyes magnified in beauty by his dark eyeliner.

There were so many highlights throughout the night. I loved hearing them play "Welcome to the Occupation." Mike Mills ran to our side during "It's the End of the World" and sang along with us. He was so close to us that I could see he was truly having a ball. The grand prize at any show from a band you love is to make eye contact with them. I think me and Mills had that for a minute during "End of the World," and Stipe and I had it a few times during the night (or at least I think we did). He came right over to where I was and looked down at me, then I reached up and touched his pant leg. I was terrified to do anything else that might piss him off and make him move away from my gaze, but he didn't, and I had a nice concert moment bonding with the person I admired most in the world.

Sometime during the show, I decided this was my chance to give Stipe the poem I wrote for him. I don't know why I thought it was a good idea to do it during this performance, but I was probably lost in the moment. When he was closer to my side, and I thought maybe he and I were making eye contact again, I took out my poem that was written in pen on a piece of paper from my notebook and threw it with what I thought was enough force to get to him on the stage. Unfortunately, I have no aim, and the poem missed the stage and went down some opening at the bottom of the stage, to never be seen or heard from again. It was for the best since I am sure it would be too embarrassing to recite now.

The night prior, before playing "Losing My Religion," Michael said he wanted people to throw their clothes at him. I was too far away on the first night to throw anything at him, but now that I was in the front row, I had my chance to throw whatever I wanted if he said it again, which he did. In the heat of the moment, I dug into my hippie bag and pulled out my sweater that I thought would be something Michael would wear. I threw it with all my might. It landed next to him, and he picked it up and pointed in my direction! Then he threw it off to the side of the stage with the other clothes people had thrown at him, including Nancy's jacket. Sometime that day, before I met them, Nancy and Sandi (being the concert professionals they were) went to a thrift store in the city and bought an orange '70s-style jacket with white stripes on the sides. It was something that Nancy knew Stipe would dig in the moment where his taste was aligned with punk kids and the retro look.

I had a moment when I touched my hero's leg and another when he looked at me with my sweater in his hands! Then Uriah had his moment at the show. Near the end of "End of the World," while the band was running around the stage and the audience was dancing and jumping around, Stipe sat closer to the audience, where most of us could try to touch or get a closer look at him. As he sang the last bits of the song, he threw the microphone into the audience, and a few people sang along to either "It's the end of the world as we know it" or "Time I had some time alone." One of those people was Uriah. He screamed into the mic Stipe used all night amidst dozens of people trying to squeeze closer to their hero.

After it was over, we were all on a R.E.M. high that we didn't want to end. We decided to go try and meet the band. Nancy was willing to drive us to R.E.M.'s hotel if we could find out where they were staying. I knew which hotel because I had asked a roadie the prior night.

They were at the luxurious Four Seasons hotel off the Ben Franklin Parkway, close to The Philadelphia Art Museum. After a quick drive to the hotel, we stood at the entrance and prepared for what I had wanted for years - to meet my favorite band. We were one of the first people at the hotel. I guess the roadie told others because the crowd got larger. About 40 people stood behind us in front of the doors of the five-star hotel while we waited for an hour.

Then, a van pulled up, and we all got excited when we realized it was Mike Mills. He got out of the vehicle, and instead of the Elvis-type suit he wore on stage, he was dressed very casually in jeans and an Iron Man T-shirt.

From all the interviews I saw with him, I assumed Mike would be down to earth and nice as could be, and that was true. I got to shake his hand and get his autograph. Eddie and I stood there in shock while we had a chit-chat about the show with Mike Mills. I asked him, "Do you remember us having a sing-along moment during "End of the World"? and he smiled and said, "That was you, wasn't it?" Thinking about it now, he was probably humoring me or making me feel like we had this moment during the show since it clearly meant a lot to me, and I appreciate that.

Mike then said goodnight to all of us and went to his room. I might have some issues with grasping reality and feeling things fully at this time, but I absolutely grasped that I just met one of the guys from R.E.M.! If the night ended then, I would have been on cloud nine from meeting Mills.

It wasn't long until the lingering crowd got another thrill. A white van pulled up, and someone said Michael Stipe was inside. My heart jumped. I looked in as the van pulled up to the hotel sidewalk. There he was, my idol, role model, and hero, Michael Stipe. I was in front of the crowd, and the security guard or Stipe's bodyguard told us to move back, and Michael would come out and shake some hands.

I saw Michael in the front passenger seat and couldn't help myself. My teenage heart took over. I didn't know if I would ever be this close to my hero again. I knew I had to tell him how I felt. I jumped in front of everyone in the crowd, looked Michael Stipe in the eyes, and said, "I love you so much, Michael." It was the most genuine thing I could have said from my heart.

He smiled, maybe just to be polite. I guess I didn't scare him off since he came out of the van. I can only imagine what he was thinking. Here I was, a kid who modeled himself off him, shaved head, eyeliner, and skinny as a rale. I hope he was flattered.

He was calm and beautiful, standing a foot away. I couldn't get over him being in front of me. Part of me wanted to reach out and touch his face. Instead, I kept my hands to my mouth in a shocking expression. I gather now that Michael could tell I was over the moon for him, and he handled it very well. The world seemed to stand still at this moment. All my attention was locked on Michael Stipe. He was the only thing that mattered. There was electricity in the air. Every second he was in front of us felt so intense and important.

He shook my hand and talked to the crowd about the show. Michael wore what he had on during the show, but one thing was added: the orange jacket that Nancy threw on stage during "Losing My Religion." She was right. It was right up his alley, and he looked really cool wearing it. She told him she was the one who threw it at him, and this led me, in my awe of being in my hero's presence, to ask him if he got the sweater I threw on stage.

It was the sweater that had instant soup mix and cat pee on it (without my knowing). There was a silent moment, and then Michael replied, "Yes, but I couldn't wear it because it smelled too bad." My heart sank, and I felt embarrassed. I was still on a natural high from being in front of my hero. Even though he associated me with a foul-scented garment, I was happy to be in his presence. I think the bodyguard laughed when Stipe said this, which made me more upset. I think Michael saw that in my eyes and said, "Sorry about that, man." I got another handshake and said it was okay. But yes, the first time I met my idol, my shitty home life came into play, and he told me I smelt bad. Only my luck.

I had more pleasant interactions with Michael over the decades, on his own terms, at meetings he was aware of, instead of an ambush at his hotel after midnight. After he went inside the hotel, we all went to a diner and talked about one of the greatest nights of my life. After the meal, Sandi asked me if I wanted to go to her apartment in New Jersey and see her massive R.E.M. collection of CDs, records, magazines, video tapes, etc. I didn't want to go home to my cat-piss couch. I was up for anything.

Nancy drove us to her place, and we stayed up till God knows when watching R.E.M. interviews and live performances. I was instantly jealous of Sandi's record collection. She had so many rare albums and singles, including the limited edition of R.E.M.'s first single, "Radio Free Europe," on HibTone records. Years later, I paid $100 for that single.

I watched interviews with Stipe from 1991 for the *Out of Time* release that I had never seen before. Michael looked so good with his short, messy hair and 5 o'clock shadow beard. He sounded intelligent, deep, and confident (everything I wish I was). He told a story about how he hated writing love songs. He said he was driving around after a breakup, and after every love song on the radio, he thought, "That's me," until he realized he was being manipulated. He thought most love songs were all the same, so he wanted to make new ones that were different. That's what *Out of Time* is about.

The interview showed me that the band's hit "The One I Love" wasn't just a song with a violent twist, in which Stipe is saying the one he just broke up with was just a prop. The repeated lyrics in every verse made it the perfect anti-love song. With the verses being the same, Stipe could be saying that all pop-love songs were the same (simple props to occupy your time). With R.E.M. songs, there are usually a few ways to interpret them (which helps them stay relevant).

Eddie and I thought it was about relationships you knew would never last and were only there to occupy your time. Maybe Stipe was saying "Fire" to all the love songs on the radio. Interestingly, he starts each verse with the most cliché thing to say in a love song, "This one goes out to the one I love."

The next day, Nancy and Sandi took me back to my residence so I could get changed. They didn't come in since it was a shack of an apartment that I was embarrassed by. My drug-addict father was sitting in the living room, and our dog was a vicious beast who would bite the shit out of anyone's ankles.

I got changed and grabbed a CLEAN t-shirt from my bag of clothes. While staying with my parents, I kept my clothes in a trash bag and carried them to and from the laundry mat. I grabbed a shirt I bought in Wildwood that I thought Michael would like. It said "Question Authority" on it. I only wore it a few times and knew it was clean. I planned to throw it at him during the last show, and maybe he would see that not all of my clothing smelled like cat urine.

I met Eddie and Uriah for the last show of the best weekend of my young life. We would pull the trick that got us to the front row the night before. Uriah and I had 2nd row (almost center stage) tickets, and we used them to sneak Eddie, Denise, and Cheryl down to our section. Sandi and Nancy had front-row tickets again, so Uriah, Eddie, and I planned to jump over our seats when the show started and hang out in the front row like the night before.

Everything worked with no problems. One of these reasons was that the security guy, Mike, working at the front of the stage, was dating Christin from Kensington. Once he knew I was in the crowd and that close, he was very cool with me getting to the front. He knew I was in love with R.E.M. and told me the first night Stipe practically had his leg leaning on him. He also said he was backstage right before they came out to play in front of 18,000 people, and all they were talking about was what they had for dinner. They were the biggest band in the world, and they didn't let it overwhelm them.

The show was just as good as the two previous nights. I was still in awe of being so close to the stage. I danced and did all my best Stipe moves to every song. When Michael said to throw clothes at him before they played "Losing My Religion," I threw my clean T-shirt with all my strength. It hit Stipe on the head. I thought, "Uh-oh, Stipe is going to be mad at me!" Instead (and I thought I was imagining this), he stared at me during the first parts of my favorite song in the world. I kept it to myself.

A week or two later, a free Philadelphia newspaper called *The City Weekly* had a review of the last R.E.M. show in Philly. They mentioned that someone hit Stipe in the head with a shirt during "Losing My Religion" and that Stipe stared down the assailant with a cool glare while singing to him. It's not word for word, but that was basically what the article said. I knew they were referring to me, and I was glad I didn't imagine the whole thing through wishful thinking.

I loved every minute of the rest of the show. After it was over and Stipe and company ended the free-for-all version of "End of the World," my ears kept ringing (another sacrifice you make as a concert junkie). All I wanted to do was be like R.E.M. I wanted to be in a band. I wanted to dance, sing, and write meaningful songs. I was still young enough to dream of being like my idols without reality slapping me down, or at least believe that deserving my dreams was enough to make them real. If only that was true.

We decided not to try to meet R.E.M. again at their hotel. We figured once was enough to bug them, and they would probably be in a rush since they left for D.C. the next day. Eddie, Uriah, me, and my new R.E.M. friends (Sandi, Nancy, Cheryl, and Denise) all hung out for a while before going our separate ways for the night.

Sandi gave me her number and told me to keep in touch, especially when R.E.M. is touring. I said I would, but I lost the paper with her phone number shortly after she gave it to me. I regretted that so much. Sandi was such a cool girl and loved R.E.M. as much as I did. But I lived in a ball of chaos and lost most things that I put in my pocket. I hoped I would run into her again at a show.

I didn't see Sandi again until 2001, standing outside MTV's NYC studio, trying my best (failing) to get into REM's 2nd MTV Unplugged performance. I begged the doorman to let me in, and Sandi was doing the same. We didn't recognize each other right away, but when we did, it was a big "Oh My Fucking God" feeling for both of us. She gave me her phone number for the 2nd time, and just like in 1995, I lost the little paper she wrote it on before getting home to Philly. I was a year or two away from owning a cell phone to store her number in for good. That was the last time I saw my R.E.M. hero, but she really came through for me that weekend.

Chapter 48:
Listen to the Radio

Now that the thing I was looking forward to for so long was over (the thing that kept me ticking and gave me a sense of direction through my mental torture and life plan), I decided to call Y-100. I wanted to let the Barsky show know that the three R.E.M. shows were exactly what I needed and wanted. I called and told the producer it was Chaz, the R.E.M. guy, and he put me on the air.

Barsky, likely thinking he could kill some time again with this Stipe nut, asked me how the shows were. I told him I didn't need their contest, and I got to the front row for two nights and met Michael Stipe and Mike Mills. He acted sincere and said he was happy for me, then said he wanted me to write a poem about meeting Stipe and call back and read it on air. I had a hunch it was another ploy to get me to read a shitty poem about my favorite singer so he could make fun of me some more. But, with my current (and long future) mental state of not fully being aware of actions or feelings like embarrassment or pride, I did what he asked.

I grabbed a yellow notepad my dad had lying around that he loved doodling on and thought about my hero and how great it was to be in his presence that weekend. My poetry then might have sucked, but I could write really fast. Lines came to me as long I focused on the subject. It was only a page long and straight to the point, more than the one I read last time. I don't remember what it said, except the line that caused a commotion on the show.

As I read my poem on the air, the morning team sat quietly listening (and probably laughing). I tried my best to focus on the words and tuned out everything else. The first line was probably about Stipe showing me how to love or some shit like that. And the very next line was, "You were the one who taught me how to give a fuck." I was ready to read the next line when I heard a bunch of noise and screaming coming from my phone and the turned-down radio I had on. Barsky and the morning crew were up in arms about me saying "Fuck" on air. All the personalities on the air yelled at me. I stopped reading my poem, and Barsky shouted that I couldn't use the "F" word on the air.

I tried to explain that I thought there was a few-second delay and I would get blurred out. Barsky said they don't have one, and he might get fined. I apologized, and he said it was okay. He told me to keep reading, but it was a ploy. Once I started reading the next line, he hung up on me out of retaliation. Barsky spent the next hour making fun of me and my love for Michael Stipe. He repeatedly said I should have known better than to curse on the air. The woman on the show played devil's advocate and stood up for me. She said I didn't know I wasn't on a delay, then Barsky put her down and bad-mouthed me some more. He was furious with me.

I didn't listen to his show often since I usually stayed up all night and slept during the broadcast hours. However, Uriah and John H told me that Barsky made fun of me again the next week while playing The Cure's "Lovesong." When the song ended, Barsky said the lyric, "I will always love you," sounds like that Michael Stipe guy. I shrugged all of it off and didn't think much about it. John H's mom heard me and thought I ruined a chance to get my poetry heard. But I doubt anything would come from a kid reading bad poetry on a local radio station. All I got out of it was a funny story at my (and Barsky's) expense.

Chapter 49:
The Spork in the Road

I was still running around with Ray occasionally the week after the R.E.M. shows. I was under the impression that the path I had to be on was intertwined with Ray and my other alt-rock friends. But the end of that irrational thinking was at hand.

We took a bus to the Moorestown mall in Jersey to hang out with Ray's "girlfriend" Janine, Katie, and their friend Mark.

We were in a bookstore looking around when Janine said Megan was in another aisle shopping. I looked over, and there was my Megan. This was the first time I saw her since Lollapalooza. She ran to me, and we embraced in a strong, comforting hug. She trembled with excitement. We talked for a bit, and it was so exciting to see her I couldn't help but kiss her. She kissed me back, and it was a nice moment to have with a girl that I truly cared about, especially since I wasn't expecting to see her.

Megan had to leave since her parents were somewhere in the mall (which made our kiss more exciting, in a Romeo and Juliet kind of way, since we weren't allowed to see each other). The rest of us wandered the mall and then went to the bus stop where Ray and I would catch a New Jersey Transit bus back to Philly.

While waiting for the bus, we sat near people offended by our presence (mainly Mark's). An older person didn't like how Mark talked in a "gay way," and I guess the fact that he was gay came up in our conversation. This person gave us dirty looks. So, Mark and I decided to freak them out by French kissing. I was not gay or bisexual (except for Stipe), but I loved to push envelopes and make bigots uncomfortable.

Eventually, I would question my sexuality, mainly because of how sensitive I was and how much I loved Michael Stipe. People said I was afraid to come out. They said I talked with a lisp. I was just hyperactive and unconfident talking to people. Most of my words slurred into each other. They thought I was gay, but the religion I grew up in was holding me back. I would ponder this and act on things. For the most part, I was straight, but I liked to make people think I was bi to make them feel uncomfortable if they deserved it. It worked well at the bus stop.

The next day, Ray told me he wanted to break up with Janine but didn't want to be the bad guy. He hatched up some plan about me calling Janine and telling her I liked her, and then somehow it would cause her to break up with Ray (all over the phone). I, regretfully, went along with this nonsense, hating myself for letting Ray manipulate me again. I called Janine and told her I liked her and wanted to date her (which I didn't). She then called Ray and broke up with him. Ray then called me. While I was on the phone, he called Janine back and pretended to be sad.

I knew at that moment I didn't want to play Ray's games anymore. I didn't want to play with people's minds and feelings. I mean, I never did before, but I knew I had to move on. I didn't want to be involved with mind games and fake relationships. I called Janine back and told her what happened. Then, I told Ray, "I never want to do that again, I felt like shit over it, and I don't want to play your games." He blew it off and thought I was overreacting. But I wasn't. It was the tipping point. I was a day or two away from cutting Ray off (at least in my heart and head).

On Friday, October 20th, Ray and I attended a dance with two girls we met in Wildwood. It was at their high school in Delaware County, PA. Amy was super laid back and cool. The other girl was why Ray wanted to end things with Janine. He had the hots for her. After that dance, I had enough of Ray and hitched my horse to the Eddie and John H. wagon.

A day or two before the dance, I hung out with Eddie and John in Port Richmond. Eddie and I talked almost daily and were closer than ever after our R.E.M. weekend. We were all wandering around the area when someone came up with the idea of getting someone to buy us beer. Someone got a runner (an older person to buy underage kids' beer), and then we went into an alleyway.

I distanced myself from alcohol and drugs for a year and a half, even throughout my summer of mental problems and anxiety. I wasn't planning on drinking that night. I was hanging out with the guys, and they bought beer, but that didn't mean I had to drink. I still believed I had to stay sober to get a handle on my life and emotions so I could continue being a better person. I thought what I was going through was temporary and a test. I was partly right. I should have kept from drinking and gotten a hold of myself and my emotions, but I was a kid, full of confusion and no one to guide me.

Eddie was drinking the beer they all got and said I should also drink some. I told him how I felt about it, that I didn't want to hide from life. I wanted to take everything head-on with a clear mind. Eddie, who I trusted now more than ever, said, "Life sucks, and sometimes you got to drink to deal with it." This made sense, and I decided to have some beer with the fellas. My thought pattern was, "Eddie's right and full of emotions. He drinks, so maybe once in a while will be okay for me too." (Hahahaha, let's all laugh at me in unison).

I got drunk with my teenage friends and had fun all night, like a teenager should. Unfortunately, I didn't stop drinking or doing drugs for quite some time. I stopped for a year or two. Then, I went right back to it. But life does suck, and sometimes (most times) you got to drink when you come from a dirt-poor, born-again Christian background.

After the drinking lowered my defenses, Eddie convinced me to hang out at the Franklin Mills Mall again (the place I had been dreading and avoiding for months). I did the next day, and we hung out with some girls I met the first time I went to the mall in February: Sarah, Amy, Missy, and Severa.

Severa and I exchanged numbers at the Live show in September. We talked on and off for a month as friends, but a romantic relationship seemed promising. She was awkward, sweet, and pretty with curly, Shirly Temple-like dirty blonde hair. We arranged to hang out at Sarah's house (in Northeast Philly, about a 10-minute ride from the mall), then we would go to the mall. I went solo to Sarah's house, and Eddie, John H., and Nick met up with us later. We were all hanging out in Sarah's backyard, eating the most delicious thing in my life, pizza fries from Pizza City, and talking a mile a minute with pure enthusiasm for being in front of four pretty girls who were actually interested in what I said and liked being around me.

I felt comfortable around the girls like I had known them for years. It stemmed from having the same taste in deep, sensitive music and an understanding that we were all going through similar situations during the early years of our lives. At this moment, at least in my head, we were all in the same boat. A bunch of sad kids attracted to pop culture that addressed our needs for comfort, sympathy, and a break from the demands to conform to a lesser version of ourselves. I was on a roll that day, speaking faster than I could think (which was my norm). I talked a mile a minute, going from one subject to whatever popped into my head next.

Everyone seemed to be entertained by my ADHD antics. Missy (a splendid soul) asked me if I required oxygen to speak since I talked so much that I hardly stopped to breathe. I had a ball.

As Sarah showed me to the bathroom, she kept looking back at me while I tried to be charming. I asked what her last name was, and she said "Uglyman" because it was really Beautyman, but she had self-esteem issues. I looked at her smiling face and told her she wasn't ugly at all. It was true, but one might not notice what others do in the looks department. Sarah Beautyman had caught my attention. A love story was about to blossom.

We took the Septa bus to the mall. At least 50 kids were hanging out near the arcade (that's how predictable we were). I recognized some kids from last winter. Instead of being separate, they were all together. They acknowledged each other but weren't on the same page yet. They were on the verge of becoming friends. They weren't so different. They just needed a little push or a common thread (which was me and Nick).

It was my first day back in the area that I thought led to my demise. I was not 100 percent there. I was weary of it and thought it was just a one-time thing, and I would go back to being a hermit, trying to figure out what to do with my life. So, I was on the defense a little.

I met up with Eddie and John H., and we goofed around with Severa and her circle until we went home. Severa asked if I wanted to hang out on Friday (the day of the dance with Amy and the girl Ray was trying to get with). I didn't know what to do, but I said I would, and we would see a movie or something. It was a dilemma for me. I now had two dates with two girls on the same day.

I was in a pickle. I had Amy, who knew more obscure Nirvana songs than me. She had a similar Jeff/newsboy hat that I was keen on wearing. With her came the path of Ray and his mind games, pretending he was a mental god. He thought he was going to be the next Charles Manson. He thought he could control anyone who came across his path.

One time, we were hanging out in a park on 8th Street in Center City, and Ray wore a Charles Manson shirt that glorified that insane piece of shit. An African-American man came over and put Ray in his place. He asked Ray why he would wear a shirt of man who murdered a pregnant woman. Ray was stumped at first and wanted him to go away. Then Ray explained that Manson never killed anyone; others did it for him. That was Ray in a nutshell. He thought he was some cult leader or guru who could make teenagers do what he wanted. Scary fucking shit, Ray.

On the other hand, I could embrace the simpler life of hanging out in the safer parts of town (Northeast Philly) with my friend and soul mate, Eddie, and some nice girls who liked alt-rock as much as I did. I didn't know what to do that night, but I didn't have to choose. Life (my shitty one) got in the way. I was supposed to meet Severa at the mall that Friday night, and all day long, Ray was trying to persuade me to go to the dance. I told him I wasn't going. Then I took a bath in the bathtub that wasn't inside the apartment.

My dad passed out due to drugs, and my mom was working at the card store. After my bath, I got dry and put on my clothes. I went to open the door to our shitty apartment and realized the door was locked. I didn't turn the door handle lock to the unlock position when I went to take my bath (a bath like I was in the 1800s). I was locked out of the place that had my wallet and shoes. I pounded on the door, but my pop was not to be awakened from his drug-induced slumber.

We only had a chorded phone, which was also in the apartment, so I had no way of getting in touch with anyone, including Severa. I was supposed to meet her in an hour, at 7 p.m. Time flew by with me sitting in the bathroom. I didn't even know what time it was since I didn't have a clock in there and I didn't wear a watch. It wasn't the easiest thing to do, sitting in a rundown bathroom for hours with nothing to occupy your already rapidly moving mind.

Finally, around 8 p.m., my mom came home from work and let me into the apartment. I tried calling Severa at home, but she left for the mall. I thought about just going to the mall but figured it would take me an hour, and I wasn't 100% sure Severa would be there. And I was still on the fence about hanging out at the mall and giving in to how I was before my breakdown (being the center of attention and always "on").

I decided to call Ray to see if he left for the dance yet. He had not, so I got on the El to meet him at the K&A stop. Ray boarded the train, and we were together again (for the last time on friendly terms), going to my first high school dance. We had to take the El to the end of the line (69th street), then catch another bus to get to Amy's school.

We got there in time to have fun and dance. I kissed Amy during the night, and part of me thought I could date her and go down this road for a while. But Ray would be involved, and he was getting on my nerves more than ever. I realized I didn't need him. He was a phony compared to my best friend, Eddie.

I missed Eddie that night, and I wondered what he was doing. Most likely, he was having a ball at the mall with all kinds of alt-rock kids and cute girls. I thought about the possibilities of being surrounded by people like Sarah, Amy (Not Delaware County Amy), Severa, and Missy. Ray thought he was the king of alt-rock and everything that came with it. He was exhausting to be around. It was almost like a competition with him over how sad and angry you were and how bad your life was. There was no progression or positiveness to come from this tired friendship. I had enough of him.

I had come to a fork in the road. Do I stay the course I was on with Ray's nonsense and all the drama that came with runaways and wandering around Kensington without a purpose? Every action leads to other actions. In 1992, I was tired of being poor and wanted to make some pocket money. I got the paper job, which led to meeting two other kids in a similar financial situation. They impacted me and represented my choice that would change my current life and consume me for years.

With Ray and that life, I was muzzled. I couldn't think or feel without thinking Ray would judge or put me down. I was more introverted and only wanted to get through the day, hoping the next day I would wake up and be back to my senses. On the other hand, with Eddie, I would be back with all these people who didn't really know me, only how wild and animated I could be. The choice was already made.

I spent seven months avoiding kids I was having fun with out of fear that I wasn't being true to my suffering and pain. I would go the other way and throw myself into the mix. Eddie, Nick, John H., the girls at the mall, and a boatload of other kids will be my world for the next few years, with all the craziness that comes with throwing caution to the wind and being as wild as possible.

Chapter 50:
When You Tire of One Side, the Other Serves You Best

After the dance party and my final cut-off from the Charles Manson wannabe, I contacted Sarah Beautyman (not Severa) the next day. I had her number from the day we hung out at her house. It was given to me to get the right directions there. I couldn't get a hold of Severa to explain what had happened to me the night before and thought going through her friend was the easiest way of apologizing.

Sarah invited me to a party (an unsupervised one) that her friends were having in the Northeast. I asked if I could bring Eddie with me, and she said, "of course," so we met up near her house and tried to locate the party house. Sarah didn't know the exact address, only what the house looked like. We never found the party. We walked around the Parkwood section of Northeast Philly for about an hour, then gave up and went to a diner. Then we went to her best friend Amy's house for the night.

To keep the Amys apart, we will call this Amy "Amy C." because her last name started with a "C" (I know, really clever of me). Amy C. was somewhere else for the night and was supposed to be home late. When we got to her home, we went around the back area where you could get into her backyard, which was connected to the furnished basement.

We sat there (on a chilly October night) until Amy C. finally came home and let us in the basement. Eddie and I weren't necessarily allowed to be over that late in Amy C.'s house. Her parents were the cool type of parents. They let us hang there a lot when we had nothing else to do, and Amy C.'s mom would throw huge parties that we would attend and have a lot of fun at. But, on this night, Amy C. said we could hang out inside the basement with her and Sarah, but when she went to bed, we would have to either go home (which wasn't going to happen because it was now close midnight and it would take forever to take Septa home) or we could hang out in the backyard since then two strange boys weren't technically sleeping over a 16-year-old girl's house.

Amy C. went to bed, and Sarah (who was supposed to sleep over after the party we never had) continued hanging out with me and Eddie. All night, we got to know each other better. I had no idea if she liked me, but there was flirtation between us. I was on my usual behavior, talking a mile a minute and trying to never have a dull moment. She was the opposite. Sarah was laid back (a bit of a pothead) and would sit back and listen to me be a loud maniac all night. I learned she was 15, and her birthday was the same day as Michael

Stipe's (January 4th)! That alone made me like her more. She was born on Stipe's 20th birthday.

She went to a different high school than Amy C., who went to a Catholic school in the Northeast called Archbishop Ryan. Sarah went to an all-girls Catholic school called Nazareth Academy. Even though they weren't in the same school, they were close as can be. Sarah had long brown hair and dark brown eyes. She kind of looked like Alanis Morissette but not as angry and sadder. She was a few inches shorter than me, which I always liked, and on the thinner side. She was a pretty girl and never had anything negative to say about anyone.

Eddie must have noticed a spark or mutual interest between Sarah and me, so he stayed quiet and let us talk to each other through the night. We stayed over (in the backyard) the entire night. Well, there was a time when Sarah got gutsy and said we could warm up for a bit in the basement, but we had to be quiet.

It must have been 2 or 3 a.m. I was a little delirious from being up so late. I was running on instincts and fumes. I was sitting at the stereo in Amy C.'s basement, playing music they owned. Sarah was sitting close to me on the floor. I was so attracted to her that I wanted to kiss her. I didn't know if she had the same feelings, but her face was inches from mine as we sat, listening to music.

Eddie read the room and knew how to pull at my heartstrings. He played a song he knew would push over the top to make a move: "(Everything I Do) I Do It for You" by Bryan Adams. It was the kick in the butt I needed. I leaned in and kissed Sarah for the first time. It was peak teenage life.

After we kissed a few more times, we fell asleep until the sun came up. Eddie was cracking jokes in Amy C.'s backyard (a side I rarely saw of him) about how cold we all were last night, and he said to the sun, "Where the fuck were you last night?" I laughed way too much, but I was sleep-deprived and happy I kissed a girl I thought I could be in a relationship with.

Sometime that morning, as we waited for Amy C. to wake up, I talked to Sarah about going steady. She said she wanted to, and just like that, I had a new girlfriend, and just like that, my new place to roam for a few years will be the great northeast and a fucking mall.

Chapter 51 :
Hung Down with the Freaks and Ghouls

I had chosen Eddie and now Sarah. I had chosen stability over Ray and his dangerous, foolish ways. Looking back, I should have gotten mental and emotional help to deal with my problems instead of masking and hiding them. But I didn't have anyone to show me what to do or where to go. I didn't even know if there was something wrong with me or if this was the way life was supposed to be: a constant struggle to have confidence and a continuous flow of guilt for the smallest of things like eating when you're not starving or looking at a girl that you find sexually attractive.

My head was a mess. My hope was that one day, everything would work out for me, and I would be in control of my mind and feelings again. I wasn't feeling so numb anymore. I had feelings, but I didn't have control over them. If I felt too much or thought about a subject that brought on negative feelings, it would be too much for me, and I would go back to my rituals and obsessive thoughts and behaviors. Saying to myself the things and people I loved and finish my little mental chants with asking for something I wanted the most and the word "forever" to seal the deal. The whole time I would have to feel everything I said and put positive energy into to proved I meant it and made sure no negative feelings or thoughts creeped in during this prayer like ritual, and if a negative thought or a doubt came in my troubled brain during it, I would have to start all over again until I got it right. This would happen countless times a day. All based on how anxious or down on my luck I was. It mostly flared up when I was alone or not talking to people. I was smart enough to know this strange behavior was odd and was obviously stemming from my Jesus loving days when I prayed constantly to make I was saved or to be in constant communication with the supreme being, to let them know what I needed. The whole time I would try to stay of pure mind so god would hear me since I was told sin and bad thoughts would block him from my prayers. Even though I knew this was what was happening, I still did my rituals for the sake of my own fragile mind.

The only things I could count on were my favorite music and friends. Eddie was my best friend, so I followed him, thinking I could trust him. I didn't believe in the Christian God anymore, but I still thought something was in control and that there was a reason for everything. I believed my chosen path would open the next chapter in my life.

Perhaps this was all because of the born-againers and their belief that God has a plan for everything and everyone. But I don't think it was just them. The concept of fate or destiny is fluid through everything I watched and listened to growing up. If I am just a consumer and a product of what I was taught and had seen, then the secular world also made me this way.

I was many years away from realizing everything is random, and only my ego (or a desire to inflate one) would lead me to believe in destiny. But here I was, the forever dreamer.

I ran from this lifestyle for months, and just like that, I was going right back to it, thinking, "Okay, let's see where this takes me." Where it takes me is to the limit. My mind was erratic and full of confusion. I didn't know what was what, and my brain was fragile. I went through a whirlwind of ups and downs, and my consciousness felt fatigued. I had months and months of built-up anxiety and anger. Instead of dealing with these things head-on, I pushed them down and unleashed them on the world like a wild child.

I was out for experiences and whatever life threw my way. If there was a group of people around that honestly liked me, a switch would go on in me. I would be the great entertainer for the moment. Something inside of me after my breakdown didn't want to face my miserable reality. I tried for months to get back to where I was on March 2nd, but nothing worked. I was just a kid with no idea what was happening to him, and instead of getting help, I spent years running away from life and my reality.

I became consumed by good times, trying hard to push out every negative thought. I found myself addicted to the attention, admiration, and respect of my peers.

In the first few months of meeting various people, I barely had alone time. I was over-stimulated by the hundreds of people I met throughout the area. I was on fire with charisma and storytelling, an animated ball of energy. I was on autopilot with everything I said and did. If I went to a normal school, this would probably be the time in my life when I was the lead in a high school play or something, but instead, I was labeled the "mallrat king." How pathetic is that?

Don't worry, I never took it seriously. I was hanging out with like-minded kids from a much safer neighborhood than mine. It was mostly a bunch of kids who liked similar music and weren't popular at school. They were freaks and misfits, and this place became a home for them. Kids aged 13-21 came to the mall and hung out with us for hours.

It was a constant battle with mall security as they chased us out of areas when we loitered too long. Each entrance to the mall had a different color. Ours was the yellow section. We hovered around that area because of the arcade. I rarely played video games, but we spent most of our time there.

We also frequented the food court. We'd order something small and sit there as long as possible. There was a movie out that year by Kevin Smith called *Mallrats*. It was like our lives at the mall, but we had much more kids and drugs than Kevin's movie.

In the movie, the main character walks around with a soda cup from a place that gives out free refills. He uses the same cup every time he goes to the mall. Most of us did this as well. We all had a cup that would get us free refills from a deli in the food court (later, it would be a place where we get our acid). We would also get someone older to buy us rum, then we'd fill the cup with coke, pour the rum in under the table, pass it around, and get drunk for cheap. Security would eventually kick us out, and we would roam around the mall until we found another place to relax.

I had several run-ins with the security guards (and the cops stationed at the mall). Once, the head security, trying to be a tough guy, had a bunch of his guards at the yellow section say we couldn't hang out there again. We started yelling at each other as we circled each other. They kicked me out for the day, and he said he would have the last laugh. My rebellious attitude made me say I'd be laughing last because he was 60, and I would live much longer than him. I know it was mean, but it was in the heat of the moment.

If we got kicked out of the mall for the day, we would either take a group of friends (usually for me, it was Sarah and her crew) and wander outside the mall until we got to one of the fast food places (McShit, Taco Hell, or Burger King) that were all relatively near each other. We would stay at one for the rest of the night in the parking lot, sometimes into the weary closing hours. If one unhealthy food place kicked us out, we went to the next one, and so on.

Once, after we got kicked out of the mall, a cop patrolling the area stopped us and searched our bags (all alt kids in the '90s wore some type of bag). I just handed my bag over to the cop. Sarah told the cop, "You can't just search us. We have rights." I followed with, "Yeah, we do have rights." But he searched us anyway and took my boxcutter that I had for self-defense in case of a mugging on my way home to the hood.

The cops were searching us because other groups of kids were spray painting walls in the mall. We might have all been degenerates with nowhere to go, but the only laws we broke were underage drinking, smoking, and drug use.

Kids came up to hang with us from all over the Northeast and suburbs of Philly. We had about 50-150 kids on any night (especially the weekends) partying for hours. We were a bunch of kids trying to make friends and find a place to belong. I think I had some part in creating an atmosphere that was accepting of everyone who wanted to be a part of the community we started.

We didn't just go to malls and fast-food joints. There were also numerous house parties. In many cases, Eddie and I slept over people's houses as much as possible so we didn't have to take buses to our horrible homes and neighborhoods. I slept out for days at a time, sometimes weeks. For a couple summers, I spent months at a friend's house who had a cool parent who didn't care what hooligans their kids were involved with.

We were kids and young adults trying to figure out life. We weren't quite ready for adulthood (especially in my case, with my fragile mind and fears of God and my future). We wanted to have fun but also take on some adult situations and pretend we were wiser and older than we were due to our outlook on life and the pain we already went through.

We did things that seemed adult that other kids did throughout history. We smoked cigarettes (even I did off and on for a bit), we drank, smoked pot, had sexual encounters, and talked about the best bands and movies of all time, like our opinions were fact, and we were critics instead of devoted fans to the medium we followed.

Most of the people were good, just looking for fun and friends. I think people were drawn to me because of my energy. I was living in the moment most days. My personality was the complete opposite of the past several months. I was always had a burning desire to entertain everyone in my path. It spawned from my genuine desire to meet new people and not be held back by religion or fear of what people thought of me.

The more positive attention I got, the more my antics would go on. I was constantly energetic with a larger-than-life persona that most kids from the Northeast weren't used to. In the 1990s, kids who liked alt-rock liked real people who faced some struggles. They liked relatable folks with tales of misery. Eddie and I were these types of people. Suddenly, it was cool to shop at thrift stores, to be poor, have some emotional problems, and not shower (or brush your teeth) daily. We were punk as fuck, without liking that style of music. I think this was also part of my appeal. We had a boatload of crazy stories and emotional baggage, but we were also full of life and wanted to have fun as much as possible.

When I say "fun," I don't just mean having a party. It meant doing meaningful things like talking about life and religion, attending concerts, etc. I also think people liked me because I remembered everyone's name and their favorite band since that was important to me. I loved music. I thought everyone loved their favorite bands as much as I loved R.E.M. (most did not).

I also just left a born-again Christian religion that was good for one thing. It gave me a sense of accepting everyone (until someone crossed me) and wanting a community. So, I welcomed everyone who wanted to join what was happening during the mid to late 90s in Philly. In my juvenile mind, I thought it was the road to being something better than I was and a part of my journey to where I wanted to go.

In reality, I was hiding from my shitshow life and not accepting I would have to move on with or without Laura. I was so delusional that I got lost in this lifestyle for way too long. Doing drugs (especially acid) didn't help much in the reality department. The more drugs I did, the easier it was to think I was doing what I was supposed to do. This way of thinking kept me in a hamster wheel of negativity.

Chapter 52:
Maybe You're the One That's Gonna Save Me

Sarah and I spent most of our time together. I would go to her house after she got done school, make out, listen to music, and eat (usually mozzarella sticks since Sarah owned a deep fryer). I would leave before her mom got home from work, then go to the mall and hang out with whoever showed up. Most days, there were plenty of people to pal around with at the mall or at their homes that I saw as rich since they had their basic needs met and then some.

Most days, Sarah and I were fine with our little window of time being teenagers in love. She knew what time her mom was usually home from work. We had it down to a science when I had to leave, then wait to come back to knock on her door and pretend we were following her mom's rules of boys not being allowed over without a parent. But one day, to our surprise, Sarah's mom came home earlier than usual.

I didn't have enough time to leave the house without the chance of her mom seeing me. Her mom would come through the front door and see me leaving that way. If I went out the back door, which led to the backyard, there would be the chance her mom would look out a window and see me in the yard or leaving the yard connected to an alleyway.

Sarah told me to wait in the garage connected to their basement. I waited for God knows how long (probably an hour) sitting behind storage boxes. I listened to my poor man's Walkman at a low volume to hear someone approaching. I had WDRE on since my batteries were running low, and playing cassette tapes would kill the battery. If that happened, I'd be really bored.

I heard a bunch of songs that were popular at the time, such as "Jane Says" by Jane's Addiction, "Rooster" by Alice in Chains, and Oasis' "Wonderwall." The latter's lyrics were similar to my relationship with my newfound girlfriend. Our intense feelings in life and how much despair we both had for it, combined with our need for each other's love, made me think Sarah might be the one who would save me from the madness. There was hope on the horizon.

Finally, Sarah came down to the garage. She was so sorry that it took so long for her mom to get a shower. I finally had a chance to escape. I was living a teenage movie cliché. It wouldn't be the last time. I didn't mind or fuss about being stuck in a garage for so long. I was just happy this pretty girl liked me. My expectations for our future made it worthwhile.

Chapter 53:
To Shake These Zipper Blues

At the end of October, I had it out with Ray for the last time over the phone. I told him he was a phony and an asshole manipulating people. I thought this would be the end of the story with Ray. I thought he would go his way, and I would go mine. Since I had Eddie, a bunch of new friends, and a promising girlfriend, I thought it was my time to shine (haha, Chaz).

Ray wouldn't go away, though. He was a thorn in my side for years, stopping at nothing to pit people against me. It got so bad that we had turf wars. I couldn't go to Wildwood without the fear of getting jumped by Ray's buddies (though I never really tried), and he couldn't go to the mall in the northeast without getting run out by my friends (which happened once). But before all that, there were a few weeks when I didn't hear from him.

I was spending a lot more time at the mall. I went every day (most days after school because I knew kids would be there to hang out with). Almost every time I went, I met someone new. It was like I entered a new town and quickly got to know the people there. They all went to nearby schools and sought companionship with like-minded peers. It was a whirlwind of events that left my head spinning.

I went from not wanting to be the life of the party and the center of attention with these people to being that all the time. It left me shell-shocked for doing what I told myself I didn't want to do. The same doubts I had before resurfaced with guilt over my fakeness, not dealing with my problems, and ignoring my feelings.

I just had the time of my life meeting and seeing R.E.M. with my best friend, Eddie. I was wrong for thinking I couldn't have it both ways. I could be the life of the party and deal with my inner demons simultaneously. But the more I entertained people and didn't deal with my problems, the easier it became to ignore reality. Drugs and alcohol helped me avoid everything even more. It was the opposite of how I was for a year and a half. I knew something inside me was wrong, and I hoped that letting loose with kids my age and following this path would lead me back to myself.

Eddie was dating a sweet girl named Nicole. We had about six Nicoles that we hung out with at the mall. For instance, Sarah's friend Nicole (her last name escapes me) and Nicole Baum, the biggest Beastie Boys fan I ever met.

We will call Eddie's Nicole "Nicole D" since her last name started with a "D." Nicole D didn't dress like she liked rock music. She was more of an "Old Navy" type of girl. She was super sweet and gave everyone a chance, no matter how they looked or dressed.

Eddie and I had girlfriends from the same circle of friends, which basically sealed the deal for us to go to the mall and northeast Philly every day. For Halloween that year, we went trick-or-treating with Nicole and her friends around the neighborhood. I went as Michael Stipe, of course, and Eddie just wore a skeleton mask.

Sarah was stuck at her job at the mall. She worked at a women's shoe store called Parade of Shoes. I spent much time there over the next year and a half. I would roam the mall with friends, then go into Sarah's work and talk to her. I usually stayed until the place got busy or her manager told me to come back later.

As a mallrat, I knew many people who worked at the mall. Many kids got jobs there. It was convenient to stay at the mall after work and hang out. During the first few weeks of hanging with new people, I got to know Sarah well.

Sarah was a lot calmer than me. She was quiet and only talked when she wanted to or if you engaged her in conversation. She had an older brother, and her parents were still together (though this wouldn't last much longer). Sarah was a sophomore at the all-girls Catholic school Nazareth Academy, which had a reputation for only letting smart girls attend.

Soon, our fast-paced relationship, marked by our overwhelming emotions and self-loathing, developed a tighter bond. Our shared sadness and affection for one another had us wanting to be with each other as much as possible. It was true teenage love blossoming. After only a few weeks into our courtship, we let the "L" word out of its cage. While listening to music and making out, feeling the security and desire for one another, we said we loved each other. I might have been a bit numb and constantly feeling low about myself, but that moment felt so good. I believed she meant the words that symbolize the highest devotion and caring one has for another.

Music was a big part of our lives. We had the same taste for the most part. She liked R.E.M., the only thing that mattered to me. She shared the same birthday with Stipe, so that was a plus. Her favorite bands were Pearl Jam, Hole, Stone Temple Pilots, Counting Crows, and Live. We listened to these bands all the time together. Often, we just tuned to WDRE. They played so many good bands there was hardly any reason to turn it off.

Another band Sarah and I liked was becoming the biggest act in alt-rock. In the fall, The Smashing Pumpkins released their double album, *Mellon Collie and the Infinite Sadness*. It was a staple in our lives. Songs like "Thirty-Three," "Muzzle," and "Zero" became the soundtrack to our lives. "1979" was an anthem for us kids who had nothing better to do than drink, have sex, and listen to music 24/7. Oh, when the Smashing Pumpkins could do no wrong.

Chapter 54:
Desperation Road

By the beginning of November, I was settling into being a full-time mallrat and spending most of my time with my girlfriend. But I was running out of money from my summer job. I needed a part-time job. Christmas was coming, and I had a girlfriend. Because that's what the holidays are for. Spending money on loved ones, and if you don't, it means you don't care about them.

The whirlwind few weeks of meeting hundreds of people and being "on" all the time made me ignore my gut feelings. I also didn't think highly of myself (and never really will), so I didn't think I could get any jobs in the mall besides what I already knew: fast food.

I didn't have other options with my low self-esteem, so I started talking to a 22-year-old girl named Michelle (an attractive ex-stripper for those who like strippers) who worked at a fast-food joint us mallrats frequented. I liked Michelle as a person, so we got along despite the 5-year age gap. She was young enough to get along with us 17/18-year-olds and talked to us when it wasn't busy at her job.

I was desperate enough to tell her I needed a job and had worked at other fast-food places. Other kids I knew worked there, so it wasn't hard to go with the flow. I was hired to work in the back, cooking up dead animals.

I ignored my gut the entire time I was back being a maniac mallrat. It was against my beliefs as a vegetarian, and I didn't want to take another job at the bottom of the barrel. But I was also a poor Kenzo with no options. I told myself it would be temporary. I would look for something better as soon as possible. I looked, but the five months I worked at this hell hole scarred me for life and made me cut out fast food forever.

While I worked there, I was the biggest bum. I barely did the bare minimum because I loathed it. The only thing I liked about working there was when Michelle was around. When she left the job, I soon followed. I had to touch meat, doing almost slave work for the minimum wage, around degenerates who settled for a shit job and were miserable because of it.

I told myself that my hero, Michael Stipe, once worked in a fast-food place (the Waffle House) when he was my age, and he lived to talk about it. So, I could suck it up for a couple months until I found something better. How hard could five months of working at a job I hated be? Haha, Chaz, haha.

Chapter 55:
The Hearts Filthy Lesson

Since I was back in the groove with Eddie and John H., John A. was back in my life as well. He was still an egomaniac, trying to belittle me and get me to think like he did. Late nights, when I slept at home (instead of random mallrat houses), the four of us (John H., John A., Eddie, and I) would talk on landline phones via three-way calling. We were back to how it was in February, talking about music and having it be almost a competition with John A. criticizing my (and Eddie's) taste in music. I put up with it because I had nothing better to do and wasn't good at sticking up for myself.

John A. was recording his self-produced and self-funded EP. He was on a high horse and thought he was breaking musical ground with his attempt at music. He would send the EP, in cassette tape format, to music labels, but no one gave him a chance. He got a letter from a record company that told him they weren't interested, which he held as a small victory that someone at the label took the time to write him a letter.

We would stay up all night talking. Eventually, Eddie and John H. would get off the phone and go to bed, leaving just me and John A. to talk about nonsense. He was nicer to me when it was just the two of us. He would make fun of Trent Reznor when the other guys were on the phone, but when we were alone, he talked about how much David Bowie was influenced by NIN on his new album and how I should get it (which I did).

Just like my first introductions to great artists like U2 and Depeche Mode, the first album I bought by Bowie was one from later in his career and not his work that made him a legend. It was his 1995 album *Outside*. I got it at a used record shop. I liked the album, so I bought his classic, *The Rise and Fall of Ziggy Stardust and the Spiders from Mars*, which I liked a lot. However, my interactions with John A. left a bad taste in my mouth and turned me off from one of the greatest acts of all time. I felt like a fraud, like I was letting John A. control or influence me too much when I listened to the bands and singers he held up high. It was full-on confusion in my teenage brain.

It wasn't just John A. Those first few months of being full of so many emotions and not knowing what was what made me feel ill and guilty, almost dirty inside. It was a whirlwind of emotions and people that I was running around with, and I was working on autopilot. I didn't know how to express myself with my foggy mind and feelings.

I was an easy target for manipulation and belittlement. The fall of 1995 and the winter of 1996 were adjustment periods when a flood of emotions and events shaped me. If I didn't already know myself before my breakdown, I would say this was how I found who I was. But this period was more about how I learned to have a comeback. Music that wasn't already dear to me got shunned for a while.

When I listened to a song like "Moonage Daydream" or "Five Years," my fragile mind quickly thought of John A., and I was turned off by it. I knew he was trying to control me and put me down to inflate his ego, and I knew he liked to influence people. I hate, and I mean I *hate* being controlled, especially when it's obvious to me what is going on. John A. talked about how wonderful Bowie is and how NIN and R.E.M. were garbage. It made me upset since those were two bands I held dear to me.

John A. also liked to talk about politics. He said the Republican Party was great, and Bill Clinton's economic success was due to the previous administration (probably a talking point from AM Right-wing talk radio that he loved). He went on about the trade deals that were hashed out by the Republicans but signed into law by Clinton when he came to office, giving way to a slight boom in the economy while sending good-paying jobs overseas. He talked so confidently about NAFTA that I couldn't argue with him even when I knew he was wrong.

I had doubts circling in my head. Whenever someone puts me down, making me feel and think less of myself, I dwell on it and have to do my rituals. I pushed out the negative feelings or thoughts to get on with my life. This was one of those times when someone made me doubt my fragile self-worth. Usually, when these things seeped into my brain, they wouldn't leave. The doubts morphed into other doubts based on people's negative opinions of me and what I liked about myself.

It was an ongoing struggle whenever someone like John A. went out of their way to make me doubt myself. I'm sure a stronger-minded person (like me years later) would have said, "Go fuck yourself." But my fragile ego was battling demons and obsessive thoughts that cut me down to size every other minute.

It took everything I had to fight these things off. I realize now that it was my maternal/paternal conflict in me and my personality. I jumped to the worst conclusion, thinking everyone was right and I was wrong. I picked that up from my dear old mom. And it was my dad in me that saw what was happening in conversations with people trying to make themselves feel superior and make me think like them.

My dad's influence also led me to drink and do drugs to relieve some of my stress and suffering. The third part of the battle was the "me" factor. The one who was a combination of my parents but had the sense to see their faults and tried to walk his own path. That one usually did well when I was alone or with people who weren't out to hurt me (like Eddie and Sarah). But in most adult and social functions, my mold that was cast by Mr. and Mrs. Charles Holesworth would dance the waltz in my mind, leaving only me to calm myself down by either giving in (like mom would) or not bothering with anyone at any time (like dad).

When I decided to party and see where this rock and roll lifestyle would take me, I took a stand on what I wouldn't do. I swore to myself many years before that I would never do a drug that would take over my life and leave me physically addicted to it. I maintained this promise.

I had an alcohol problem for a bit, but it was my way of self-medicating my high anxiety. I always knew when to pull myself out of the gutter and try harder. I tried most of the "harmless" gateway drugs, but I never let them take me over. I watched too many others fall down that rabbit hole and use harder stuff, only to lose everything, including their lives.

Chapter 56:
Secret Destroyers Hold You Up to the Flames

One night, after a late shift at McShit, Michelle invited me to her place to drink beer and crash. She lived in an apartment in the Northeast with another manager from McShit whom I hadn't met.

The other manager, who I will find out was a piece of shit, (POS for short) met Michelle when she was a stripper at the club he worked at. He took her in when she left to find a job that didn't require her to be naked and groped by Northeast Philly's finest pieces of trash.

I thought nothing of it since I was sleeping out most nights. Whether it was in the car of one of Sarah's friends on Halloween night when Eddie and I didn't want to take the bus back, or at any mall kid whose parents were cool with some poor kids crashing at their house.

The apartment was in a huge complex with numerous buildings. I wasn't one to judge someone's living arrangements, but this place reeked of white trash and dysfunction (and this is coming from a white-trash, dysfunctional kenzo). It was a cesspool of filth. There were roaches all over the kitchen and dining room, dishes piled up all over the ground and sink with dried food on them, and a smell that was a combination of shit and body order.

The apartment was a refuge for those with no plans for the future and were just trying to get by, but not in a good way. It wasn't like my friends at the mall or Eddie and I crashing anywhere we could find to not go home to our bad neighborhoods. This wasn't like the romanticized living in Jack Kerouac novels or the punk rock lifestyle I sometimes saw. There wasn't a community or bond, just desperation living.

These degenerates had no ambitions or reasons to be better than the fast-food workers they were. I was 17 and very impressionable, and I went over to the apartment several times, mainly to hang out with Michelle. She was a better person than this toxic environment but was desperate and had nowhere to go.

I put on a polite attitude there and tried not to judge out loud, but constantly thought I didn't want to wind up like these people. I didn't want to settle for a shit job and live in filth with numerous people living and sleeping anywhere they could. It was an example of what I didn't want to be. It was the only good thing to come out of hanging out there for a month or two.

It was like a squatter place with one person on the lease, and the rest crashed there in pure desperation. Michelle and her kid lived there, and a 12 or 13-year-old girl who I didn't know. It was fucking weird, and I didn't stick around long at this den of despair and lost souls.

The place was full of dogs and cats, and they shit and pissed all over. There was no order. They would just put down newspaper so the dogs could shit all over the floor. Even at the tender age of 15, I knew to clean up the shit my dog pooped out.

One thing my mom did right while I was growing up was to make sure our house smelled as pleasant as possible. So, the awful smell in the apartment was another red flag My home was covered with roaches too, but we were poor kenzos, and that came with the territory. In the northeast (especially the far northeast), an apartment should be clean of things like roaches due to the high rent.

These people weren't from poor backgrounds. They could have stopped living in filth if they didn't settle for the environment they created. It was not like they couldn't help being so pathetic. It was almost like they didn't care about how bad their living area was. It was like they chose to be poor. My mom at least washed the dishes after being used.

I was only 17 and might have been more experienced than other kids because of my poor life. But I was surrounded by "adults" in their early to mid-twenties who were doing things I never saw other people in their 20s do. Even in my 20s and 30s, I never saw anyone act in such low-life ways.

I only lingered there for a handful of nights, mainly because I had to spread out my options of places to sleep. I didn't want to ruin my welcome at places that would pass a health code check. I would only go over when Michelle was around. Sometimes she wouldn't stay there because of how fucked up it was.

I became closer to Michelle. It wasn't a sexual attraction, although she was an attractive woman with large breasts and a tight body. Most men would crave her attention. Our relationship was more of a brother/sister thing. She was roughly the same age as my sister, and since I had no intention of communicating with her, Michelle played the part of big sister for me. But it only lasted a few months since our situation was utter chaos.

Looking back, I realize how young Michelle was and was probably going through so much. I was a teenager, full of confusion, and Michelle was a few years older, trying to figure things out and take care of her kid.

Michelle was drifting through life, trying her best to get to a spot that would level things out. She seemed to know how fucked up her living situation was, but she also knew this was what she had to do. She did finally get away from the POS who let her live there and moved on to what I hope was a more positive scenario. Unfortunately, I'll never know since we lost contact the following year.

Some of the times I spent at this hellhole made me think this was what the Christians were trying to hide me from. It was the sinful people who were dangerous. POS (I will not say POS's name due to not wanting to give POS any credit or acknowledgment by name) claimed he was bisexual. I gathered that he was just a sex fiend who was so perverted from his strip club haven ways that he had to get his kicks from sex with men.

When I first heard he was bisexual, my inner Stipe tried to find common ground with him. I tried, as I did with most gay or bisexual people, to be the voice of encouragement for being different in this society. But POS didn't want to hear it and was a cocky asshole who belittled me every chance he got. He was like John A. but a lot worse and mean about everything. POS gave off spoiled brat energy.

I asked how he knew he was gay, and he said he wasn't gay; he just liked sex. He had a threesome with his guy friend and decided he enjoyed whatever sexual things he did in the scenario. He even told me he would go down to local Philly gay bars and verbally abuse gay people.

I saw him as a weak person. He was taking the self-hatred for his own acts out on innocent people he thought were beneath him. He thought he was better than being gay. But he didn't go through the life choices and pain that most homosexual men had since they were born the way they were and not just looking for a new thrill.

Maybe POS was gay the whole time but in denial, but his actions made me not give a fuck about his struggles. He was perhaps the worst person I ever met. I never met Donald Trump, but POS reminds me of him. He was a bit of a narcissist.

POS was so full of himself that he was hard to be around. I don't know much about his background and the way he thought. He was toxic and had red flags shooting out of. That's how terrible of a person he was. Once Michelle moved out of that toxic environment, I also cut off POS (as much as I could since he worked at my hangout for years).

I didn't know how much of an asshole he was until November 1995. I was still fragile and trying to give people the benefit of the doubt. I was trying to relate and fit in as an adult most of the time and went along with hanging out at POS's place while he put on gay porno like it was the nightly news (in front of 17-year-old me and the 12–13-year-old girl who stayed there). Michelle came out as bisexual. She walked around naked with her girlfriend, who also worked at McShit, and was on the road to nowhere.

The apartment was dingy and dark, with smoke from all the chain cigarette smoking fogging the place. Drugs and alcohol always flowed there, and I would take whatever was handed to me by Michelle since I trusted her like a sister (since my sister didn't give a shit about me).

One day, Michelle gave me a muscle relaxer, and I mixed it with the beer one of the older McShit workers got for me. It led to me being out of my 17-year-old senses. I didn't know what was going on. I was still trying to fit in or pretend I was an experienced adult. I thought I knew everything due to my rough life, but I quickly figured out this was not the adult life I wanted.

We were talking about how small my penis is like it was a normal conversation. Then Michelle's girlfriend grabbed my dick through my pants and said, "It wasn't that small." I didn't give a fuck about how small my penis was, only how big my heart was. I'm not saying I was sexually assaulted, but it was weird to have a stranger grab my member out of nowhere. It was another red flag, warning me to stay away from this place.

The intoxication from the muscle relaxer and the beer took over, and I started to lose consciousness. I passed out in a room full of fast-food employees who were more experienced in mixing drugs than me, and I woke up to just me and POS in the room.

I don't know if something happened to me while I was in a drug-induced sleep, but POS said I was a sound sleeper and made weird sexual comments about me. It gave me the creeps. I realized that I should cut these people off (including Michelle if I had to) and get back with kids my own age who were more positive.

Chapter 57:
Little Trouble Girl

I was eating food with my dad in our living room. It was a weekday afternoon, and I planned on going to the mall to hang out with my friends. One thing that kept me from fully embracing life and reality was the fear of what bad things would happen next. It seemed like I was jinxed, and something terrible was always lurking around the corner and this is how I felt when I got a phone call that day from Ray at the beginning of Thanksgiving week 1995.

It had been weeks since I heard from Ray. After our last conversation about how I didn't want to play mind games with the girls we knew and how much of an asshole I thought he was, I thought that would be the last I heard from him. But it wasn't. I was taken aback when I heard his voice. My stomach sank when he told me why he called.

Ray told me there was a problem we had to deal with. Megan from New Jersey decided she had enough of living under the strict rules of her parents and (much like her friends) ran away from home. I had cut off this part of my life and was trying my best to have a normal relationship with my girlfriend.

Sarah and Eddie were my entire life, and I didn't want the drama that came with Ray and girls running away from their suburban homes. But it was partly my fault that she decided to leave her house at the tender age of 14.

When I started going out with Sarah, I told Megan I couldn't see her anymore because her parents hated me and wouldn't let us see each other. I didn't want to hurt her with the knowledge that I was with someone else. I figured this would be the best way to let her down, and we could all get on with our lives.

Megan decided that her parents were too controlling when it came to me. They made her go to therapists and doctors to get over her depression. She was on heavy doses of drugs (stuff I had no idea about, like lithium). She said they made her feel like a zombie. It made me not want to try any medicine that would help my mental problems (though I think my problems weren't just chemical imbalances but were caused by trauma).

Ray said it's up to us to help her. I fell right back into the lifestyle I was trying to run from. Looking back, I think Ray convinced Megan to run away from home and used her to get to me so he could throw a monkey wrench in my new-found life. I was so upset that I couldn't eat the dinner I had in front of me.

Megan was quite unhappy at home, and Ray and I still had this understanding of taking care of those with bad home lives who needed our support. So, I caved and agreed to help Megan find places to stay. The saddest part is that we thought running away would lead to something better. We believed we could keep Megan away from her parents long enough for her to get a job or move in with someone. It was teenagers being teenagers, thinking about the now instead of the future. But this was the life I was given.

Ray and I came up with a plan. We would take shifts to keep Megan safe. For some reason, I took nights while Ray took days. He had it easier since he could sit inside a fast-food place or a mall during the day. I had to find places for her to sleep. Ray took care of her the first night. Then, I met up with both of them at a fast-food joint in Frankford.

I didn't even want to talk to Ray. He looked like an idiot with his newly bought trench coat and fingerless gloves. He was pretending to be upset about his life, trying to get me to feel for him and perhaps be his friend again. But I didn't trust him and never would again.

I took Megan off his hands for the night, and we crashed at a mallrat's house whose parents didn't mind random kids sleeping over. The next day, Ray met me and took Megan for the day. I told him when I was ready, I would come down to Kensington and take her off his hands. I asked him not to bring her to the mall since I would see Sarah there before she started work. Sarah and I would walk around for an hour or so before she started her shift, and then I would pal around with friends during the night until Sarah got off work. .

Unfortunately, Ray, being the troublemaker and asshole that he was, brought Megan to the mall, and she saw me holding hands with my girlfriend. I saw the awful look on her face. Her fragile teenage heart was set on me. She thought she loved me. I knew I didn't do anything wrong, but I felt guilty for letting Megan down.

I still had feelings for her, and if things were on our side, I would have loved to have a relationship with her. I was a crazy teenager going through growing pains, but I knew the smart move was to stay with Sarah, if only out of convenience, since her parents weren't against our courtship. I panicked but got myself together. I acted like I didn't know them as all three of our eyes met. I kept walking with my girlfriend. Then I realized that I had to communicate with Ray about what would happen that night with Megan.

I walked over to them while Sarah and my other friends went outside to smoke cigarettes. I quickly told Ray I would meet them somewhere in the mall after Sarah went to work. I also gave Ray a look that said, "What the fuck are you doing here?" and then I went outside with my friends.

I told Sarah what was going on the night before, so there were no worries there. She knew how much I hated Ray, and she knew that I would help a friend who needed me. So, I "relieved" Ray of his duties that day of watching the beautiful soul that was (and is) Megan. This is when Ray leaves this story of taking care of Megan during one of the worst weeks of my life. He went home and I decided to rely on those I knew at the time. I felt I didn't need Ray and still wanted nothing to do with him. So, I took over sole protection of my little trouble girl.

I I had off the next few days at McShit, so I could stay with Megan as long as she needed me. I was sick of dealing with Ray and his fake bullshit anyway, so I was glad to get his toxic persona far away

I had to rely on everyone I knew to deal with this drama. That night, I asked Amy C. if Megan and I could sleep in her basement. She said we could hang out, but we couldn't spend the night since it was a weekday and I was a boy. I had to take what I could. I knew I had to stretch out my options because I didn't know how long Megan would be on the runaway train. I took everything as it came. I knew other people that would let her sleep over, but I didn't want to wear out that welcome too soon.

We stayed at Amy C.'s for a while and left around 11 p.m. It was a cold and windy night in late November, and we needed somewhere to stay. I saw a house around the corner from Amy's that was also a family doctor's office. It was a row home in the Parkwood section of Northeast Philly, but it had an area attached to the practice that was like a shed. It was an aluminum structure, about four feet wide, with a tiny roof and a screen door. I figured it was better than being out in the open with the strong winds and hidden from the eyes of any cops that might drive by.

We spent the night in this makeshift shelter. It was so cold. We alt-rock kids did not dress properly for the weather (thin coats and thrift store sweaters). But the wind got blocked, and it was warmer than the streets. We also huddled together and used our body heat to stay warm.

So, here we were, two depressed teenagers holding each other in a stranger's outside walkway, trying to stay warm. We talked about our feelings and things of that nature. I got lost in the moment and gave in to my teenage heart (and hormones), and while feeling all these crazy and dramatic emotions, Megan and I kissed for the first time since I saw her at the bookstore in NJ in October.

Our faces were only a few inches apart, so things were bound to happen eventually. The part that I found strange was I just cheated on my girlfriend (Sarah) a stone's throw away from where I kissed her for the first time a month prior. I got swept away in emotions and the pure excitement of the situation. I had no idea what would happen, but I was not in the mindset to figure that out.

I did what I always did: I went with the flow. I would see where the chips fell when they eventually did. I gave in to my urges, and I knew I would regret it, but I chalked it up to everything that happened to me. Hopefully, it would work out, and I'd live with it (haha, Chaz, you fool). My fragile mind couldn't comprehend what I was doing or what was happening. I still believed I was doing what I was supposed to.

The next day, Megan and I roamed the mall until that night. It was the night before Thanksgiving, and the mallrats all had off from school the next day. Nicole Baum had a party at her house in the Northeast, and her parents said people could sleep over. I told her that I had to bring Megan. Since I didn't want to explain the runaway situation, I told Nicole that Megan was my cousin from out of town. It was a go for us to sleep over, and we had a great time that night as normal kids with 10-15 others who liked the same music and movies. I had a moment of security for the night for me and Megan. It was the only time I felt that during this chaotic week.

Chapter 58:
Black Sheep Got Blackmailed Again

This Thanksgiving was the 2nd straight year I wasn't home for the holiday dinner. I didn't really care about holidays, especially one about eating a bunch of food and being thankful for my shit life. The year before might have been the best Thanksgiving (seeing NIN and meeting Ed and Venus in Virginia). This year was the worst.

I had to figure out where Megan and I could sleep that night, so I wracked my brain and thought about Michelle and the hellhole she lived in. I knew it was an option since there were no parents to keep order, and there was already a weird thing going on with the 13-year-old girl living there. Also, most of the mall kids' parents wouldn't let the likes of us over on a holiday night. It was utter chaos at Michelle's place, but I was desperate and thought this could be a spot for a couple days until something else came up.

Michelle said we could stay for a couple nights. POS said it was okay since he couldn't say no to the lively and fit Michelle. I regret many things in my tormented life, but bringing an angel like Megan to this shit hole is one I regret the most. That night, for our bullshit holiday about a bunch of white men pretending they deserve this land, it was Megan, me, Michelle, Michelle's main female squeeze, Michelle's son, the POS, and the random young teen who never left the couch, all stuck in this despair central apartment eating a meal POS made.

The place was full of the usual disgusting dirty dishes and fecal matter all over the floors. Michelle and her girlfriend were lying around naked like it was normal behavior. POS was moping around about how he made us dinner and let Megan stay there, and I wasn't showing him any gratitude. It was odd for a grown man to say this to a teenage boy. It seemed he was trying to hint that I owed him something for letting us stay there.

I did thank him. And it wasn't like I was asking to move in. I was desperate and needed a place to hide for a couple days. I wasn't going to do sexual favors for a place to stay. POS was a big-time pervert and probably wanted me to get him off somehow. Even if I was gay, POS was the ugliest person I ever met (inside and out), so, sorry bub, it's a hard no.

I am not trying to slut shame anyone. But POS was a disgusting pig. He only cared about himself and what he wanted. I think he might have been a sociopath or something along those lines. I don't really care to know; I just knew he was no fucking good. It was my gut feeling from the moment I met this monster of a person, and like most times, my gut was on to something.

Another strange thing happened while we were there. POS took pictures of Megan and me sleeping on his couch. I took my shirt off and let Megan wear my trusty R.E.M.'s *Automatic for the People* shirt. I let her wear my favorite shirt because she was almost out of clean clothes. Mine weren't very clean, but she wanted to sleep in it.

Megan and I were making out, and POS took a picture. It was creepy and bizarre. He took pictures of Megan and I embracing while we slept and a few more when we were kissing, thinking that no one was watching us in another room in the apartment. POS knew I was dating Sarah and made comments to make me feel bad about cheating on my girlfriend. He was gathering evidence to use to control me.

I realized I had to get Megan and me out of this situation pronto. But first I had to get the film from POS' camera. It was 1995, and people were still using film and taking their cameras to a film development place. I waited that second night until no one was around, and I found the camera and took the film out.

A few days later, POS confronted me about stealing his film. He said he needed pictures on the film, and if I didn't give it back to him, he would tell Sarah (with Michelle and her girlfriend as witnesses) that I cheated on her with Megan. My plan to destroy the evidence went out the window, and I handed him the film.

POS blackmailed me throughout the time I worked at McShit and had a year-and-a-half relationship with Sarah. It put stress on our relationship and my mental health. I know it was my mistake to cheat on Sarah, but I was swept up in the emotions of taking care of a girl I had strong feelings for, and let's face it, my mind wasn't the strongest at the time.

I should have come clean with Sarah and told her what happened, but I was too scared to lose her. I thought the guilt would just go away. It didn't. It doomed our love. But the fact that some creepy loser blackmailed me with pictures of me sleeping was way beyond the limits of my understanding at the time. He used to say things to get me to squirm. He said I would never marry Sarah (after I said that I loved her and wanted to marry her). He also said, "The girl who Chaz cheated with Megan on just came in McShit" when Sarah came to visit me at work. He was playing with my head to make me feel like shit. And I didn't do a thing to deserve it.

One time, I decided I had enough of the McShit job and was going to walk off and quit. POS ran over and said if I quit, he would tell Sarah that I cheated on her and show her the pictures. He was blackmailing me and controlling me to stay at a job I fucking hated. It was insane. I realize now that it was because he was a grown man who had a loser's job and was ugly as fuck, so he took out his misery on people like me, people who still had joy in life.

I had to pretend none of his threats and control tactics bothered me (even though the one thing I hated more than anything was to be controlled, especially by fear). I had to pretend we were friendly and that I didn't hate his fucking guts. It was the hardest thing I had done so far in my life. I was in total survival mode to protect my relationship with Sarah because I was too scared to tell her the truth.

I probably would have saved myself a boatload of worries and anxiety if I were brave enough to tell her the truth. But I was an emotional wreck and a coward, so I kissed POS' ass and pretended that I could stand his company. I wanted nothing but to tell him to fuck off.

A year later, I was on acid and fell asleep near the end of the trip. I had a dream that I stabbed POS in the heart and was happy doing it. This is how much I hated the fuck. He was an ugly and obnoxious person who preyed on the weak and young. He was the first person who made me doubt humanity or made me scared that enough bitterness could make anyone that ugly and mean. He was a bully and a scumbag.

Shortly after these events, Michelle and POS had a falling out. POS was talking about how bad she was (like he had any room to talk and like I would side with his fucked-up self). She moved out, and I didn't see her much after that. I stayed as far away as I could from POS. It was tough since I worked with him until next year and hung out with people in the McShit parking lot. I finally had enough balls to quit the fast-food hell job I was blackmailed into keeping in early 1996. I rolled the dice, and POS didn't tell Sarah anything (that I know of) about me cheating on her with Megan.

Once, I dared to say something mean back to him. He had me thinking I didn't know what love was, and my feelings and struggles weren't real. I tried to ignore it all like I did with most people who told me how I should live. But one time he said something that pissed me off, and I replied, "Fuck off, you piece of shit." I instantly regretted it since I was terrified he would try to ruin my teenage love story. I apologized right away.

POS said he wanted to drive me home to my shit neighborhood that night. I was too scared to say no, so I let him drive me down to Frankford (a 20-minute drive from the mall). The whole time, he told me how much of a loser I was and how I had potential, but I just wanted to hang out with other kids. He thought I was better in his shit-filled apartment with his pornos and him being able to control me and take pictures of me in compromising situations instead of having normal teenage fun.

POS made fun of me for being like every other kid at the mall but also for wearing make-up and nail polish, which was one of the things that only I did. He wouldn't let me out of his car when we got to my place. He circled the block, telling me how much of a loser I was. All of this from a guy who dropped out of high school, worked in bottomless-pit jobs like strip clubs and fast-food places, and was an overweight sex addict with a fucking mullet.

I didn't care what he thought of me. He was the moral compass of what I never wanted to be. I would make sure that I would never be so cruel and ugly to anyone, no matter how bad things got for me. I wouldn't turn to that way of thinking or being.

I wouldn't attack teenagers for being happy and full of life. It wasn't just me. There was another girl who worked at McShit named Katie, who was a very nice teenager. POS did a shady, perverted thing by photoshopping her head onto a naked body and passing it around the fast-food joint. He was a fucking immature child. He was more toxic than Ray and any Xian I had ever met.

I saw this experience as a life lesson. Not everyone is going to be good. I went from meeting the most beautiful person I met so far, Laura, to meeting the worst person a year later. Part of me (the panic-stricken part) thought that this interaction with POS was due to my backsliding ways. Maybe if I hadn't rebelled from the church, I wouldn't have run into such a terrible person. But then I tell that small part of me (that sticks around for the rest of my life) that I was meeting tons of people after I left the cult, and I was bound to run into the lowlifes of the world sooner or later. Add the fact that I was working at a going-nowhere job and came from nothing with no education, and it almost guarantees I would run into some asshole like POS.

Not everyone at McShit was terrible. I got along with Michelle and some other kids. There were even some bosses who weren't bad people, like a gentleman named Isaac. He told me I could be with Megan legally when I turned 18, but I wasn't planning on doing that. I didn't have a plan, but I wanted to stay with Sarah.

This Thanksgiving week dampened the excitement and fun I was blindly having. I was too paranoid about Sarah finding out what I did. It did a number on my conscience and mind.

The next morning, I left POS' place and had to find a place for Megan to stay. I was stressed out and needed a break from the drama. I called John H. and asked him if he could take her in. He said he would, which surprised me, and I brought her to his house via the bus.

By this time, Megan was without her lithium for five or six days. Her hands were starting to tremble from withdrawal. I didn't know how psyche meds worked and had no idea how dangerous it could be for her to go without them. Michelle told me Megan would need to get some quick, or something awful might happen.

I thought the best action was for Megan to go home, but she wasn't ready. I let her spend the weekend with John H., and I spent the weekend with Sarah and my friends at the mall, blowing off steam. I said we would talk on Monday about her calling her parents.

I don't know how (I have a hunch it was Ray), but Megan's parents found out where I worked and that I knew where their child was. The buildup of stress and figuring out what to do next had come down to this weekend. Her parents were on a rampage and heading for the mall.

They showed up Saturday at McShit, only to find I was gone for the day. Little did they know I was still in the mall, just a stone's throw away. I got wind of this from other mallrats who worked with me. Megan's parents found out I was working the next night and told someone that they would be back.

I called John right away and told Megan what was going on. She said she would go home if I got in trouble. I said, "Let's see how this plays out first." The next day, it played out. It was a drama-filled night. I was working the late shift with Michelle (who had my back) when Megan's parents showed up with fire in their eyes. It was a normal night of us mallrats and slackers hanging out at McShit, so a bunch of my friends were there, including Sarah.

Megan's dad started yelling at me, asking where she was. He was making a scene, so Michelle had me talk to him outside. He demanded to know where she was. I didn't want to give her up yet, so I said I hadn't seen her in days (which was true) and that I would tell her he wanted her home.

He got in my face and started threatening me in his "voice box" voice (due to having a voice box for a medical condition) sounding like a robot, asking, "Where is Megan?" I replied (in a mocking robot-like voice), "I don't know!" Then he screamed he was calling the cops.

The cops showed up a little later, asking me where Megan was. I told them the same shit I told Megan's parents. There wasn't much they could do to me since I didn't have her with me, and I was a minor.

Meanwhile, Megan's parents were yelling at my mallrat friends, telling them how much of a bad person I was and how they should stay away from me. My pals stuck up for me, especially Sarah and Kevin (the guy Sarah was dating when I met her). I appreciated that.

The cops left, and her parents said Megan needed her medicine or she might die. It seemed a bit dramatic, but what the hell did I know? They also told me they wouldn't stop coming to the mall until they found Megan. I couldn't have this nonsense happening at my place to let loose.

I called Megan and told her the situation. She agreed to go home the next day on a NJ transit bus, and I never heard from her parents again. I didn't hear from Megan for a few months. After she went home, her parents said if she wouldn't be in contact with me, they wouldn't be so strict and let her do the things she wanted, and they wouldn't just shove medicine down her throat to feel better mentally.

They blamed me for all their home life problems, even though they existed before I met Megan, three months before she ran away. I never told her to run away from home. But they had a scapegoat they could blame their lack of parenting on, so why not me?

The good news was that Megan got some freedom and is a beautiful person I still talk to. We have gone in and out of each other's lives (dating again here and there), mainly as friends, knowing we had an emotional bond and a crazy, fucked up Thanksgiving week in 1995.

Chapter 59:
No Future

Now that the drama of caring for a runaway was behind me, I felt relief. Most days, I was a nervous wreck, but this week was extra nerve-wracking. Megan was home, and I could breathe easier, thinking I did my best for her. Now, I had to pick up the pieces left behind after the runaway train came to a stop.

My mental health issues were swirling around, and I had not one (Ray) but two people (POS) who were enemies out to get me. I was used to everyone liking me. I thought people were good at heart. Now, I saw the ugly side of humanity. It became a constant struggle to justify situations that clashed with my idea of right and wrong. I wasn't sure if I made the right decisions or was on the right path. These were intense things for a 17-year-old to think, but I lived a pretty intense life.

I spent most of my time trying to calm my irrational mind and feelings. I had to balance my life with Sarah and my growing group of friends with my thoughts on life while protecting myself from Ray and POS. I was still drinking and doing drugs, and meeting new people was a daily routine.

During the week I took care of Megan, I met Jim. His nickname was "Nazi Jim" because he wore a green army jacket that looked like it was from World War 2 Germany. He was not a Nazi. He was a couple years older than me and from the Bridesburg section of Philly (near Frankford but a lot nicer).

Jim and I quickly became friends. He was around for most of the party that was my life in the '90s. The guy lived with his grandma in a row home about a 5-minute drive from me. He was a music fan, especially punk rock. Jim was the first punk rock guy who wasn't condescending to me about his taste in music. He showed me punk bands I had not heard and made me tapes of his punk rock CDs, including bands like Rancid, Operation Ivy, and the Sex Pistols. He also liked top 40 music and rap, but punk was his favorite and went along with his persona.

Jim was one of the only guys I knew who had a car, and he didn't mind driving me, Eddie, and Nick around. He was obsessed with the rap group NWA and played their debut album, *Straight Outta Compton*, nonstop. He was the driver, so he got to pick the music. After the 5th or 6th time listening to NWA, I realized I liked the album and learned some of the lyrics by heart.

Jim also showed me singers like Jim Croce when he was in a '70s folk rock singer mood. Sometimes, he would even leave the radio tuned to the latest hits from artists like Celine Dion. This prompted Sara (not Sarah, my girlfriend) to say, "You know, for a guy they call

"Nazi Jim," you sure listen to some pussy music." That comment made Jim drop us off at the party we were going to for Halloween and leave us there for the night. He was a sensitive soul.

Jim went through mood swings, so I was careful not to piss him off or upset him. He was a good guy and helped me a lot, but he took things to heart too much. He looked like Robert Downey Jr. but shorter with a small frame but had a temper that forced some of us to walk on eggshells around him.

Jim was dating one of Sarah's friends from high school. Once he and I became friends, he showed up more at the mall and house parties.

Once, in a desperate attempt for fun, a bunch of us got a motel room off Roosevelt Blvd. in Bensalem, just past the Philadelphia city limits. The Neshaminy Inn was your typical trucker stop motel in price and quality. It was 60 dollars for the night, and we would all chip in to have a place to drink and play music all night.

Me, Jim, Sarah, Eddie, and some random girls were all in the motel. There was also an older guy Jim was friends with named Chris who didn't say much, but when he did, it was the craziest shit. We drank shitty beer and talked about whatever nonsense came to mind. It was a Saturday night, and I had to wake up early to work at McShit. Sarah and I tried to sleep in the corner of the room while everyone else kept drinking.

Nazi Jim was talking to one of the girls we invited to the motel. They were hitting it off and ended up hooking up in Jim's car during the night, with Sarah seeing and taking note of his cheating ways. The next morning, Jim asked Sarah if she would tell his girlfriend about his cheating. She said, "No, but I am disappointed in you," and gave him a judging look. I thought, "Fuck, I can never tell her that I cheated on her with Megan. I never want to see that look towards me." Jim and his girlfriend broke up soon after the party, so no harm was done, but Jim told me for years how awful he felt when Sarah said what she said and gave him that look.

Usually, we hung out at a diner or in his car and talked for hours about music, movies, and the love of our lives we missed so much. He had a girl who broke up with him earlier in 1995 that he was still not over, and I was still in love with Laura and hoped, at any moment, we would be together again. Jim and I were both hopeless romantics and loved the opposite sex to a fault. We both talked about how much we missed 1994 when things seemed hopeful. We wished that some genie would show up and grant us one wish - to return to that year when we still had hope and (for me) a sound mind.

Another funny thing about Jim - he was obsessed with ex-girlfriends. On a few occasions, Jim took me and Eddie on a drive to sit outside someone's house. We didn't know what was happening. We thought we were just sitting in a car talking (which happened often with Jim).

Suddenly, in mid-conversation, Jim would stop talking and listening and become attentive when someone came in or out of a house a few doors down from where we parked.

He suspected girls of cheating on him. If they broke up with him, he wanted to see if they were seeing anyone else. Eddie and I were 18 or 19, still figuring out who we were. We just went along for the ride only to find out we were on a stakeout for the girls who did Jim wrong.

Aside from the moodiness and occasional stalking of ex-lovers, he was a stand-up guy you could count on. Jim was a few years older than Eddie and I, so he had a few more years of heartache and being burned by people and girls to be more skeptical about life. He was cynical and bitter but also a go-getter.

Jim played the bass and tried to start bands with other kids. After 1995, many people we hung out with were either in bands or trying to play an instrument. Jim was like the rest of us - in limbo, wanting something more, be it romance or a band or something to erase the miserable experience that was our lives.

Jim drank and did drugs with us sometimes, but usually, he was the sober, responsible one witnessing our antics. One night, I was drunk and on some downer pill, walking around a pole in the parking lot of the mall during a snowstorm. I was going around and around saying, "I just can't find it," (whatever the fuck that means) when Jim pulled up and saved me from freezing my face off since I was barely dressed for the weather. This was an ongoing situation from 1995-2001. I would be off doing something crazy on drugs or alcohol and get rescued by a more responsible friend. I was a big fan of getting drunk and trying to walk home or find an adventure somewhere. Eddie was the same way, including trying to jump into the Delaware River naked.

Jim was now a fixture in all the lives of us kids from the neighborhood. It started with me and Eddie, then grew to Nick and John H. Then, somehow, John A. got involved and tried to recruit Jim into his band "Sparkle" or whatever it was called.

Jim and John A. lived near each other so they got together a few times to jam until Jim realized how annoying and cheesy John A. could be. After a few weeks of the two palling around with each other, Jim had enough. He said John A. was the type to get on you and never leave like spackle, and he should call the band Spackle instead of Sparkle.

These two people floated in and out of our lives, especially Jim, who only left our crew for a break and would return for more antics. John A. gave us a break by finding someone else to deal with his gigantic ego.

Chapter 60:
Cupid de Locke

The rest of 1995 was mainly me and Sarah spending more time together and me trying to make sure POS didn't spill the beans to her about Megan. I spent Christmas and New Year's Eve with Sarah. We were in the "I love you" stage. I was a mixed-up mess in the feelings department, but I knew I cared about her. At this age, you think these feelings are love, and who's to say they aren't?

We were in teenage love, and I was happy when it was just me and her together. Although, I was always scared that she was going to dump me at any moment because of my outlook on life and how most things are taken from me. Some people (like POS) said we wouldn't stay together and we were too young to know what love is. Then there was all the negative garbage that people who didn't get what they wanted felt the need to bestow on the youth.

I was very impressionable, and these thoughts got filed away with all the other ones that rampaged through my head. I always felt guilty about the Megan thing but soon cut myself some slack. It's not like I wasn't trying to be a player or have sex with other girls all the time. It was my ex-girlfriend with whom I shared an emotional experience for a week of hell. I was barely with Sarah then, and I was only 17.

I wasn't planning on trying to be with anyone else (except Laura since she was more like a soulmate). I was more than dedicated to Sarah. We were a happy couple (mostly). Even as sad and depressed teenagers full of worries, we worked well together with our insecurities. Our joint outlook was that life was mostly a torture chamber. We were a good fit. She was the introvert to my extrovert.

Chapter 61:
The Bends

By the end of the year I finally owned *The Bends* by Radiohead. This album was instantly my favorite of the year (sorry, Smashing Pumpkins). I loved every song on it and listened to it nonstop for a year. Eddie and John H. also loved it. I even got Uriah to listen to it. Radiohead had become all my friend's favorite new band and obsession. The album was a beauty and 100 times better than not just every other band on the radio at the time (besides R.E.M.) but better than (and different) than all the other Britpop that was getting popular in America in 1994-96. It wasn't Britpop at all; it was Britartsypoprock (I just made that up).

Every song was worth listening to, no skipping. Each lyric struck a chord with my mental and emotional state. It made me feel like I wasn't alone in my despair and emptiness. It felt like I had been through too much, and there was still more to come, so be ready. Musically, it was miles ahead of the band's first album. It was them reinventing themselves from the "Creep" stardom they received in 1993. They did it with the cunning ways of a David Bowie type of artistry. Throughout the winter of 95-96, I listened to that tape more than any other, besides R.E.M., of course.

Thank the gods for Radiohead and Thom Yorke for knowing what it's like to suffer and creating beauty from it. With his pain and anguish, he wrote songs that were clever, creative, and poetic to their core. It was a much-needed rest for my brain and the exploding emotions at all waking hours. That year was full of extreme ups and downs, and *the Bends* summed it all up for me and gave me the ultimate comfort.

My friends and I knew we were onto something better and more important than other music and art we came across. The album starts with a song called "Planet Telex," which sounds dreamy with just the right amount of sonic explosion and ends with "Street Spirit (Fade Out)," which is also dreamlike and haunting, taking you through a spectrum of emotions. There were lines in all these songs that I could relate to. Whether it be songs about what haunted me via depression or anxiety or ones about alienation and feeling like you are going to burst with emotions from what is happening (sometimes all at once).

Throughout the album, I wouldn't just think about my struggles emotionally but also the love of my life so far, Laura, and how losing her brought me to a state of constant fear of something negative happening. Paranoia was in my brain, and apparently Mr. Yorke's as well. He seemed to be inside my mind when he wrote about the CIA being used to stop him. A figure of speech that hit home with me and how the Xians blew me away with their actions. The highlight for me was how the last song, "Street Spirit," tackled the one thing that plagued me throughout my life (and I am sure most people's lives) - the grim reality that death was always around with its beady eyes. Thom took me on a journey of dark emotions over the fears of the unknown but ended it most positively. He told me to not worry as much and that the only thing one can do is "Immerse your soul in love." Whatever happens in this life of misery, love will keep you sane. File that one for long-term use, Chaz.

Chapter 62:
High and Dry

I only had mental issues, doubt, and OCD when I was alone. But I was rarely alone. I had plenty of things to distract me from thinking about my real problems. It was easy to go from place to place looking for nonstop fun and something to occupy my mind. While I was running around like a nut job party animal, ignoring the underlying pain and decay of my mind, I only saw my mom and dad every so often. I was still mad at them for my life. I was upset that I had to move back in with them in a small apartment, but I was also in denial that it was happening. I was running from being stuck in this rut of poverty and everything that was piled up against me.

My dad's drug habits were still lurking around. He got high as much as possible and passed out on the hand-me-down chair, watching TV. He was chain smoking like crazy, and his intake of food was slim to none. He did, however, drink a half case or two liters of the store brand cola he liked daily. Since he had not worked since 1992, he spent most of his days watching daytime TV and sleeping. It was the mid-1990s, so the programs he watched were game shows and sleazy, pitiful talk shows like *Jerry Springer*.

Dad still went to his day program at the nearby Mental Hospital called, "Friends Hospital", to help him with his mental health and substance abuse issues. He was trying to get clean and get himself declared disabled so he could start collecting Social Security Insurance (SSI). This meant going to a psychiatrist connected to his day program. For the rest of his life, he went to the program. At this time, he was denied SSI (he first applied in 1994), and we were as broke as ever since the only income coming in was from my mom's minimum-wage Hallmark job.

My dad had to get money to feed his drug addiction. There wasn't much left for him to steal from the house to sell for drugs. The only thing we had was the 19-inch T from the house in Kensington that no one would want. Plus, it was his only source of entertainment. He had to figure something out, and robbing people for money was beneath him, so he applied for credit cards. After he was approved and received the cards, he would take out cash advances on them or buy products he could sell, and then he would buy heroin.

His scheme worked for a bit until he maxed out the cards and couldn't use them anymore. His next move was more devious. He started opening accounts under my mom's name and social security number without her knowing. Well, she knew that they had a Sears store credit card in her name, and he used that card as well to buy products to sell for drugs. Long story short, he ruined his and my mom's credit for quite some time by maxing out all those cards with no intention of paying them off.

All of this happened without me knowing. Then, the Holesworths caught a break. My dad kept applying for SSI and hired a lawyer (who gets paid once my dad got paid from SSI) to sue the government over all of his denials. He jumped through all the hoops and got doctors to say my dad was too sick physically (Hepatitis C) and mentally (ongoing list of conditions). He was playing the waiting game. Seemingly, when most people first apply for SSI, they get denied and have to hire a lawyer to get the ball rolling. By the fall of 1995, my dad got approved for SSI and received back pay for all the months he should have collected while waiting for the appeal process to finish. He got a huge check (around 5,000 dollars after lawyer fees). He also received a monthly check, and Medicaid covered his medical bills. Medicaid was one thing he always had to jump through hoops for. Every year, he would have to prove he needed Medicaid and was worried he might lose the coverage that paid for his numerous medications.

Now that my dad had a big chunk of money, the sky was the limit that Christmas. I don't remember exactly everything they got me that year, but one thing was a new stereo. It was just what I needed since the only thing I had to listen to music was an old-fashioned clock radio and a poor man's version of the Sony Walkman. My last stereo broke during my move from Wildwood to Philly. After several months without a CD player, I could play my CDs again! Things were looking up for us on Paul Street. My dad bought my mom a brand-new microwave! We had cable TV. We were slowly (but not so surely) catching up with the rest of the lower-class people who had these things, like Uriah's family (although they also had cars, a house, a VCR, extra money, and a working shower).

Chapter 63:
On New Year's Day

1995 (the most chaotic and life-changing year for me yet) was over, and the new year would bring a comeback for me. In fact, 1996 was the first of what I call comeback years (I had some few and far between throughout my life). I spent the end of the year with Sarah, Amy, and the rest of our little crew at a party. I smoked "wet" for the last time and puked my teenage guts out.

I spent the changing of the year at 12:00 am with a kiss with Sarah (something I will do on a few more New Year's). I was hoping things in the new year would work out for me, and I would be my old self with a clear mind, maybe even start a band. Some of these happened.

I embraced every year as every day. Yes, my life was in shambles, and my mind was plagued with irrational thoughts. But today could be the day I came back to my senses and woke up from my mental and emotional coma. I could return to my old self, ready to take everything life threw at me. Maybe this would be the year things started making sense. I hoped to be on the right path.

That first day of the year WDRE premiered the new single, "Caught a Lite Sneeze," from Tori Amos. It was haunting and beautiful. It was different from anything on her first two albums, in my opinion, but still a great song. 1996 was already better with a new Tori song on the airwaves.

The album *Boys for Pele* took Tori from cult status to mainstream. People knew who she was from now on when I mentioned how I loved her. I thought it was great for her. She deserved it, and I was glad to see her popularity grow so she could help more people and push change with her thought-provoking songs. On the downside, Tori became so popular that all the "Negative Nancys" of the world started giving their two cents about how she wasn't good or overrated. It was similar to what I heard going forward about my favorite thing in the world, R.E.M.

Tori announced a tour for that year, and I felt confident I would see her for the first time. Things were looking up for this leap year already.

The next day, I turned 18 and was now an official adult in the eyes of the law and society. I spent the day driving around the city with Sarah and her friend Genevieve. I sat in the back seat, thinking I didn't feel much different from the day before. There was no big reveal now that I could legally vote and buy lottery tickets in Pennsylvania. I did purchase cigarettes for Sarah since I was able to do so legally. I guess that's something I gained from becoming an adult.

There was no big reveal to life, but I did have the sense I was getting older, and other adults I was surrounded by growing up (my parents and church folk) would start judging me for not having a high school diploma or a career path. I was still young enough to goof around, try to be in rock bands, and experience things that would shape me for years (some in bad ways). But I sensed I was running out of time and getting old.

I still hoped my dreams could come true and fate would drive me to a positive place. I thought I had time to get it all together and make something of myself that I would be proud of. Later, in my teens and early 20s, I felt that my life was over and I should give up and stop trying to get better. I now realize that was my depression talking and my self-defense mechanism telling me I had enough and needed to get help. But I waited too long for that realization and suffered for many years, not knowing where to go, what to do, or if anything was wrong with me.

I believed these things happened to everyone, but they didn't. It was because of my traumatic experiences. I spent too much time in my head reliving experiences I didn't like or being so self-conscious over everything I did or was done to me. It always led to me trying to be the center of attention or drinking and taking drugs.

Sarah and Michael Stipe's birthdays were both two days later. Sarah was now 16, and Stipe was 36. I just thought it was cool that they shared a birthday.

Chapter 64:
The Blizzard of 1996

In late January, Philadelphia had such a bad snowstorm that the whole city shut down for three days, including Septa and the mall. The streets were packed with snow. I had no transportation out of my neighborhood, so I was stuck in the one-bedroom apartment with my parents.

One of my issues growing up was that I barely had privacy. I only had an enclosed, secure bedroom for about five years in Kensington. I had a corner in the apartment where I kept my clothing and CDs. This is where I listened to music and tried to have "me" time. Those three days in January were rough. To make things worse, our landline phone broke on the second day of our lock-in.

I liked to talk to my friends as much as possible and was tempted to walk to Port Richmond to hang out with Nick and John H. Instead, I stayed in, listening to the CDs and tapes I got for Christmas, including Sophie B. Hawkins' second album that Sarah got for me.

After the second day, I was losing my shit, sitting in that apartment with the cat piss smell giving me a headache. My mental anguish was always at its worst when I was alone and not in good spirits. My demons seemed to work overtime when I couldn't get distracted by entertaining people or just talking to people to make the day go faster. That's what usually got me through the day. The night was my favorite since I could fall asleep (the only time I had pure relief from life).

I got restless, which made my mental and anxiety problems go haywire. It was a test of my will. We only had basic cable. There is only so much TV one can watch. I did see a good film called *Midnight Express* that came on one night. Oliver Stone wrote the screenplay. I liked some of his movies, so I gave it a shot. It was an intense movie with some great acting from the stars. At least I killed two hours of those three days.

I only left the apartment to find a pay phone to call Sarah. I climbed over mountains of snow to get to a phone under the El (now that's teenage love). Soon after, the city reopened. Septa announced they were back up and running, and I was finally free to see my girlfriend and friends. I ran to the bus stop on the corner of Womrath and Frankford Ave. (a few feet from the site of my mental breakdown the previous winter) and hopped the bus to Sarah's.

Chapter 65:
Love is the Higher Law

In February, I decided to call Laura to see how she was doing. It was a few months since I had heard from her, and in my mind, we would still be together forever. Even though I had feelings for Sarah, she was not my soulmate (when I still believed in souls and soulmates). When Laura was free from her parents, I would drop everything for her.

I know it sounds terrible that I was still with Sarah and thinking about Laura. But much like the U2 song "One" said, "Love is the higher law." I wasn't thinking clearly. I was going with what life or fate was handing me, and Laura was my end fate. I knew we were in love. I knew Laura was different and the most beautiful person I ever met (besides Stipe). So, calling her to see how she was doing did not seem wrong. I didn't call her much because I didn't want her parents to think I was trying to do something that would get her in trouble and make them madder at me.

Megan's parents were already furious with me for being a bad influence. I couldn't have that with Laura. I wanted her parents to know I respected their rules and wouldn't sneak around to see her, even if that's what I wanted to do the most. So, I took the gamble and called her. If her parents answered, they would want to know who the boy was, calling for their daughter. There was a chance they would say I couldn't talk to her. I timed it right, though. I knew she would be home from school, and I had a good chance of getting her or her sister on the phone instead of her parents.

When Laura picked up, she was crying. She told me it wasn't the best time to talk. I asked what happened. Getting burnt too many times by people, I had a rush of doubt that she was saying this to get off the phone with me. This is what it's like to have such low self-esteem you think everyone you love wants to avoid you. But she said her parents went too far. They physically abused her during an argument about her not listening to them and not living for Jesus. She told me they hit her and that she was moving in with family outside of Pittsburgh, PA. I happened to call when this was all happening (strange timing). I told her I was sorry and asked what I could do. She said while crying, that she had to go. It was the last time I heard from her until the summer of 1997, but my love for her was carved in my mind the whole time.

Chapter 66:
Break on Through
to the Other Side

In late February, I was introduced to the drug LSD (acid) by that best friend of mine, Eddie Maurer. There were talks about trying acid for a while since we met all kinds of kids who tried it already. We liked classic rock bands like The Doors and Pink Floyd, and we associated them as experimental and how LSD was a big part of their creativity and opened "doors" of the mind.

I didn't know what to think of acid, but I looked at it like I looked at most things since leaving the Christian world. It was there to make you more creative and help you go deeper into your thinking of yourself and your existence. I was all about it.

I watched Oliver Stone's movie *The Doors,* and acid had a big presence, along with how cool and poetic Jim Morrison was. I saw the film for the first time in 1994 when I lived with my Grandma Peggy. I asked my cousin Billy, who I knew had done acid, if it made you more creative and understand life more. He told me the creator of the '90s cartoon *Ren and Stimpy* was on acid when he made those characters. This was not what I was hinting at, but I kept this conversation in mind, like most things that happened to me. I wanted to be more creative and clear my head of the nonsense (Christianity and the doubts that kept me from being my best self) that plagued me.

I was still in the crazy thought pattern that my soul was damaged from being weak and giving up on that day in March of 1995. I thought taking acid would clear away the muck that was holding me back from feeling like I did before my breakdown. I hoped I could find the meaning of life (Tammy from Kensington warned me to leave that one alone).

One usually did acid to see things, listen to music, and watch "trippy" things for a thrill. I did too, but was foolishly under the impression that acid was some magical potion that would wipe the slate clean for me. .Eddie was like me in this way. He was a sensitive, thinking man, so he was all about taking this drug and expanding his mind to see the bigger picture of what life is really all about.

The things that I knew of LSD came from old wives' tales and what I had seen on TV shows and movies. I remember the urban legends that adults who tried acid told us to scare us straight.

When I was about six or seven, I got a temporary tattoo from a coin-operated machine. I got it without my mom knowing. We were at a store on Front St., and she was distracted looking at something. When she was back with me, she told me she didn't want me to stick the tattoo on my skin because that's how people in the '60s took a drug that made them hallucinate.

Her words scared the shit out of me, and I threw the tattoo away. I eventually bought other temporary tattoos and put them on my skin, a little fearful some evil sinner might have put a drug on the tattoo before it went into the machine. But nothing happened except the part of my body marked by the tattoo would show you how I didn't bathe much since it would be on for weeks.

I also heard about the person who took acid and then somehow got stuck in a closet. She was so high she didn't know how to turn the doorknob. She freaked out and clawed at the closet door until her fingers fell off, and she was a bloody mess.

Then there was the story of the kid who had acid in his pocket. It was a hot day, and the acid melted through his pants and into his skin. There was so much acid in his system that he never came back to reality. His brain was fried for the rest of his life.

There was also a tale of someone who thought they could fly (either like Superman or a bird, depending on who was telling the story) while on acid, and they jumped out the window to their death.

These stories were made to scare us away from LSD. Most of the parental figures around us were ex-hippies or knew ex-hippies, and acid was a big deal for them during their youth and the counter-culture world they grew up in.

Some even compared acid to the story *Alice in Wonderland* by Lewis Carroll, in which people took the drug and went down crazy rabbit holes, seeing shit that played with their minds. I watched a show on PBS called *Degrassi High*, a Canadian teen drama set in the late '80s/early '90s. In one episode, two kids took acid, and one of them fell during their trip. The kid was never the same and had to be cared for by someone for the rest of his life. So, these stories (along with the movie *The Doors*) were in the back of my mind when I decided to start using acid to expand my mind.

Some of the negativity about doing the drug started with the stories planted in my childish, undeveloped brain. Obviously, I was not a great candidate to become an "acid head," but this was the road I was going down. I already had anxiety, OCD, and a self-loathing depression that I couldn't tame. Instead of getting help from a professional (since I didn't have insurance or anyone to show me how), I decided to see if acid would cure my problems. I think one can see where this will lead me. Here we go down the rabbit hole, just like Alice.

Now that I was trying other drugs and my stance of staying sober was behind me (for the time being), I was eager to give it a go when Eddie brought it up. He was the one who found the source and got us four tabs to use on one February night for me and my three friends I loved so much, including him, Nick, and John H. The first time doing a drug like acid, you don't really know what to expect. I placed the "hit" of acid onto my tongue and waited for it to kick in.

It would take a while to enter your system. Then, suddenly, you would start feeling a tingling sensation and a warm, buzzing feeling. That was when you knew the drug was taking its course through your brain waves. There was always the fear that the acid tab you bought was fake or very weak, so the first feeling of it kicking in was assurance that you purchased a legitimate product to expand your perspective.

Acid is a drug one should have no obligations or responsibilities for 8-12 hours (depending on the strength or type of acid) when taking. There are several ways to "trip" on hallucinogenic drugs. Most days for us, we put a little tab of paper dipped or sprayed with lysergic acid diethylamide (LSD) on our tongue. You could also buy a bottle of acid and take it in liquid form. Then there were microdots, which were speed pills dipped in LSD to give you an extra shot of adrenaline. Some people put the liquid in their eyes to have it kick in faster. I never tried that, but I tried all the other methods.

Other hallucinogens never did it for me. I tried shrooms that people had once in a while, but I liked the kick that acid gave me. I liked the speed part that made my brain work overtime. Shrooms were more of a mellow high, probably better for those who want to chill and listen to The Grateful Dead or The Beatles. I was out to think about life and the existence of God. For me, acid was an 8-hour shift I would go through in which I had to find something out about myself and life in general.

It was 75% learning and 25% fun for me while doing the drug. In the middle of the trip (around the 3rd or 4th hour), the drug would peak in your body's reaction to this foreign chemical, making you see, hear, and think more clearly. The chemical interacts with one's body and brain, causing the senses to react to every stimulating thing with more perspective and awareness. It made sounds and sights more detailed. It made all the senses feel young and new again, making it seem like you were hearing, thinking, and seeing things for the first time.

There were times when I was peaking, and it was nonstop senses being overloaded by my situation. No matter what I was doing, whether it was talking to my friends and listening to music, watching movies, having sexual encounters, or riding in a car, during the peak, it was impossible to not be overwhelmed (in a good way) with the environment I was in. I heard everything around me so intensely, not just music or other media we were indulging in, but sounds from distant places, like police sirens, fans blowing, and water going through pipelines in whatever house we were at during the trip.

When we tripped, we usually had a plan set up for day or night. Eddie and I took acid over 100 times in three years. There's no way to remember exactly how many times. For a while, it was a weekly thing, often triweekly. After coming down from the trip (my favorite part because I could think more clearly and better understand my existence), you would feel like a car hit you. It was like being hungover from drinking, but the whole body felt tense and achy from the drug doing a number on the nervous system. It required a few day's rest from being so tensed up. You could try doing acid again the next day (I have a few times), and it would get you high and give you an experience, but it wouldn't be as intense as if you waited a few days (in my experience).

Unfortunately, there is such a thing as a "bad trip." It's when your trip goes sour, and you freak out or panic. Once this starts, it's tough as shit to get out of the negative way of thinking once that ball starts rolling toward sudden panic. It usually only happened if I was in a bad mood, something happened to make me think of bad things, or if I was in the wrong type of environment. I only had four or five bad trips. It was usually preventable if I planned the night better or wasn't already upset about something.

The bad trips I had were terrible, but I kept sane enough during them to keep myself from having an acid freakout. During the first bad one, Eddie had to keep me calm and focused on the good things in life. But the first time we did it, there was no chance of having a bad trip since it was all new to us, and we just went along with the ride.

Out of all the drugs I consumed through my young and dumb years, acid was my favorite. I would compare everything that I try in the illegal drug world to acid (ecstasy, pot, and shrooms all fell short of the glory of LSD). I wanted to take acid to expand my mind and kill the constraints that kept me in the rut I was in (mainly the born-again shit), but the first time was more of me and my best friends having a fun night in Port Richmond.

Eddie and I lived every day like it was Saturday night, so I don't remember if it was just Saturdays when we took acid, but every week, we left the mall and went to the small section of Port Richmond where John H., Nick, Jay O'Hara (another part-time mallrat) and Dungeons & Dragons dungeon master Matt lived. We usually took acid when we first got to Nick's house, and when it kicked in, it was party time.

The four of us would take the drug and then run wild around the neighborhood, bouncing around from house to house (John's, Nick's, Jay's, and Matt's). We would stay up all night, tripping and roaming around for hours.

Usually, after peaking, John and Eddie would call it a night and go into John's house and listen to mind-bending music. It was a nice place to finish their trip. They left two wild children (me and Nick) to our own devices for the night. Eddie had one thing over me. John (I can stop referring to him as John H. since John A. isn't in this part of the story) was Eddie's good friend who would do anything for him. It will be a big part of Eddie's development and how he stayed sane and a valued member of society after coming from such a terrible background.

John was the sensible one. He had the most structured home life. His mom worked full-time at Temple University and was loving and caring to her only son. John's dad moved to a nearby house after he divorced John's mom, so he was still a father figure. It led to them raising a good, trustworthy person who one could always count on. It all came in handy when John took Eddie in and became the rock he needed through those troubling teen/early adult years.

I joked with John many years later about how he and Eddie would go in after their peak and leave the two people alone who needed hi attention. He said it wasn't me he was getting away from, but Nick and his wild ways. I don't know how true this was, but if I went in with John and Eddie and listened to Pink Floyd or The Beatles all night while coming off acid in a safe room, I would have settled in for the night and had a great come down. Instead, I got caught up in the madness of Nick (I'm a sucker for peer pressure, and we would be nutty teenagers in the inner city of Philadelphia until dawn.

Once, when Nick was going through his pyro phase, he set some old washing machines on fire under I-95, covering a large section of Richmond Ave. in Port Richmond. He smiled with a spark of pure joy in his eye, seeing them all catch on fire. We all ran when we heard fire engines coming. He also lit up some abandoned used tires later that year, and the fire was so bad it made the local news.

We once stayed up all night on acid and wound up at a playground (across the street from where Uriah lived on Aramingo Ave.). We met up with a girl we knew from the area who liked alt-rock (who had a crush on the sexy and rebellious Nick). We played a game while swinging on some swings to see who could remove the most clothes before getting too scared to go naked. I lost when we were both in our boxer shorts, and Nick was about to take them off (he might have removed them for a moment).

During a quieter night, we were at Nick's house, and he put together a playhouse for his little sisters. His parents told him to do it right before we dropped acid. I just played with his family's brand-new golden retriever puppy for hours, thinking it was the purest, most beautiful thing in the world (this is pretty much how I thought on acid).

One time, we all took acid on the bus. Acid makes your mind see patterns even when they aren't there. Humans look for patterns in life. On acid, your brain and all the nerves are firing off so rapidly that the patterns become a matter of fact. We looked at the Dunkin' Donuts at the El station, and there was a huge sign for their new slogan that said, "It's Worth the Trip." Of course, we thought this was a hidden code for us. It isn't the best example of the patterns and revelations my brain conjured up while tripping, but the thought crossed all our brains. When you come off the drug, most things like that seem trivial. I usually chalked it up to coincidence and didn't mention the absurdity to anyone out of fear of embarrassment.

We put on the radio and tuned into WDRE because nothing is better than listening to music while tripping. I was friendly with one of the DJs, Lee, a very attractive woman in her early to mid-20s. I would call the station and talk to her about music during her overnight shift. I also hung out with her at concerts (when she was working and as a fan).

Once, it was me, Sarah, Lee, and her boyfriend at a show, having a good time. I was so friendly with her that I gave her a picture of me and Sarah from when we went to Sarah's junior prom. She took it, probably thinking how weird it was that some kid would give someone she barely knew a prom picture. She probably accepted it just to be nice.

Anyway, I called Lee and told her we were tripping and asked if she could play some good acid music. By now, which was my 3rd or 4th time tripping, I assumed everyone was doing the drug or had at one point. It was another misconception my acid-filled brain came up with. I figured Lee knew about "trippy acid" music since she was a modern rock DJ. She played a song that night and said it was good to go on a trip with.

I called her back and asked if she was dropping a hint when she said the thing about a trip. She wasn't. It was just another coincidence, and my acid brain was looking too hard for signs (a big part of my acid journeys).

My mind played tricks on me while tripping, and some of those tricks followed me when the trip was over. I began thinking further about my destiny. I figured everything was meant to be, and I was on a path to better things. It was the Christian way of thinking, without the Christ or judging God.

I didn't realize it yet, but it was basically the most imputed info and belief system I knew in another format. I believed a higher power, like fate or a supreme being, was guiding or setting a path I had to follow to get where I wanted to go. Except I wasn't following the bible. I turned to my favorite albums for insight. This thought pattern had its pros and cons. It gave me hope when I was at my uttermost worst but made me keep people around for too long, getting into sticky situations along the way.

One time, we all got some acid called "Jerry Garcia's." Dealers often gave their product a name to separate it and show how strong it was compared to others. The paper the acid was dipped in had a logo printed on it. The dealer would cut the picture into smaller pieces, and the name of the batch would often be the picture from the sheet of acid. So, we knew it would probably be strong and create a good trip.

Sometimes, the acid might be weak due to the mixture or age, or the paper might not be soaked in LSD long enough to get you going into the rabbit hole. Occasionally, the paper would be dipped multiple times after being dried out each time, making the acid trip more intense (or so I've heard). That's another thing about acid and hanging out with a bunch of people that don't know shit and love to spread hearsay. You hear the craziest things about everything from existence to what acid really does and everything in between without a way of fact-checking since the internet was only for well-off folk in 1996.

We all took the hit of acid and were starting to feel fuzzy and energetic when Eddie said he didn't feel anything and maybe it didn't work on him. John laughed and said, "Yeah, you just put a chemical in your body named "Jerry Garcia" and you alone are immune to it."

Then Eddie described a scene where Jerry Garcia is in his mind, saying, "Oh, excuse me, Mr. Eddie's brain wave, let me move by you there." He acted it out. I was already feeling giddy from the acid (when you are in a good mood, it gets amplified, and things tickle your fancy more than usual). I laughed so hard at my friend John's face and him calling Eddie out for thinking he was somehow immune to the acid while everyone else was already feeling it. I felt pure joy and happiness in that moment, innocently poking fun at our friend. It was a moment I could rest a bit, let my guard down, and be happy. I laughed so much that I peed my pants and had to run to the bathroom!

John was one of my favorite people to trip with. He was smart, witty, comforting, safe, and trustworthy enough to be around during an acid trip. John was more structured and surer of himself than me. I wish all my trips involved him, but sadly, there were plenty he wasn't there for. Eddie and I took a lot more acid than John, and I continued running around like a maniac with whoever crossed my path.

Eddie started to feel the effects of the drug soon enough (since he wasn't immune after all), and we all started "tripping balls" (that's what the kids called it when you were so high you didn't know what was going on).

While the acid made us feel alive and in awe of life, Nick wanted to walk to Wawa at Richmond and Allegheny Avenues. It was a 20-minute walk, mainly under the cover of I-95. The walk was never my favorite at night because of the neighborhood kids. I was still afraid of getting jumped or fucked with by them. The stretch was ten times worse dressed the way we were (dyed bright colored hair, nail polish, and long hair) and on a heavy dose of LSD.

During this part of the "adventure" of tripping with other people, someone is always coming up with something to do that will take you out of your comfort zone. You had to go with it since you were on the trip together. So, we went to Wawa. We got some drinks, and everything was okay with the kids we saw in the nearby playground. They seemed preoccupied with whatever sports they were playing to worry about some alt-rock "freaks" walking down the street.

Being inside stores like Wawa when you're on acid, everything seems so much brighter. You think everyone is in on the things you see (like the dirty floor since it's extra noticeable), or they're on to you being on acid (like you have a tell), so you better play it cool until you're out of the store. This is when I would try to whisper to my friends and over-analyze every interaction I had with the workers and customers at Wawa.

Orange Juice was said to be the best thing to drink while tripping because vitamin C enhanced the effects. Once again, this was never fact-checked, just passed down by others who tripped with us. We bought a bunch of OJ, and I drank it like it was blood and I was a vampire. It tasted so good and felt like the nectar of the gods.

Speaking of vampires, the movie *Interview with the Vampire* always reminded me of tripping. It's a good example of explaining what tripping is like to someone who never did it. In the scene when Brad Pitt's character becomes a vampire for the first time, he wakes up, and everything is new to him. He sees and feels everything more intensely. Tom Cruise's character explains that he is seeing things in the night for real for the first time. That's how acid is. Once it kicks in, you see things with different eyes. Everything looks and feels new like you just discovered something worthy of telling others (even though you forget the big revelation you came across or it wasn't that big of a deal).

After we started walking home from Wawa, my worrywart/PTSD mindset thought this is when the bad stuff happens (like getting jumped). Too bad I wasn't too far off. Things were fine at first. I kept my fears at bay, singing songs loudly with my friends. Our teenage voices echoed off the enclosed area under the highway. We loved to sing songs by Queen, R.E.M., and The Doors while tripping balls.

We were two blocks from the safe zone of Port Richmond (where my friends lived) when we passed a bunch of cops parked in one of the lots under I-95. We did what every kid did when they saw cops lingering - we stopped talking (and singing) and tried to act like we weren't doing anything suspicious.

We turned off Richmond Ave. and thought we were in the clear. We were only five minutes away from Nick and John's homes. Suddenly, 4-5 cop cars and a paddy wagon pulled up, sirens and lights on, surrounding us four kids. Panic ran over all of us. The sort of panic that only the taxpayer-funded police force could bring on some troubled youth.

The cops got out of their cars and started talking loudly and forcefully to us. They accused us of writing graffiti on the stone pillars that hold up I-95. We carried bookbags (like any real alt-rock kid did in the '90s), and I had my multi-colored hippie bag. The cops assumed we had magic markers or spray paint cans in our bags to "tag up" anything that caught our eye.

Like most inner cities in America, there were loads of graffiti done by kids throughout their neighborhoods and beyond. It was a badge of honor for kids to tag their names on as many places as possible. Ray was a big tagger until he decided he wanted to become an alt-rock god overnight (I tagged once in my life with him). I found it redundant and didn't want to do it again.

There must have been a sting or a stakeout for kids committing this crime under 95 that week. That would explain why all those cops were there. Real crimes, like murder and drug dealing, were happening on most corners of Kensington. But hey, let's harass some teenagers walking down a busy street instead.

The fuzz made us bend over and place our hands on their cars. They frisked us and went through our school bags. They were probably hoping to find the jackpot of evidence of us graffitiing landmarks (but would probably settle for finding drugs or beer). It would make their harassment worth it. They only found CDs and a change of clothes in my bag and Eddie's.

The cops got upset that they were wasting their time. They didn't give a fuck about wasting our time and almost making us shit our pants on acid. They screamed at us while we were lined up on the cop cars. It happened right when we were all "peaking." We all kept our heads and didn't freak out, but Eddie told us later that he had no idea what was happening.

One cop asked Eddie in an aggressive manner, "Where is the paint?" Eddie thought they knew we were tripping, and it was a test to see if he was on acid by seeing paint move on the cop car. This is what it's like on acid. The irrational seems rational, and your imagination can carry you away. Eddie asked, "What paint?" thinking that if he didn't see anything "melting," he wouldn't fall for the cop's acid test, and we would be on our way.

Melting is when your vision plays tricks, and things appear to be melting or dripping. Sometimes, you will see shadows in places you never noticed, like your face, and your imagination will take you on a ride, making it look like you are a different person. In my case, with my hairy face, I would see myself as a werewolf while staring in the mirror. They say to never look in the mirror, so I always did.

The cops had nothing on us. They asked us our ages. Eddie and I turned 18 that winter and John was 19 or 20, so they couldn't get us for curfew. The only thing they squeezed out of their bullshit taxpayer-funded waste of time was a citation to Nick for being under 18 and out past curfew (even though cops barely gave a shit about that). We walked back to the safe zone with a funny story to tell about surviving a cop raid while tripping balls.

Those were some of the early good times on my drug of choice, but of course, like everything in my life, the bad times with the mind-altering drug were only a few trips away.

Chapter 61:
You Got to Roll With It

S ometimes, it was okay for me to sleep over John's after a night of tripping (Nick wasn't always around or couldn't have me stay). I loved sleeping at his relaxed house. During the winter, the heat was blaring. It was so comfortable dozing off on the bed with friends. The alarm went off at 6 am to get on all the buses to go work at McShit.

I was nearly suicidal going to the place I hated most in the world. I was still scared to quit the job because of the sociopath POS blackmailing me to stay there so he could fuck with my head. Acid gave me the courage to finally quit that shit job.

After a few weeks of tripping, I realized I was tired of living in fear of POS and being controlled. I didn't want to live a second more doing something I felt was below me or holding me back. So, I didn't show up for the morning shift and prepared myself for the aftermath.

I expected POS to tell Sarah about Megan. I was ready to be unemployed and broke until I found another job. It turned out I didn't have to prepare for anything. POS never told Sarah. I think he knew his power over me was fleeting (at least physically). I got another job at a telemarketing place in the northeast shortly after quitting McShit.

I worked at RSVP Telemarketing and made a whopping five dollars an hour for twenty hours a week. I called up businesses and interviewed them for companies that hired the telemarketing company. The main account we had, and the one I called the most, was Brooklyn Union Gas. I called random warehouses all around America and asked them numerous questions about how they felt about their interactions with Brooklyn Union Gas. It was as boring as it sounds for an 18-year-old acid head.

I worked there for seven months, though there were droughts due to a lack of clients. I also wasn't the best employee there. I was only 18 and didn't have the urgency in my voice that demanded those I called to give me their attention for twenty minutes for an interview about their satisfaction with their gas company. I sat in a room with ten people (mostly pleasant, elderly, retired women who needed extra money since social security wasn't enough to pay the bills).

We were in cubicles (like the born-again Christian schools), facing a wall, calling companies from 8 am to 12 pm. Sometimes, I worked a night shift for another company, ringing people at home. I was tired as fuck during the morning shifts. I was up all night (or close to it) hanging out with friends, doing whatever we could to pass the time. I probably didn't fall asleep (pass out) until 2 am, then I'd wake up and go to my new shit job. I often fell asleep on the phone. I'd take my lunch break early to get some coffee to stay awake. I was so bored that I made personal calls to friends and did other non-work things to pass the time.

Once, I found the area code for Athens, GA (Google wasn't a thing, so I called the phone company and asked them for it). I called random numbers in hopes of getting a member of R.E.M. on the phone. I found the phone number for a vegetarian restaurant that I thought Michael Stipe owned (I found out later he owned the building and rented it out to the restaurant). It was called The Grit (I eventually ate there several times and loved every meal).

My love for Stipe was strong as ever, and I thought I could get lucky and find him and tell him how cool he was. I had no idea what I was doing, but I was going with it. I called The Grit, and when someone answered, I felt a rush of excitement. Maybe I was talking to someone who met R.E.M. I panicked and asked, "Can I talk to Michael?" Maybe I caught lightning in a bottle, and Stipe was in The Grit at that second.

The person who answered said, "Hold on, I will get him." My stomach dropped. I was both excited and scared. What if Michael got on the phone and told me to fuck off for being a creepy stalker? At the same time, I would be on the phone with my idol. Imagine that level of getting what you wanted while playing around to pass the time at your shit job. I waited patiently with my heart pounding until a man on the phone said in a grunt tone, "This is Michael." "Michael Stipe?" I asked. "No, Michael the cook!" I laughed at myself and gave Michael the cook a half-ass reason for calling him.

I called the legendary Athens, GA music venue called the 40-Watt Club. R.E.M. played there throughout their career. I went to the venue several times during my mecca trips to Athens (including one when I hung out with Mike Mills in 2011). But in 1996, it was a mystical place that was part of the R.E.M. legacy I read about in numerous books.

I was straightforward and honest with the person I talked to. I told the poor soul exactly what this nut-job teenager from Philly was up to. I explained to him that R.E.M. was my favorite thing ever. I said I was a poor kid from Philly and wanted to meet my idols and tell them how much they meant to me, especially Michael Stipe.

I thought he would tell me to get a life or that they were just people who wanted to be left alone (which might be true, but that's the last thing acid-head Chaz wanted to hear). Instead, he gave me insight on how to meet the fab four from Athens, Georgia.

He told me Stipe lived in Athens when he wasn't touring or working on art and that it's common to see him around town, walking around, or checking out live music. He said he is a down-to-earth guy who likes his privacy in Athens, so if I came down and saw him, I should treat him like another resident, and he would probably talk to me.

I also got info on the places Stipe liked to drink or hang out at. I don't remember the places the guy on the phone told me about, but I was happy that Stipe was down to earth and approachable as long as you don't invade his privacy. I had no intention of doing such a thing (besides being outside his hotel with a bunch of fans after they played in my town like it was Beatlemania). I never wanted to make my hero and role model feel threatened or uncomfortable. If I never met him again because it wasn't on his terms, so be it.

I wanted to go to Athens more than ever. It was always my dream to see all the R.E.M. landmarks. It seemed to be a place of legend with all I heard and read about over the years about their hometown and earlier music (especially the *Fables of the Reconstruction* era), displayed musical postcards of this mystical college, art, and music town.

I thought (during my isolated and financially stranded days in Kensington, in my drafty and doorless bedroom) that Athens was the place to go. I even foolishly thought when I ran away from home in 1994 that Ray and I should go to Athens to start a fresh life. But it was just an impulse thought of teenage fantasies. Eventually, the reality of having two dollars to my name snuck in.

I wish I had gone to Athens then. Instead, I kept randomly dialing numbers with the Athens, GA area code, asking for Michael Stipe, and getting mainly college kids who liked to talk about music with me after I told them what I was up to. No one told me this was crazy behavior. They seemed amused or understood how someone from hundreds of miles away would be infatuated with someone so beautiful and amazing as Michael Stipe in 1996.

The other reason I made these calls during work was they didn't give a shit about long-distance phone calls, and in the '90s, calling someone long-distance was pricey. After a while of not getting in touch with the biggest alt-rock artist in the world, I switched my attention to people I knew personally.

I rang Laura's house once, but no one answered (she was living in the suburbs of Pittsburgh anyway). I also dialed friends from the mall who I knew might be up in the morning (either for school or later in the summer for work). Whatever I could do to pass the time until I got off work and could be with my friends.

Chapter 68:
Chaz's Introduction to a Pyramid Scheme

While I worked at RSVP, I was always looking for a better job. I should have been thinking about getting my GED, but school was the furthest thing from my mind. It wasn't easy to find a job for someone with no high school diploma who didn't want to work in fast food again (and I never would).

I saw an ad in the local paper that said "Hiring for jobs to help the environment." I was intrigued thinking that maybe I could get a job doing something important and see where it would lead me. I called and scheduled an interview a few days later when I was told that no high school diploma or experience was necessary.

I walked into the place in the far Northeast and was greeted by a woman in her 30s who seemed overly nice. Her wardrobe and persona were professional. As she explained the details of the "job," I started realizing why they didn't care if I had a high school diploma or not. It was the first of too many run-ins with pyramid schemes.

Truthfully, my first job selling newspaper subscriptions was a pyramid scheme. Still, I didn't know it at the time and I was so far down the bottom of the pyramid that it was just a job to me. This, however, was the first time the schemers were directly out to recruit me to build their income. Luckily, I was smart enough not to bite.

In this case, the product I would have been pushing was environmentally friendly cleaning products. The office looked professional but lacked the furniture and employees for such a large space. That was the first red flag. Then, a woman put a video on going over the details of the job and what was expected. I would have to buy a kit of these cleaning products, then sell them to people I knew because I must know tons of people who would be interested. At least that's what they told me to make me think it was easy to sell their bullshit.

If I got paid hourly and commission, I might have tried it. However, not only did I not get paid hourly, I would also have to pay some outrageous price ($200-300) for the supply of cleaning products. Then, I was encouraged to find other people to help me sell the products this woman was trying to sell me (see how this goes?). She was scammed into buying the kits and was now trying to scam me. Then I would get people like Eddie or Nazi Jim to help me get rid of the product no one wanted.

I nodded when the woman talked, pretending I was all in. I had to act interested to save face and bide my time to get the hell out of there and never return. When the interview ended, I got the fuck out and ignored all calls from the woman until she gave up.

I would love to say this was my last encounter with a pyramid scheme, but I had several more. I think it was because I was such a people person for a while and would talk to anyone any time, giving many of the "prey on the weak" types an in. Every time I get cornered by someone trying to sell me their scheme, I have the same thoughts of, "Great, how the fuck am I getting out of this one?"

It was easy to escape the first scheme since I didn't know anyone there and could make a clean getaway. Pyramid schemes that involve people you know are tricker to get out of. A few years later, I ran into a kid I knew from the newspaper job in Kensington. He was another go-getter. I was always in competition with him for that college bond we told people we were trying to win.

Joe was nice but had the salesman personality a pyramid scheme was made for. I saw him when I was about 20 at the Roosevelt Mall. It was the first I'd seen him in years (since I left the paper job), and he looked the same with his boyish looks. He asked me what I was up to, and I told him not much. Then, I made the grave mistake that those in a pyramid scheme wait for you to make. I asked what he was up to with his life, and boy, he wanted to tell me.

He was making so much money with a company selling . . . something. I don't remember what because I tuned out what he was saying like he was an adult figure, and I was Charlie Brown. He was saying how much money I could make, too. Then he laid it on thick, telling me I looked like I could use some extra money. I was still dressing in my thrift store best, but it was cool to do so in some circles, especially the ones I was haunting. Joe said I could succeed because of my skills in selling newspaper subscriptions.

I politely replied, "Oh wow, that's how much you're making weekly?" and told him I would think about it (I already thought about it, and my answer was no). This interaction struck me as the life I would have accepted if I stayed in Kensington with the paper job until someone decided to branch off to another selling scam.

I knew I didn't want the life of a salesman, especially one who treats the "opportunity" as if it's a cult. I had so many of these offers because I had no filter and met so many people that I was bound to run into schemers. I was also poor and these scams prey on the poor.

Sometimes people with stable jobs tried to talk me into attending a "seminar." I would laugh it off and walk away once I saw the same pitch, business model, and the same sureness they had pitching the scheme. It reminded me of the born-again preachers I grew up around and of Johnny M. He would have been a champion of the pyramid scheme. John A. would have been great, as well. Both had a used car salesman approach to life.

My favorite pyramid scheme story happened at a place I thought was a haven during my youth: a rock concert. I loved live music in clubs and small to mid-sized venues. I'd go to pretty much anything aside from metal and country music. I didn't care if I only knew a song or two; it was great to be in a room with music blaring out of the speakers. Concerts were my new church, and I loved the entire environment.

I won tickets from some radio station to see The Sundays. I liked them but wasn't a superfan, but I thought it would be a fun night out and something to do, which is how I lived most of my life in the '90s.

The show was at the Electric Factory, a mid-sized venue I frequented. I took a friend to see them, and the band was so good I wanted to meet them and tell them how they impressed me. The usual thing that happens when trying to meet a band at these venues is you go to the back or the side door of the venue, depending on where the tour buses are parked. All of us concert junkies know the band has to go onto the bus at some point that night, and we innocent rock star stalkers patiently play the waiting game for hours.

I was waiting by the side door, where I spent many nights waiting for some of my favorite singers and bands, just minding my business with my friend. Every time I wait to meet bands, a crowd from all walks of life and age groups with the same common bond of loving an artist shows up and waits with me. It becomes an unspoken bond between the other fans. I felt this bond with people hundreds of times for R.E.M., Tori Amos, and Radiohead especially. But, this time, I was barely a fan. I was just there for the experience and didn't care too much if I met them or not. I could give up and walk away at any time.

My friend and I (who was in the same mindset) were waiting for about a half hour. About ten people were waiting for The Sundays. In comparison, I've waited to meet bands and singers with hundreds of people, all pressed together, pushing the lucky ones at the front of the line next to the wooden or metal barriers.

Comfort and proper breathing aren't as important as seeing your favorite artist in person. Knowing they are only a few feet away (sometimes inches) creates a sudden rush, making you feel alive with the electricity and excitement that the unbelievable is happening. Time stands still, and the only thing that matters is that moment. Moments that get built up with pure dedication and love for these other human beings who made something so wonderful and amazing that they become the most important thing in one's life.

Seeing them in person is so surreal that the only thing that matters is if you can get a word in, a glance, or a touch from them to help you get through another session of misery until the next encounter with them. And it happens while surrounded by like-minded people you can be yourself around. But it wasn't like that this time.

This time, a guy loudly bragged so someone would pay attention to him. He was in his mid-20s with a friend who was probably in his 30s. I knew right away what was happening. I could see the setup happening, the con game taking place. The team effort was in full effect. The bigger friend asked the louder, shorter guy (the one pitching the scheme) in a louder-than-normal voice, "Hey, man, who are you getting for your birthday party?" It was the pitch the small guy needed to brag loudly about everything in his life.

The short guy loudly replied, "Oh man, I'm having my party on a private island, and I got Hall and Oats to play!" The bigger guy answered, "No way, how did you get Hall and

Oats to play your party?" (as if he didn't already know these details). The short guy said, "I am making so much money, I can afford that, and I am getting them helicoptered into the island!"

This led to more bragging about the short guy's car collection and other nonsense I didn't care about since I was poor as fuck and didn't care how rich some asshole was. But the short guy kept looking at everyone waiting, trying to see if his pitch and yelling were catching fire.

After ten minutes of this guy repeating how much money he was making and how Hall and Oats were playing his island party, I took the bullet for everyone, made eye contact, and asked, "How are you getting Hall and Oats to play your party?"

This gave him the "in" he was pathetically desperate for. He and his friend started trying to sell their scheme (and their selves with how successful they are) for the rest of the time we waited there. I did the usual nodding and pretending I was intrigued. They thought they had their mark and circled in (too bad for them - I was the poorest person there and already had a few run-ins with their type).

I had enough of waiting for a band I half-heartedly liked, so I called it a night. The shorter guy said, "Hey, man, if you give me your CD cover or ticket (or whatever I had for them to sign), I will get it to you if you give me your number." Now, the dance of the con continues. I said, "Okay," and gave him my number and thought, either he would never call me and have two autographs from The Sundays, or I would ignore him if he called.

A few days later, he called, saying he got the autograph. For the record, I don't care much for autographs. I would rather have a conversation or picture with the artist I love. He said he could bring it to me the next day. I said he could bring it to me when I was working (at the mall in an office setting). I thought he would just bring it to the busy mall on his way home, but that wasn't the case.

He showed up at my place of work with another friend, a different one from the show, and tried to sell me more bullshit about an investment thing. I brought them into a back room, and they pulled out all these papers about how much money I could make and all that jazz. The worst part was they "forgot" my autograph from The Sundays. This was a ploy, of course, to try to get another meeting with them, but I wouldn't fall for it. I was fine living without the signature from the band. Sorry, conmen, find another mark.

He smirked when he told me that he had forgotten the autograph and said he would bring it the next time we met (which was never). After I got them out of my work (and life), I held an unjustified grudge for The Sundays, thinking, "These guys are your fanbase? Really?" It left a bad taste in my mouth for the band that I never got over. So, sorry to The Sundays for not being able to separate these conmen from your music.

Chapter 69:
Caught a Light Sneeze

1996 was one of my comeback years. After the traumatic and draining 1995, this was the year I started getting my head together and gained confidence (as much as I could).

I was always busy, having fun with friends and tripping so much that life was starting to seem exciting and promising. There was always something going on, someone new to meet who liked the music I liked, and concerts to go to.

I received the news I was waiting to hear for years. Tori Amos announced three dates at the Tower Theater in May of that year. I was so excited. This time, I would stop at nothing to see my beloved Tori. On the previous tour in 1994, I didn't get to see her due to not knowing when tickets went on sale for her shows in Philly and not knowing how to get into a sold-out show.

She was touring for her newly released epic album *Boys for Pele*. It came out a few weeks before tickets went on sale. I was still digging into the album and discovering the feel and the lyrics. It was different from her previous two albums (which are still my favorites), but it was still a beautiful masterpiece. It didn't seem to have the intimacy that her first two albums had, but in return, it was longer and more collective in the styles and sounds Tori used.

I didn't know it yet, but this would be the album that launched her from a little cult following to a much bigger cult following. There were a lot of songs on the album that reminded me of Laura and everything that happened in 1995. The album was very comforting in ways, and songs like "Hey Jupiter," "Putting the Damage On," and "Doughnut Song" still make me tear up decades later.

I decided to camp out for tickets at West Coast Video on Cottman Ave. where I camped out for R.E.M. tickets in '95. It was a cold winter night with snow lingering from the blizzard a few weeks prior. I didn't care. Nothing would stop me from getting good seats to the woman I loved the most in the world (after Laura).

I got there and was about third in line. I was happy with this since I was only getting a ticket for myself (I didn't have friends who liked Tori Amos besides Eddie), which usually meant a better chance at a good seat. Most people go to shows with other people, and there is always a single seat available closer to the stage; the ultimate goal of camping out for shows.

Camping out for shows was a favorite thing for me to do for years until the bastards at Ticketmaster employed a rule that people couldn't camp out at their locations. I met so many other fans with the same taste in music as me, and the sense of community rivaled the born-againers' sense of belonging.

The Tori Amos fan community made sense. Her music was my biggest escape and place of refuge for my struggles of being raised as a born-again Christian. Those I encountered through a common bond and love for her had a similar attraction. We needed her intense and intimate songwriting and her persona as a beautiful, strong, wise, and genuine icon.

I soon discovered Tori Amos shows weren't just seeing her perform a spectrum of emotionally fueled songs full of passion and intimacy. It was an event filled with like-minded, kind, and beautiful people I was excited to see at every show. The night was a taste of things to come, with good people I would meet at future Tori shows and some I've known for the rest of my life. It's the best part of loving a musical artist - bonding with those who feel the same as you.

Eddie and John H. showed up early to keep me company for a few hours. Eddie was also a Tori fan (because of me), but, for some reason (probably because he didn't have any money), he couldn't get a ticket. I didn't have money to buy him one. Besides, I wasn't letting the guy who made me miss Kurt Cobain live keep me from getting a good seat.

After they left, it was just me hanging out with Tori fans, talking about how great she was and how much we loved her first three albums (in my opinion, her best). Tori fans, like myself for most of the '90s, are usually sensitive and see the best in people. They give people the benefit of the doubt (which got me in trouble until I wised the fuck up).

It was the first time I met people who loved Tori Amos as much as I did. I met some people who liked her, but these were fans through and through. Tori Amos was the artist I loved that no one else I knew felt the same way. Camping out for her show was one of my favorite days of the year since I was surrounded by people who felt the same way about this woman I would love for the rest of my life.

Usually, when I camped out for shows, I slept the bare minimum. I might doze off here and there since I was sitting on cold concrete with whatever I wore at the time (eventually, I got wiser and brought pillows and blankets). Sleep was hard to come by. I was also too excited to sleep, knowing I would get a Tori Amos ticket soon (it was like trying to sleep the night before Christmas).

One guy told me he wanted to make love to Tori, and I thought that was odd. I loved her so much, but not in a sexual way. Others told me it looked like Tori was having sex with her piano bench. This also struck me as odd since I never thought of such an image. I thought she was just passionate about her music.

As the night went on, more and more people showed up to get tickets. In the morning, 80-100 people were waiting for 10 am to hit so we could buy tickets. I was in a position to get a good seat for the show since I was one of the first in line. Then Chaz's shitty luck came into play.

Sometime before the doors opened at West Coast Video, a man showed up who didn't seem to be a Tori Amos fan. Without sounding too prejudiced, he didn't dress the part. He wore Nautica clothes and appeared to be a rap fan. He was also in his 40s or 50s. He asked us exhausted fans who we were in line for. We kindheartedly told him it was for Tori Amos. Of course, he had no idea who she was.

He said he was there for *Sesame Street Live*, which was coming that summer and also on sale at 10 am. We thought nothing of it and assumed he would have to wait until this long line of cult-like Tori fans were done getting their tickets. I was incorrect.

He hovered near the front of the line on the side. Seemed to be up to something. My kenzo sense was tingling. Then, this asshole walked in front of us at 10 am, pushed his way through the door, and told the Ticketmaster saleswoman he wanted to get *Sesame Street Live* tickets, and he asked if he could go first.

This woman, who I will never forgive for this, let him in to buy the tickets he claimed he wanted while the clock was ticking on getting tickets to Tori. When the on-sale time hits, every second matters. It's a sudden rush to score the best seat possible, along with the anxiety (a healthy anxiety) that someone else at another Ticketmaster location can get a better seat than you. It was a race against time and fellow fans.

So, this son of an asshole ate up 5 -10 crucial minutes that we Tori fans could have used to buy better seats than what we got. The person first in line probably would have gotten the front row, or at least close to it, and I would have ended up most likely in the top five rows to see the woman I idolized. Instead, I had to settle for a ticket 20 rows away in the farthest seat to the left of the theater. I was devastated knowing I would probably be looking at Tori's back the entire show since she played the piano in the center of the stage.

The worst part, though, is something that makes me so mad at the asshole who bumped in front of us and mad at myself for not being more vocal about the wrongdoing. The jerk came out while us sensitive, young Tori fans just witnessed this tragedy of events in our pursuit of good tickets and showed us eight tickets he bought for Tori Amos!!!! He had front row! This asshole was a fucking ticket scalper!

He said, "You guys got me interested, and I think I am going to check her out." Which was a lie. Then he tried to sell the tickets to people further down the line (I don't know if he succeeded but fuck him). I was so outraged and wanted to do something about it, but I was a scrawny kid. I looked around and saw no one else there who would do anything, so we took the defeat and settled for less than what we deserved for Tori Amos.

When the shows came around, I went with girls I met hanging out in the Northeast who went to the same catholic schools as my friends. During the months before the show, I went to parties and met kids who were Tori fans.

There were five of them. They gave me a ride to the show, which I appreciated because it would have taken me a while via Septa. They were all pretty girls. Four of them sat together, and another sat by herself in a seat (since her friend canceled on her). They were 40 rows back but dead center.

I sat in my seat for the first few songs until I realized my view was restricted. I was next to the wall and could only see Tori if I leaned over to one side and looked past the stage speaker.

I went back to the girl with the solo seat (who was quite lovely) and sat with her. This seat was much farther back, but I had a clear view of Tori and everything she did on stage. It was a great first Tori show experience.

There is nothing like seeing Tori Amos play live. It's an epic, emotional rollercoaster. She plays songs that are planned but also changes up the setlist (it's easy to do since she's calling the shots) with surprise songs stretching from rarities to cover songs from Bruce Springsteen, Elton John, and Neil Young, incorporating a Philadelphia theme when playing our region.

Tori is also the most personable music artist. She held meet and greets so fans could tell her what her music meant to them. It was different than waiting around to meet my favorite singers because these events were encouraged by Tori. She wanted to be connected to her fan base.

Tori nicknamed her fans" Ears with feet" since many of us travel to see her all over. It was like the Grateful Dead's following of Deadheads, except we had a love for more trauma-filled, emotionally charged songs. The meet and greets were the equivalent of the purest Catholics meeting the Pope (except more intimate and real). People could request a song they wanted to hear that night and explain to Tori what it meant to them. Her fans aren't just people who like a catalog of popular music.

Her songs tackle unique perspectives and life experiences that attract fans who can relate to and find comfort in her lyrics. Her music is a soundtrack for people who have dealt with traumatic moments. Tori's songs make it a little easier to deal with negative experiences. For me, her songs were like a guide to get me through life and everything that tries to kill my spirit and hope.

The meet and greets were almost as important as the live show. It was a chance to "kiss the ring" of the woman who meant so much to you. In 1996, I was a newbie and didn't know the ins and outs. I wasn't sure what time I should line up before a show or how early I should leave during a show to be the first in line to meet her. At this one, I had to settle for being in the middle of a large group after her show. I was content that I could sort of see her talk to those in front (if I leaned over the right way and stood on my tippy toes since I was short as fuck).

After the show I camped out for sold out in under an hour, three more shows were announced within days of the first one. Acts usually leave dates open for a big metro market area like Philly in case tickets sell out fast. My ticket was for May 1st and a show was added for May 2nd and two on May 3rd (one at 7 pm and one at 10 pm).

I didn't have much money to go to the other shows, but I would try in May. When I got my next paycheck from my telemarking job, I thought about paying as much as possible to get tickets, but I could only afford one or two. I decided to miss the May 2nd show, thinking I would just see Sarah that day before she went to work. I wish I had gone to that show, though. It was the only night Tori performed R.E.M.'s "Losing My Religion." She didn't play it often, and I didn't see her play it until 30 years later.

On May 2nd, I was at Sarah's house on Morrell Avenue and went home when she left for work. I hopped on the 20 bus across the street. Her house was visible from the bus stop, and I spent many days on the bus going home or to the mall, wishing I was back in the house with Sarah.

On this bus ride, I saw one of the girls I was hanging out with the night before at Tori. She was with a bunch of teenage girls at the front of the bus who acted like it was their first time taking public transportation. They were confused and unsure about what to do when they got off the 20 bus that took them from the comforting Northeast to the rundown, sketchy area of Frankford and the end destination - the borderline of West Philly (two harmful neighborhoods).

Being an expert Septa bus passenger, I helped the girls by telling them how to interchange from the bus to the El to get to 69th and Market, where the Tower Theater was. The ride was 45 minutes to an hour from the first stop at Frankford terminal to the last stop at 69th.

At the girl's high school, there was a buzz about Tori coming, and they went to the show in numbers to be safe. This included taking the bus with people from their school they barely knew or didn't know. I knew a couple from my area and the girl who went to the show the night before with me.

One girl I didn't know was Liz Dollarton. We became good friends and still have our Tori bond decades later. Liz is two years younger than me. She worked in the mall at JCPenney, and her younger sister Caitlin became a regular mallrat a year later. Liz had an outgoing personality and could talk to anyone about almost anything. She is the type that's not afraid to step on toes and tell someone when they are wrong (especially over politics and women's rights), and she loves a good time.

We got along right away during the 20–30-minute bus ride. Then I walked everyone to the El entrance so they could get to the Tower Theater. Liz's hair was red (like Tori's), but she dyed it brighter to be like her idol. Liz is also attracted to both sexes, so I am sure if she had the chance, she'd marry Tori. She was head over heels in love with her and was the biggest fan I knew (even over myself). Our friendship spawned from this common bond.

We made out once a few years later, which led to a chance for a romantic relationship. However, I think we both realized we were meant to be friends and would probably have killed each other if we dated too long (we both have strong, stubborn personalities). She became like a sister to me, which was fitting since I met her on my estranged sister's birthday, May 2nd.

Liz and I traveled to numerous Tori shows throughout the U.S. during our friendship and even some overseas dates when we wanted to get more of Tori than the one show she plays in Philly.

For these rows of shows, Liz only went to the one I saw her on the bus for. She saw Tori again that fall on her second leg at Penn State's campus. I wish I had gone with her to that one because Liz met Tori for the first time at a meet and greet. Liz told Tori how beautiful she thought she was, and Tori said Liz was beautiful as well. I was jealous but happy that she experienced this interaction with Tori.

I had to see Tori again that week in May. Alisha, another fan I met in Northeast Philly, had an extra ticket for May 3rd. I jumped at the chance and bought her ticket.

The tickets were closer than the first night and more in the center. Alisha was friends with the girls from the first show, and one of their boyfriends drove us to the theater again. The show was amazing. I was so happy to be around thousands of Tori fans and didn't want the night to end. And it didn't have to end yet. Tori was playing two shows that day; one at 7 pm and one at 10 pm. Our ride was staying for both sold-out shows, and Alisha and I only had tickets to the early show.

We hoped we could find tickets for the 10 pm show. Otherwise, we would have to wait for our ride for a couple hours. Right after the first show, we knew we didn't care how much it cost to get into the later show. We needed to see Tori again.

We stood outside, hoping a little concert luck would fly our way. I learned a lot about concert luck throughout my days. Concert luck is being at the right place at the right time when someone is giving away tickets or selling them cheaper than other scalpers. Or, in some cases, walking up to the venue's box office and finding out they had released tickets for sale that were previously spoken for by the band or someone in the business. This was the best and almost the surest way of getting in and usually getting great seats. But, at this time, I was still new to the deals of sold-out shows. Luck found us almost right away.

A nice human came over to us at the entrance of the Tower Theater and said they had two extra tickets and we could have them for $20 each (half off). This was good news since I had a net worth of around $100 every two weeks.

We jumped on this chance. We were excited and almost in shock that we could see our Tori again on the same night. It made us happy to be in the same space and room as her. We went from not much hope of getting into the show to getting in for a deal! It was a whirlwind.

The Tower Theater is my favorite venue to see a show. I have seen over 300 shows in my years of being a concert junkie, and the sound quality and intimacy of The Tower is hard to top. It only seats about 3,000 people, so almost every seat is good (except the one I had for the first Tori show). The acoustics in the venue make an artist like Tori Amos sound even better. Most of the shows I have seen at this venue have been Tori shows, which makes me associate my memories of the place with seeing one of my favorite artists. I saw Tori many times after those first shows, but nothing will ever top the first three I saw in May 1996.

I'm not sure if they are still the best because that tour was mostly songs from her first three albums (which are my favorite) or if it's the fact that nothing will ever top the first time seeing such powerful performances. Regardless, that week was one of my favorite times, not only because of the Tori shows (the main reason) but also because things seemed to finally be working out for me. I felt a weird sensation of optimism about what was coming next (oh, Chaz, how foolish thou art).

Chapter 70:
Still Just a Rat in a Cage

I was still in a crazy spot mentally. I thought my feelings and old identity (the one that was more confident and could deal with my lousy life head-on) would suddenly return, and I could live life to the fullest. I was in denial, of course, mainly because I did not know what was happening. I had nowhere to turn to help me figure it out.

I still had irrational thoughts ramming into my head from what I thought was external. They were internal, and I couldn't control them due to my anxieties and fear of the unknown, especially the big unknown of that god thing they made me fear. I was trying to push these thoughts out of my head with things I considered good or pure (friends, love, and my favorite music). I had to think in order about the things I loved and feel that love, so I felt that I earned the right to love them forever.

I know now what was going on, but then (and throughout the next ten years), I didn't know shit. It was mainly when I was alone, especially at night in my parent's place, when I felt the worst about my life and self-worth.

I overthought everything and tried to figure it all out on my own. I regularly jumped to conclusions, and those conclusions went from simple ones to the most extreme, disturbed, and outright ridiculous thought patterns. I had no boundaries to my anxiety-filled thoughts that seemed to be out to hurt or mock me. If I thought something (like I love R.E.M.), my next thought came as mockery, belittlement, and negativity. I would think I didn't deserve to love R.E.M. because I was a weak person who went numb at an early age. I thought, "R.E.M. thinks you're a fool, everyone thinks you're an idiot, and you're not good enough for R.E.M. Fucking insanity, man.

The negative and doubtful thoughts overwhelmed me to the point of numbness. I wasn't able to make any progress in healing my life and mind. I would toss and turn on my cat piss-stained couch in our apartment, with a massive headache from the smell, and suffer when I couldn't sleep.

My mind raced with thoughts, trying to figure out what was happening in my head and trying to keep above water long enough until something showed me the way to go. Whether it was with a band or Laura, I was playing defense against all the negativity I collected in my memory banks that wouldn't let me live the way I wanted. I was restricted by my lack of self-esteem and everyone who made me feel inadequate. I was in a battle for independence and wasn't properly fitted for this battle.

If this was before my breaking point the year prior, I could have handled everything. If only I didn't have that one moment of weakness that led to losing my confidence and having doubt wash over me. I thought it was just what happens in life and that I was in denial. I had to give up and become a typical human without passion or the strong spectrum of feelings I thought would never leave (but they did).

My feelings didn't go away; they were just out of control. It was like I was this intact person, and then someone shook up all the insides, and I went haywire. Confusion was now the norm. I knew who I was at the core. I knew what I wanted but struggled with my inner thoughts and overwhelming feelings. I had major demons that put me in survival mode most of the time, which is why I never wanted to be alone for long.

I felt that if I wasn't doing something, I was a loser. The demons would creep in and make me feel terrible and try to get me to give up on everything. It was a combination of things that were haunting me. I had a negative-energy cocktail roaming in my brain. It stemmed from my depression and anxiety and was fueled by my self-loathing and uncertainty about god and life.

I hoped these constant struggles would end on their own. I hoped that once things so floating my way, everything in my head would go away too, and I would be the emotionally confident person I was before. I was so terrified of the next blow to my feelings.

I was trying my best to figure things out and get a handle on life. I needed to figure out how negative feelings vs. positive feelings worked and how things flowed around me. I was seeing patterns and trying to figure out if they were brought on by the universe or god.

Acid helped to find these patterns. I went down rabbit holes in my brain, trying to have a big revelation and crack the code of why so many bad things happen to me and good things also happen.

I still thought there was a battle of good vs. evil (negative vs. positive feelings or impulses). I thought all the religions were onto something when it came to their god vs. the anti-god, but they dumbed it down and made it an easier concept for the masses. I believed the universe was full of energy flowing around everything, making people good or bad. I also thought these energy waves were locked in with the energy in our brains (our life force), and we have an equal chance to be good or bad. If one goes down the negative path (like giving into anger and hate), they will be doomed to feel that way and have negative things happen to them.

These thought patterns led me to conclude that every action has a reaction, and one has to choose how to react to things that happen to them. If you give in to anger and act out on that anger, more negative things are bound to happen. This has nothing to do with an external energy source, but at 18, I was far from this realization.

I never put all my eggs in one basket. I was constantly thinking and putting almost every situation into my theories and my think tank. I thought things happened to me in waves of good and bad, and it was all for me to learn or help me find what I was looking for.

1996 was an uplifting year for the most part. I was flying high by the summer, but then a wave of misery and terrible events occurred during the fall and winter, putting me into one of many downward spirals. I thought it was how the universe worked, and I had to deal with these negative waves until the positive ones came back. I thought these negative and positive things happened for reasons I couldn't understand yet.

In these days of being dirt poor and seeing the internet as something that might be just another luxury (much how I saw cable TV most of my childhood), I did not have much to go on with my thoughts on existence. I had to go with what I heard from people I met through my travels around Philly, those who wanted to talk about deeper things (especially on drugs). The problem was that most of these people were clueless and going with what they heard from others (usually on drugs) as well. But at the time (and for decades that followed), I assumed these people were either on to something or were all in on the big picture, and I was the one trying to catch up in my perspective of life.

I wasn't totally falling for everything people said to me. I still took everything they said to my think tank to process it, but some of it leaked in and I used it to figure out this shitstorm life of mine.

People say the yin and yang is a balance between negative and positive (good and bad), and the universe needs both to function and keep things moving. A situation or series of events can't happen without both forms of energy being involved. One has both energies inside them, and they can't exist without the other. It is a push-and-pull thing that makes us do what we do. This made sense to me, and I spent many years pondering and trying to make sense of my unfortunate life.

These thoughts (or my attempt to make sense of them) stemmed from my born-again background. I was running with all the info I was subjected to or implanted with and doing my best to make sense of it. Unfortunately, there was no guarantee that I was on the road to figuring it out. My logical mind knew this, and it helped me maintain some sense of a reality-based perspective (thank the gods for this).

I thought another reason these bad situations occurred was due to me thinking positively and being happy. I was scared to death that a god-like figure or fate would slap me back down since this was the pattern I saw throughout my life.

When I was about 10, and still in the Jesus club, I was so thankful for my eyesight. I thought about how some people couldn't see. Then my eyesight turned to utter shit that year, making it impossible for me to see objects over six inches away.

When I was 14, I jinxed two appliances we owned my entire life. I asked my mom how old our fridge was. She told me it was over 14 years, and I thought it was amazing that it lasted that long. It died a few days later. The same thing happened with our 13-inch black and white TV. I asked how old it was, and a few days later it stopped working.

Yes, this is all just a coincidence, but during my young Jesus stage, I thought I caused this stuff to happen by taking notice of them. Like my energy caused a reaction with the universe.

Later in life, when I was dating girls, whenever I let my guard down and thought I could rest easy: BAM! I got dumped. I was terrified of thinking happy thoughts. I tried my hardest to think about the worst possible situation instead. I thought it would keep god or fate from taking positive things away. If I thought of the most negative scenario, it would cause that thing to happen because I braced for it and expected it, so in my fragile mind, this could cause it to not happen.

The craziest part is I didn't base everything on these theories (which was often worse). My mind was constantly analyzing, and most times it was so ingrained in my subconscious that I didn't realize I was thinking the most negative things.

If I rubbed my eye, I would have a sudden thought about someone banging into me, causing me to poke myself in the eye so hard I would go blind.

I thought about eating and touching things that I never would, like bleach or a hot stove because it was absurd and would get the negative thought out of the way so I could function. They were compulsive thoughts that I couldn't control.

I also thought the worst about Sarah and my friends. I would think she was cheating on me, and my friends didn't like me and would mock me when I wasn't around. These weren't daily thoughts; it was just so god/fate wouldn't get any crazy ideas that I was happy and take away the things I needed. These thoughts were quick impulses. I didn't dwell on them for long. It was my obsessive compulsion trying to cover all my bases of life and external forces.

While dealing with this nonsense, I also thought the complete opposite. I was a confused-as-fuck teenager (not all my fault). As my inner self thought of the most negative things to prevent them from happening, my sensible self tried staying positive about my hopes and dreams. Then my negativity made me panic, turning my insides into an emotional tug of war. I eventually learned to not feel or think about anything and go with the flow. Still, my brain always expects the worst.

I also let in the demons and negative images of those who harmed me throughout most of my life. I tortured and hurt myself for several reasons. Most importantly, I could not control my irrational thoughts that were hurting me. In a way, the thoughts and feelings attached to them were trying to protect me from feeling too much and keeping me grounded.

I thought the negative waves were coming to kill my spirit and send me back to the born-again faith or down a drug-addicted path. I constantly checked myself to prove I wasn't going down those paths, ensuring I wasn't slipping or losing my love for certain things.

I also let the doubts of Christians, Ray, and POS in, so I could battle them off with my self-identified person who was better than people who manipulated me and made me feel like shit. I believed every thought I had was a test from an external place (they weren't) and I had to prove myself and bear the cross given to me.

All of this happened while I was poor as fuck with man boobs and no future. And acid didn't help with the anxiety and panic that came from thinking about this stuff, and the constant struggles of trying to figure out the patterns. Acid gave me clarity on certain things and more confidence in being who I wanted to be. But it left me more self-conscience than ever. The anxiety I felt during "bad trips" became a reality for too many years.

I foolishly thought things would work out and make sense. I was still new to these mental battles. I was trying to make sense of the tragedies in my life without confidence and control of my feelings. I still thought this was what everyone goes through or a part of my journey, and one day I would be myself again, like magic.

I surrounded myself with people who seemed to love how energetic and alive I was. When I was with people, at shows, or being the life of the party, my inner demons were in the back of my mind and easier to deal with. I became popular throughout Northeast Philly and the suburbs over the year. I had something to do and someone to hang out with almost every occasion. This partying and chaotic lifestyle was the norm for 3-4 years. I was living in the moment, hoping the chips would fall into place. I was running from reality, clinging to the belief that there was something good worth living for on the horizon.

Chapter 71:
Forever Young

Eddie started going out with Severa early in 1996. We were dating two girls who were good friends. We spent most days together, at the mall, Sarah's house, or parties. Sarah and her friends all started doing acid with us during this time.

We started tripping in Port Richmond every weekend, usually staying up all night and taking the bus back to the northeast the next morning after the acid had run its course. Then we would sleep at someone's house for a few hours or go to the mall and party all night. We often took more acid to stay up during the day.

The number of kids at the mall kept expanding. We had close to 100 kids hanging out during the weekends and summer. They were all into rock music, and some were into punk, ska, goth, metal, rap, and, of course, alt-rock. It was a melting pot of popular music tastes. Most kids felt their favorite band was bigger than life. Some were obsessed with the Smashing Pumpkins, NIN, Nirvana, Tool, Hole, etc.

Thanks to my acid-filled, born-again Christian brain, I felt that I was meant to be in this music community. I thought I was part of some new counter-culture movement like the hippies. In reality, we were just a bunch of kids who liked music and drugs and happened to live in the same region.

Things seemed to be going okay. However, I didn't get too confident because I feared fate would send bad things my way if I showed I was content. But I did feel a little at ease, thinking maybe this was the beginning of everything I wanted.

Eddie was a constant comfort and reassured me when I needed it. I had a girlfriend I cared about and was now dating her longer than I had ever dated another girl. Another childish fear was thinking I was jinxed to have a girlfriend for than four months since that was the longest so far. When I wasn't alone with self-destructive thoughts and had people to hang out with, it felt like everything was going to be okay. In the spring of 1996, one of my teenage dreams came true - I got to attend my first high school prom.

I always desired to attend a girl's prom since I was a full-on fan of shows like *Beverly Hills, 90210*, and *Saved by the Bell*. As a delusional, poor kid in my early teens, I watched heartthrobs having a blast at their proms. I loved how normal and fun it all looked. When I met teenagers around the neighborhood and in Wildwood who all went to normal schools and had dates to take to their proms, I was more intrigued by the idea of going to a prom than ever.

My school was against dancing and popular music, and they were so low-budget that they wouldn't have been able to pull off a thing like a prom. Some born-again schools had a Christian version of a prom (a banquet followed by preaching and no touching your date whatsoever) to make juniors and seniors feel like normal kids. Bensalem Baptist had its banquets, and I was planning on taking Laura to the 1995 one if I could graduate.

I loved music and dancing. I was surprisingly a great dancer at the proms, especially for a guy with no rhythm. Thanks to my born-again schooling, I craved the normalcy and excitement kids felt on prom night.

By early 1997, I had the splendid idea of going to as many dances as possible while I was still young. I was friends with hundreds of girls from the area, and they wanted to go with someone who was fun and wouldn't try to sleep with them. Most of the time, I had a girlfriend who was okay with me going to proms with other girls. It was the '90s, and I had very understanding girlfriends.

I went to about twenty dances from 1996-1999. I went to a few with girls I was in a relationship with, but most were just friends. We met with other friends at the dance and had normal high school fun. Sometimes, I knew so many people at the dance it felt like I went to their school. Years later, people said they didn't realize I didn't go to certain schools because I was at so many dances.

I loved the fun, pageantry, buzz, and excitement of the one night every kid felt special and got to play adult in their fancy clothes. After a couple years of going to so many proms, I bought a used tuxedo since it was cheaper than renting one for every dance. I bought it in 1997 for about 100 dollars and wore it until 2003. I also wore it at weddings (including my sister's) and concerts. I wore the tux to some of my favorite shows, like R.E.M. in 1999 and a couple of Tori Amos shows in 1998. I got my money's worth out of that tux. I was the only kenzo I knew who owned a tuxedo.

I got ready for some dances at home in the Frankford apartment and took Septa (with the tux on) to my date's house. I got some stares. Nothing says ghetto fabulous like taking public transportation in a tuxedo.

A few years later, I will watch a movie called *Trippin'*, starring Donald Faison and Deon Richmond. It's about a kid who wants to go to the prom with a pretty, smart girl. This movie hit home as Deon Richmond's character was a poor dreamer who wanted to be more successful.

The scene I loved the most and identified with was when his character took the bus in a tuxedo to get to his date's house. He had to stand up on the bus (much like I had to due to not having an available seat) with a look of determination on his face. I didn't have the same look; I had one of embarrassment. I was too self-conscious to be proud of myself for taking a bus in a tuxedo. I thought people thought I was a fool, or they felt bad for me for being the poor kid on his way to a prom via Septa. It's a good thing I was too all over the place mentally to care what anyone thought of me (at least not enough to hinder me from doing outrageous things).

The first prom I went to was with my girlfriend Sarah at her Junior prom in the spring of 1996. Nick went with one of Sarah's friends, so it was even more fun since I had one of my best friends with me throughout the night. Sarah wore a long gold dress. I wore my dad's suit that I borrowed. I wore it to a few proms and wore the pants hanging out sometimes because they were similar to the ones Michael Stipe wore on the 1995 Monster tour.

The suit smelled like mold for some reason. I'm not sure how my dad came into possession of the suit. It was just something that was there for the taking. It still smelled even after I took it to a dry cleaner before dances. But thanks to the popularity of alt-rock and grunge, no one cared about how I smelled or looked. Being this poor gave me some street cred in this misery-filled popular music scene we were living in.

Nick wore a Three Stooges tie with his trademark dyed green hair in full force. I've always been a hat guy, or I would cut my hair so short that I wouldn't have to worry about making it look presentable. For some reason, I decided to let my hair grow a bit, and I tried doing a pompadour (like Morrissey and/or Luke Perry), but it didn't turn out well.

I waited downstairs for Sarah as she got ready for the dance. She was usually a low-maintenance girl (which I liked since my maintenance was even lower), comfortable in any clothes she had around. She let her hair flow with its natural bounce.

I was in the living room when Sarah came downstairs. I saw her in a way I never had before. She had her hair curled at the bottom and had makeup on that she usually didn't wear (she usually stuck with eyeliner or mascara). She looked stunning in her long gold dress, and I felt proud to be her boyfriend and date for the dance.

I don't remember much of the dance itself. I'm sure we danced to prom usuals, like "Forever Young" and "Grease Lightning," and Nick and I acted like fools at some point in the night, but I can't recall everything. After the prom, we got into the limo or bus we rented (it made us feel like responsible adults) and drove around Philadelphia, looking at landmarks. I had seen them a hundred times before and would again since we did the same thing after every prom. We went to the Liberty Bell, City Hall, and, of course, the Philadelphia Art Museum so we could run up the "Rocky" steps like every other kid has done since 1975.

It was a chilly April night. Sarah was getting cold in her sleeveless dress, so I let her wear my suit jacket. Then, we got to the top of the Rocky stairs, and someone took a picture of us embracing, with gleaming smiles on our faces (which was not a thing we did a lot, mainly because Sarah wasn't a smiler). It was the happiest picture we ever took together and was the peak of our innocent love.

After the night of pretending we were important enough to drive in a limo, Sarah and I went to an after-party at her friend's house. Nick and his date went their separate ways. It was just me, Sarah, and four other couples Sarah was friendly with. We had some beers and lived free since their parents weren't home.

The lights went out, and all the couples slept in the living room (some on the floor, some on couches). Sarah and I were in a love seat, and soon after, we heard all the couples having the old sexual healing from their respective places on the floor.

Sarah and I had been going steady for about six months. We had not had sex yet and kept things at a PG-13 level. People always said going to a prom was almost a sure way to have sex. I didn't care about that or didn't expect us to have sex that night. It would have been Sarah's first time (and basically my first time since the other two were negative experiences filled with panic).

She told me (surrounded by lustful teenagers in puppy love having sex) that she didn't want her first time to be in this situation. I agreed, and we just made out a little until we fell asleep in each other's arms. It would have been awkward to have sex in a room with strangers also having sex, even if Sarah and I had sex plenty of times. I was happy just being with her in the moment.

It was a couple months later when Sarah and I finally had sex. It was during the day at Sarah's house while her parents were at work. Previously, she told me she was ready to "make love," and since I was at my peak of being a gentleman, I told her I could wait as long as she needed.

Now, she was ready. We put on some music, including Bryan Adams' "(Everything I Do) I Do It for You," and we had sex for the first time together. I cared about Sarah and loved her (with all the knowledge of love I had in my teenage brain), and this time was different than the other ones. I wasn't panicky and didn't feel like I was being bad. I didn't feel guilt for doing something wrong in the eyes of the lord. This time, I felt like I was where I was supposed to be, doing what I was supposed to do.

It lasted longer than the other times, and I felt closer to Sarah than ever (which is the real reason for the act of lovemaking, at least in the eyes of a teenager who still had some innocence). I felt calm and satisfied being with a person I cared about for a long time (in my teenage sense of time). I felt like I had structure and stability in my life for once. Of course, this would lead to bad things happening; another piece of evidence for my theory on negative things happening to me when I'm content or happy (like a magnetic attraction).

Chapter 72:
The Lizard Kenzo

Eddie also lost his virginity to his girlfriend, Severa, around this time. He seemed very happy about the relationship and said typical "Eddie" lines about Severa, such as, "Oh my god, I just love her so much. I think she's so great." It was what Eddie said about everything he loved with his whole heart. From R.E.M. to Queen to whatever girlfriend he was with, it was "They are so great" and "I love them so much." He truly did with his whole heart, but it was funny to make fun of him for using the same lines when he wanted to express his feelings.

Something happened to Eddie about a month after he and Servera lost their virginity together. It was the transition of spring to summer, sometime around June, when Eddie started to go down what I liked to call the "Jim Morrison" route.

We were full-time acid heads now and thought we were riding a wave to our fate and destiny and becoming "in tune" with the universe and all that nonsense. We started to develop all these notions on life, love, relationships, our place in the world, and what we deserved.

I don't know what caused it, but Eddie started getting a bit wild. He didn't stop until he met his next girlfriend, who calmed him down until the next round of wildness came about. Eddie was out to sow his wild oats, and Severa would be left in the dust.

Eddie cheated on Severa first, then broke up with her (probably for no reason) and started to get with girls we were friendly with. Eddie had a wild, sexual summer, acting like he was the lizard king, while Severa went down a path of self-loathing. She borderline hated guys because of Eddie. I felt bad for her, but I also loved Eddie like no other, so I had to stick up for him whenever Severa brought him up in front of Sarah.

Once, we were all tripping in Sarah's basement. There was a huge flag (about 8 feet tall) of Jim Morrison with an American flag behind him, posing in his iconic Christ-like pose. Severa looked up at it and said something about it being a shrine to all the dicks (meaning Eddie being a dick for hurting her) and ran into the other room in the basement to be alone. I somewhat understood where she was coming from. But in Eddie's defense, he was just an 18-year-old kid who had a rough life and started doing this wonderful drug that made you feel like you were special and opened your mind to new ways of thinking.

One of our idols while on this drug of choice was the Lizard King himself, Jim Morrison. I am glad to say this idolization of Morrison was short-lived by Eddie and me.

Eddie was on an acid ride to fulfill his "at the moment" desires, and nothing could stand in his way. I was jealous in ways. I could not lose myself and give in to the hurt and ego part of the brain. I wasn't ready yet.

Chapter 73:
We Don't Have Any Real Friends

I decided to bring two of my worlds together (for some fucking reason) in the forms of Uriah, Johnny M., John H., and Eddie.

I was with John H. and Eddie most days in 1996, but I also saw my oldest friend, Uriah, when I could. He was in love with all the rock music of the time like I was, including R.E.M., The Smashing Pumpkins, Oasis, The Flaming Lips, and Radiohead. But he did the one thing I could never do - he learned how to play the guitar. I can't remember how long he was playing for by the spring of '96, but he was getting the hang of it so well that he could play songs in their entirety.

Uriah and Johnny lived about a five-minute drive from John H. in Port Richmond. I always thought all my best buds should hang out since we all liked the same music and lived so close to each other. Now that I was an acid-head hippy, I thought everyone should come together and be in harmony through love and music (far out, man).

One day, when I was at John H.'s, I called Uriah and set up a day for everyone to hang out. John H. and Uriah hit it off so well that they started a band and became each other's lives for the next two years. I thought it was great at the time. I was all about getting people together, and now that my two worlds of friends merged, we could all be friends and do things together (haha, Chaz, haha).

It wasn't like that at all. I loved John and Uriah and wanted them to succeed, but after they started a band, I rarely saw them. I thought it would be the beginning of my best friends together against the world. We would love music, hang out, start bands, and whatever else came about. It was going to be awesome. Instead, I was the odd man out.

After introducing John and Uriah, they barely had time for me. I took this personally. I felt like I did in the CIBA days, like I wasn't good enough, and they didn't want me around. I didn't feel like this right away (I'm not that sensitive), but after getting left out of many events, I saw they thought of me the way Johnny M. did in CIBA (like I didn't matter). Since Uriah did whatever his brother did (Johnny was also hanging out with my friends all the time), I was now out of most of the fun events and things my friends did the next couple of years.

I was occasionally invited to things like their band's shows, and sometimes I went to a concert with them. But for the most part, my two groups of friends merged and lived on without me. Eddie was basically living with John H. and went with the flow.

I understand that bands are like family, and it's a bonding relationship. So, I get that John H. and Uriah were glued to the hip. Their lives were intertwined, along with their girlfriends and family. They drove around town to the movies, bowling, concerts, etc. All without the guy who introduced them.

I brought this up to John H. and Uriah on different occasions. They both blew it off and made some notion that I was the most popular guy they knew, and I had so many friends that they didn't think I needed them. It was utter bullshit. There were many kids I hung out and partied with, but Uriah, John H., and Eddie were my friends. They were the ones I trusted and loved like no others.

I eventually got over it, but the biggest blow, and the one that made me feel like I made a mistake bringing them together, was when they made an impromptu road trip to Cleveland, OH, to see the Rock and Roll Hall of Fame.

It was sometime in the winter of 1996/97, and the newly formed friends (John H., Uriah, Josh P., Jonny M., and Eddie) all decided to have fun without me. It was something I would have loved to have been invited to. I would have dropped my plans (of doing acid and hanging at the mall) and gone in a heartbeat. But they didn't bother to include me, and that really hurt.

It was a tough time, and I felt like I lost my friends. I was happy they started a band together. I just wished I was more involved than going to their shows. When I did show up, I felt like I wasn't involved in their inside jokes and the closeness I used to have with them. When the band became a full-time gig, they had a family atmosphere, and I was slightly jealous. It led to more feelings of isolation.

Eddie started playing bass in their band as a fill-in until they could get a steady bass player. Eddie didn't want to settle for being a bass player. Like me, he wanted to sing and be a frontman. We foolishly thought we deserved to be frontmen and it would all work out since we wanted it so badly. Unfortunately, we didn't know a thing about singing or being in a band.

We were still green and loved songs based on our overly emotional states of being and our tragic lives. I had no idea how pitch, staying in key, and timing worked when singing. I don't know if Eddie had the same ignorance, but we both knew we had to do this and believed things would fall into place for us.

I hoped one day, after trying my best to listen to music for its structured purposes and years of trying to teach myself to sing, it would all dawn on me, and I would do what I loved so much. Until then, I used my lack of caring about what people thought of me and my "go with the flow" mentality to my benefit. I put myself out there, singing in bands or trying out for them, without a lick of experience or knowledge. I used my numbness and crazy persona to my public singing advantage. I didn't want to accept that I couldn't sing, so I threw it all to chance, believing that if I truly wanted it, I would clear all the hurdles.

Eddie had a good tone to his voice. He could hit notes I couldn't, and his voice sounded fuller than mine. I don't think he knew much about staying in key and correct pitch, but the guy had chops. I thought he had what it took to be a good frontman/singer in a rock band.

I didn't have a natural singing voice. I was sometimes lost when it came to what I should sing and when. I panicked singing with people. I felt out of my league and thought I was a fool for trying to be something I wasn't. But I pushed these thoughts out and tried harder since it was what I wanted most.

Eddie could also play some instruments but lacked confidence (except when drunk or on acid) and was the shyest guy you could meet. I didn't know what an introvert was, but Eddie was definitely an introvert. He could stay inside for days, stay quiet for hours, and know when to listen and give his opinions. I was the opposite. I was an extrovert. I could grab a room's attention and had no problems talking to anyone about anything at any time (which got me into a lot of trouble).

I always wanted to do anything that didn't involve sitting in my shit-show house or apartment. This had been our personas since we met each other in 1992. I was the one who needed to be doing something, and Eddie was fine staying in his house playing video games. I was the one who wanted to see Nirvana and would risk my safety doing so, while Eddie was cool being safe at home and maybe seeing them one day. I was the one at our paper job who never wanted to go home after work, especially on Saturday afternoons. Eddie sometimes didn't want to come to work, let alone hang out afterward with our coworkers.

Even in our teens and adulthood, I traveled anywhere feasible to see a band. Eddie would rather listen to music at home. If he only saw his favorite bands once, that was enough (which sounds like a crazy way to live to me). I think our friendship worked so well because of our similar homelife and overly sensitive emotional states but also because we balanced each other. Eddie grounded me when I was a raging lunatic ranting about random topics or girls I was head over heels for. I think he liked that I was the outgoing one doing anything to entertain or make people laugh. I was good at getting Eddie out of his shell and bringing people in and out of our lives.

I had my writing. I wrote shitty poems for years, and then I wrote not-so-shitty lyrics to ones that I thought were pretty good. Eddie did not do this. We both had the potential to be a frontman. If we could have morphed into one person, we would have made it as a singer in a rock band. Instead, we both crashed and failed at our only dream in life.

It wasn't just about making it in music. It was also about experiencing anything in our reach that made sense to explore, including acid, books, and other music. However, writing songs with Eddie opened a pandora's box of trouble for me that lasted decades.

Chapter 74:
The Dream Child

Many shops in the '90s catered to the counter-culture/alt-rock lifestyle. They were all around the city, from the mecca on South Street to stores like Hot Topic in malls. They sold rock music-inspired clothing and other things on the fringe of the mainstream.

One store in the Roosevelt Mall was called Way Out. Way Out had a skateboarder feel, but they also sold t-shirts of bands we liked and movies like *A Clockwork Orange* and *Pulp Fiction*. The store also sold pipes and bowls to smoke pot in, and, of course, black lights to get in the right mood in your room for the smoking of the pot.

Way Out was a cool place I went into when I was bored and in the area. It had a board in the front of the store set up for musicians to find each other. You could post a piece of paper stating what instrument you played and what you were looking for in a music partner. Bands would also say what they were looking for.

People would state who their influences were and what style of music they were trying to make. Eddie and I answered one of these ads looking for bandmates. Two girls from Kensington were looking for people who liked R.E.M., Nirvana, and Hole. We didn't join their band since they weren't looking for lead singers, but we hung out with them a few times. Sarah (I knew many girls named Sarah in my day) was obsessed with Hole and Courtney Love. She even got a Hole tattoo on the back of her neck.

They lived around D Street and Allegheny Avenue in Kensington. I always thought it was weird that two girls around my age who loved alt-rock lived only a few blocks from me, and I didn't meet them until I moved to Frankford. Such is life.

One day, Eddie noticed an ad for a guitar player looking for a singer to write songs with. Eddie thought I would be a good fit for him. Eddie felt bad that John H. and Uriah started a band, and he knew I was itching big time to sing in a band. So, he gave me the number and told me to call the person and see what happens.

It's weird calling a stranger and telling them you're looking to jam. It's like answering a dating ad. You dance around the conversation to see if it's a good fit. I didn't know what I was doing with singing. I hoped for a miracle or the right fit to get me where I wanted to be, so I tried every avenue available.

The guy seemed like a well enough fellow on the phone, so I invited him to hang out with me and my huge group of friends at a channel 12 (our local PBS channel) talent show. Chris (who dated my friend Rose) invited us to see his band play. Sarah, Sevara, and Amy C. were also friends with him.

It was a fundraiser to make money for PBS. If bands sold a certain number of tickets, they would get to play the talent showcase, possibly winning a prize and getting on PBS TV. The showcase was held in downtown Philly in a studio PBS owned in an auditorium. It held hundreds of people. It was the second time I saw Chris' band (I think they were called the Kingsmen) since I started dating Sarah. We also saw them play at St. James church in Frankford, with other bands at an all-ages show.

I was a full-on hippy guru now and wanted everyone to be a part of my friendship circle, as long as they weren't an asshole. If I knew how my life would change after meeting this one person, I would have lost that number Eddie gave me from Way Out.

I met people later in life who said I should read Jack Kerouac's On the Road because it's similar to how I live my life; going from place to place and seeing where the day takes me. I gave it a shot when I was 19 (during my acid days) but didn't quite like it. I preferred books from Kurt Vonnegut. I returned to it and other Kerouac books (like I was supposed to) later and got the concept.

If I had more money (and guts), I would have let the day take me farther than the Philadelphia metro area. I would have seen the country I was born in and had more adventures with nicer people. Instead, I stuck to my usual haunts and traveled in my mind on acid, getting lost in my thoughts.

Maybe I was living a similar life as the one illustrated in On the Road, but since I didn't go that far, my book would have been called On the Septa Route. In this fictional book, I met my version of Dean Moriarty (from On the Road), thanks to the Way Out ad. His name was Nate, so I will call my first guitar player/songwriting partner Nate Moriarty.

We met on a Septa route in the late spring of 1996. Nate was a white male, similar in height and weight to me. His look was a mashup of a rocker (he was full of tattoos, including one in his ear) and a rap fan (baggy jeans and name-brand sneakers and clothing).

He seemed like a nice, tame, laid-back guy. Usually, when you meet a fellow musician, you meet in an established area meant to practice or play music, and the parties involved see if things flow or if everyone is wasting their time.

Me being me, I invited this stranger to my way of life, showing him who I was and the people I cared about. I was looking for someone who got me and what I wanted to sing about, not just someone looking for another singer (I wasn't that). I was a guy with a message, looking for a background for that message. Little did I know I would never get the message out. Haha, Chaz.

He came off as knowledgeable and passionate about his music taste and what he wrote. He seemed genuine and someone I could get along with. We went to the Channel 12 show, then to someone's house or maybe the mall. Nate came with us, and I showed him a good time with all my friends and my antics.

After that day, Nate was all in for whatever I had and was up for writing songs with me. For some reason, I felt comfortable with him from the start and took this as a sign. It was important since I had performance anxiety when it came to singing. I felt a (sometimes misplaced) bond with Nate Moriarty and felt I could tell him my insecurities about singing and not knowing if I could do it but how much I wanted to. He had a familiarity I couldn't place and took it as another sign. He kind of reminded me of Ray.

Nate was from a broken home. He was raised in the Olney section of Philly (another rundown neighborhood with low-income, working folk) but lived in the lower Northeast in a row home with his mom. His dad still lived in Olney in a home Nate frequented after our "band" started that year.

Shortly after we met, we tried to write and play music together. I went to his mom's place, and we sat in his bedroom, trying to get creative. He had an acoustic guitar and showed me some riffs and songs he had.

I felt a kinship with him from the first time he played, and I felt comfortable enough to try to sing along with some of his music. I was not a musician, and I had no idea if someone was good. I knew he was better than me, though, and he could play a song all the way through. I wasn't picky and didn't think I was better than anyone, so I was happy that someone gave me a chance to sing and put my words to music.

He played a few songs I liked, and I thought I could write lyrics to them. The first one was a song called "Soul Trip" (and yes, I took the word "Trip" as a sign since I was all about acid). He told me he had been working on it for years and that it was in "Drop D" tuning. I gathered that it was on the lower end of the music scale. The song was melodic and had a good rhythm to groove to.

The song reminded me of R.E.M.'s "Undertow," the one they debuted on their '95 tour. It had the same dark overtone, so I used that as my inspiration to write the lyrics to "Soul Trip" (which I think is a terrible name for a song, but I didn't know any better).

I wrote the lyrics in one day while Nate Moriarty played the song over and over so I could capture the feelings it sparked in me. After I was done, I had verses and a chorus. I wrote my first lyrics to a song, and I thought they weren't bad for my first time. The lyrics were basically my state of mind from the traumatic year I had before and my hopes that I would return to my own self and be the person I wanted to be. It focused on the Christians and how they left me to fend for myself.

"Soul Trip":

Left alone and drained of all I know, I'll never give in to your demands and reasons
Withering away on my doubts and fears, I'll break my cage and laugh at your treasons
I am the god of my hopes and dreams, I am the only one I'll believe in
I have already chosen to be the one that will win
So, laugh at me now, but I'll be alive again

Chorus:

"All they'll say is have a nice trip while on your way
And all I do is laugh at these fools and all their moves
And as you try to block me to fly, I laugh at you

Cause you'll never take my pride"
Alive and kicking will I presume
Youth in control I'll be all that I choose
I look at you and cry to death
Seeing what your fake ways and lies have left
Gave me your fears and drilled in your doubts
Glad to say you'll never be what I'm about
Soul tripping my way to glory and fame
Killing myself to cleanse all your pain
This is my life and I'll be the king of all I am
So, get out of my way, as my soul trip just began

The words flowed out of me so well; my acid-head brain already thought this was the guy I was meant to play music with. Then I pulled out a couple poems I wrote (while listening to *The Bends* and *Boys for Pele*) that I hoped to put to music. Nate came up with a couple riffs, and the next thing I knew, I was singing my words to music. Things were going well.

We had two songs. "What's with Today, Today?" was a slower song, more my style of music, and "I Want To" was the only heavier song we had because Nate was fond of metal and rap/rock like Korn, which I despised. But I let him have his headbanging moment.

"What's With Today, Today?"
Drive-thru drive-byes
Leftover drugs are a good high
Kids are immortal
Kids are dumb
Kids are king
So, who's going to help us out of this one
Wave it all - Goodbye
Dust is so thick how can we fly?
Left our minds in Nam
Forgot our pride with the moon man
So don't blame us for what you do
We don't have enough pity to use
Chorus:
"Sweet Mary Jane, we live in vain
Everybody's high, everybody's dead walking
Everyone lives a lie and or tired of being nothing"
Pulp Fiction is my dream come true
The desire is in check and the killers swoon
Human eyes judging for the sky

196

And god is used as the trial
To judge and curse our lives
From men who live in denial
And what do you know what god wants
You're not god, so why judge me

"I Want To"
Rebels are dead
No one is real
Left me shy of my goal line
And now child wounds refuse to heal
Every dumb boy is cashing in on sad thoughts they thought 12 years ago
Not too cracked up to be in what they show
Ouch my toe
Leech is leeching my soul
And doing all that I saw
And I want to
Chorus:
"I want to...
I can't see what you want me to be
I don't believe in what you see
Saying I'm the one without a soul
I'm the one who's out of control
My only leak is I'm not free
I want to.
Bring back my soul."
Jesus fucking Christ and Mary too
I am still lost and longing to be renewed
Lies are the blanket for the weak
And people are the products of their own disbeliefs
Never asked to be born
Never wanted to be harmed
So don't throw it all back at me
I'll make you smell your own defeats

These were the first three songs we wrote. I didn't know what the fuck I was doing when it came to singing, but I think I had a knack for writing lyrics. We wrote eight songs over four years. The lack of output was due to my lack of confidence in singing with anyone else and Nate being a guy who would regularly pawn off his equipment for cigarette money.

I had it in my deluded head that I was supposed to make music with this guy, and it would all work out in the end. It was obviously a mistake and counterproductive to what I wanted from my creative outputs. I was loyal to a fault, and my faith in my dreams and what I thought was "meant to be" was a double-edged sword. I wasted a lot of time and energy on this failed attempt to make art from my misery and traumatic events that plagued me. I only accepted these terrible things that happened to me because I thought I could turn them into songs or something else creative.

Unfortunately, I wasn't the most confident guy and knew I wasn't good enough to join another band (I tried, but it didn't turn out well). It was more embarrassment and emotional muck to bury deep inside after realizing I didn't know how to sing and the musicians knew it. So, I stuck by my (guitar) man like an abused wife who doesn't know she could do better than her abusive husband.

The first three songs were written on Nate's acoustic guitar. We focused on crafting them to our best abilities until fate or life sent us other band members to complete my tragic life's dream. I hoped it would not just kill my demons and heal my emotional wrongdoing but also be a place for me to express what I felt and thought about my experiences.

People came in and out of our poor excuse for a band through the years (including Nazi Jim and Nick M. on bass at different times). Almost every time, it fizzled, leaving me and Nate with our eight songs that weren't good enough to make it. I kind of knew it at the time but was still an idiot dreamer and thought fate would make it all work, and we would write better songs, or my persona and story would carry us to the limelight).

The one thing we had was a band name. Since this was my dream, and I thought the universe was balancing out the negativity I had dealt with throughout 18 years, Nate let me name the band. I was a hopeless dreamer under the mindset that this band was the start of my dreams. I could only think of one name that fit. It was the name my dear Tami from Kensington used to call me a couple years earlier since I was a hopeless dreamer even then: Dreamchild.

In my mind, everything was coming slowly coming together, which was exactly how I wanted it. I was fine mastering our 3-5 songs until we had a full band. But Nate Moriarty had different plans.

Chapter 75:
Tripping On LSD is Better Than Being Alone

Since I was completely ignorant about starting a band, I went along with whatever my new songwriter partner wanted. I was under the assumption that he knew best, and whatever happened from this creative partnership was all part of what I had to do to be what I wanted to be. In retrospect, I was a fool, being led by a bigger fool.

The first thing Nate did wasn't that bad and made sense. He was supposedly in a band before Dreamchild and wanted to use some of those songs and riffs for our band.

Nate brought in his old guitar player/lead singer so he could keep the songs they wrote. Neil came over to jam and said it was okay to use them. The first one was a song called "LSD" (which made me think the entire world was in on how great acid was). Neil had a catchy riff with one lyric written for the chorus. The line was, "I'm a crazy person, and I want to kill you." I kept that part and wrote around that frame of mind.

It was our trippy song, mainly about me taking acid to forget about my religious upbringing. I added a second part to the title that was based on a code word I used for LSD. I would say we were hanging out with Larry Samuel Davidson, so if the wrong ears heard it at the mall or a friend's house (like their parents), they wouldn't know about the mind-altering drugs we often took.

Neil was a character and a half. He was charismatic, looked like Freddy Mercury (including the mustache), and had a solid singing voice (way better than mine). He was also utterly insane. He had a lot to say and was very bright, but he had done acid one too many times, enough to make him crazy (like Syd Barret from Pink Floyd crazy). He was in his 20s and had been an acidhead longer than I.

Neil told me stories about how often he tripped at a party or a concert. He was a borderline hippie, so all the jam bands were his thing, and he took way too much acid at these events. I was more of a lightweight acidhead. I never took more than two hits. Most times, I stuck with one hit or sometimes half of one. Once my mild trip started to wear off, I would take the other half to keep it going. This way, I could get a clear mind and better perspective that acid gave me but still have control and some sense of what was happening. I was more of a thinker on acid and didn't care about hallucinating and all that jazz.

Neil told me he once took 15 hits of acid at a jam band show. I was impressed. He told me he bought them for a dollar or two each, so he figured they weren't strong. He decided to take them all at once, and about two hours into the trip, he realized how strong the acid was. He told me that his vision was impaired by a big black circle in front of him whenever he looked at something. For eight hours, he couldn't see anything in full view. He said it was like a black hole, like the world had a hole in it everywhere he looked (something that scared the shit out of me every time I tripped afterward), and it was not fun.

But that wasn't the time he lost his grip on reality. One would think that if 15 hits of acid made you see a black hole everywhere you looked, you would stick to a smaller amount. Soon, Neil started selling acid. Something happened where he had to eat all the acid (either because of cops being around or a dare), so Neil ate 60 hits of LSD. It's insane to even comprehend what he saw and thought.

He had such a bad trip, and his mind played so many tricks on him that he thought his only way through the horrors of such a strong acid trip was through Jesus Christ. Neil became a born-again Christian, thinking the world was hell and he needed to be saved. This is the bad side of acid. It makes you think of things stored in your mind already, and you will cling to them to save you from a freakout. It didn't end there for poor old Neil. His mind broke. He was forever tripping after reaching this point. He needed Jesus to keep him from the 24/7 bad trip that followed.

When Neil joined our band, he told me he was Christian, and when he told me his 60 hits of acid story, I realized what I was witnessing. It's what happened to all the preachers I grew up with who were hippies in the '60s. They did drugs, found Jesus, and became born-againers.

Neil wasn't that preachy (yet). He was more of a Jesus fan. I could see in his eyes and how he talked about Jesus that he needed that security. Neil was still dealing with the negative effects of the 60 hits. He really needed a psychiatrist, but instead (like the rest of the poor slobs, including myself), he tried to fix himself with some Jesus and his hippie girlfriend, who was five years younger than him. She was with him every second we were all together. She was also completely into Jesus and being a Christian, all because Neil was.

We would jam at Nate's house, and I tried my best to sing while Neil sang harmonies and played rhythm guitar with his acoustic. It was going well until we mall kids had a party on a hill behind the Northeast Philly campus of Community College of Philadelphia. We had dozens of "hill parties" consisting of 80-100 of us hanging out on the grass where local folk walked their dogs. It was surrounded by row homes near the mall.

A few kids lived in the area. Derm, Tim, and others frequented there at least once a month. The parties mainly consisted of us doing acid or smoking pot, but others drank beer or took pills to have a good time. Many crazy things happened, including random rap fans showing up and pretending to be friends with us and then stealing our friend Missy's purse. When we realized what happened, it was too late. They were long gone. I guess not everyone agreed with my hippie mindset that we all should get along.

Another time, 50 of us were hanging out on acid when the unthinkable happened. It was getting dark, and I was tripping pretty good. Suddenly, a cop on a motorcycle shot up from the community college parking lot onto the hill where we were sitting. He said there were more of us than he thought and told us to not move and lay on the ground because we were surrounded. Out of nowhere, there were cops on motorcycles, mopeds, in cars, and on foot, coming from every angle possible to keep us from running away.

They were so loud, and so many lights were shining on us that I thought, for a moment, there was a helicopter over us as well. They set up a sting operation to bust kids hanging at the hill for drugs and underage drinking. They were waiting for a group our size to catch in the act. I guess the people in the neighborhood were tired of kids being rowdy and leaving a mess on the hill (we weren't the only ones who used this area to party).

These cops picked the wrong group of kids to bust. They were looking for normal teenagers who would be drinking 40 ounces of malt liquor or Mad Dog 20/20 (most teenagers have not developed a taste for good alcohol and will drink whatever is put in front of them, including me) or smoking a bunch of pot. They wanted something that would make their efforts worth it. But we didn't have anything on us that would have warranted an arrest.

Out of the 50 or so of us, 80 percent were on acid, and the others were waiting for someone to come to the hill to bring them pot or beer. The head cop asked us, "Where is the beer?" and "What the hell are you doing out here?" We said we were just hanging out.

We said we were bored and had nowhere else to hang out. The cops were pissed that they didn't hit the jackpot (and probably were tied up with us instead of fighting real crimes). You can't smell acid, and you can't really tell if someone is on it as long as you play it cool and don't act nuts (which we all did). We all got through what seemed to be an hour-long ordeal without getting into trouble.

It wasn't easy. I was tripping balls and had to reel in all the crazy thoughts I was having. This was during a time when I was on a big alien kick. I was going down rabbit holes in my head, while on acid, about aliens being the answer in life, that they might know more than we know about existence and more possibly the reason for our existence.

It was all teenager on acid nonsense, but when you're on acid, surrounded by 10-15 cops, your mind will jump to conclusions. There was the possibility that this sting was really about rounding us kids up to be given to the aliens because they know we are on to them. We were opening up our minds to something universal, sending out wavelengths or energy when tripping, and the aliens wanted to study us or stop it. Man, that sounds insane, but acid is one hell of a drug.

You would think this would be enough to put me on a "bad trip," but I kept my cool and didn't panic (not on the outside). My friends kept me calm, especially Ken Carbone, by making jokes, being a rock, and staying headstrong.

After the cops realized we didn't have any drugs (besides the ones in our system) or beer, they made us get in a line and empty our pockets onto one of the cop cars. I'm not sure if any of this was legal, but this happens when you don't know your rights and assume authority figures are in the right.

The whole time, I felt the same way I did when Eddie, John, Nick, and I got stopped by the cops while on acid in Port Richmond. I knew to keep calm, and I knew this was serious (even if I had a hunch the cops were tight with the aliens). I had to say as few words as I needed. I was a nervous, fast talker, and being on acid made it worse. I could hardly put a string of words together to complete a sentence. My mind would go too fast for my mouth to process what I was thinking.

The cops asked for identification. Most of us didn't have a driver's license, and we didn't need a state ID. Cigarettes were a constant in our lives. I liked how smoking felt during my acid trip. Some people only smoked when they drank alcohol; I pretty much only smoked when tripping. The cops told us we couldn't have them since we had no proof we were over 18. That was pretty much all they got out of their big sting - a bunch of kids' cigarettes and a couple knives we carried for protection. I used to hold mine covered by a long-sleeved shirt or jacket (even in the summertime) for protection when I got off the El and walked to my place in Frankford.

My friends Brian R. and Mike F. had acid hits on them during the shakedown. While we were all lying on our stomachs on the ground (following police orders) after being told not to move, they both reached into their wallets and successfully pulled out the extra hits. Because they were in a baggy, they buried them in the dirt hill. The next day, I went with them and tried to find the acid, but we couldn't since it was such a big area. At least they didn't get caught with an illegal substance.

Neil lost his shit a few months earlier. This day was the start of what I thought was a hippie revival. We had over 100 friends on the hill tripping balls. The energy in the air was magnetic and alive, with the possibility that anything could happen. There was a sense that the bond we shared through music and our struggles would last forever (haha, us, haha).

Everyone was having a good time on their drug of choice (mainly acid and pot) when Nate showed up with Neil. Neil, who brought his guitar to jam with (another thing that happened since we hung out with so many musicians), seemed to be in good spirits. Our parties usually started at dusk and would go all through the night. Neil came in the early part of the night and told me he hadn't done acid since his big 60 hits debacle.

We were still jamming, and I guess he looked at me as a voice of reason. He asked me if he should drop some acid that someone at the party had. He said it would be the first time he tripped since he lost his shit. I, being a nice, comforting soul, said, "Man, I think you can handle one hit of acid since you've taken so much in your life." So, he took the hit of acid, and he was fine for a good part of the night until he wasn't.

Part of hanging out with large groups of kids was there would be a bunch of side groups that talked to each other about their interests. I kept them all together by going to each group through the night to give them a common thread. It was like being at a wedding and going to each table to talk to all the relatives and friends.

Neil was playing his guitar and hanging out with a group interested in his songs and energy when he had his breakdown. In the middle of playing music, he stopped, looked around, and said, "I am in hell, and I am going to die for my sins." Then he ran off from the hill to the residential neighborhood it surrounded.

I was talking with other people in another sub-group that wasn't far away. I wasn't fully aware of the situation. I watched him drop his guitar and run away towards the entrance of the hill, and then Nate ran up to me and said we had a problem. We had to go after Neil. We searched high and low for him, but just like the time that some assholes stole Missy's purse, Neil was long gone.

I felt partially responsible since I was the "leader" of this clan and the one who said Neil would be okay if he took one hit of acid. Unfortunately, Neil was stuck in a mindset of constant fear and anxiety from the 60 hits he foolishly took once. He was at the mercy of whatever strands of sanity and reality he had left. One hit of acid amplified the anxiety and made his mind find patterns that were familiar to him in religious themes.

Neil felt guilty for taking the acid. The same thing happened to me when I had bad trips. I wasn't in the right mindset and felt the one thing you never should while tripping: regret for taking it. That's when all hell can break loose in your mind. Nate and I went all the way to the Parkwood section looking for Neil, but he was nowhere in sight.

Eventually, we went back to the hill party and hoped for the best for him. None of us poor kids had cell phones or even pagers yet, so we couldn't find out if Neil was okay. We had to wait till he popped up again.

Three days later, Nate and I were coming down from a night of tripping. We were lying in his room, drifting in and out of sleep. For some reason, there was a couch in his room that I was lying on, and Nate was on his mattress on the floor. Sometime during in and out sleep, Neil walked into Nate's room. It was late morning or early afternoon, and the bright summer sun was blindly coming through the window in Nate's room. It almost made Neil being there dreamlike, like it was in my head or a hallucination. But Neil was there, and we got to hear all about what happened the night he ran off.

Neil said he was doing fine on the acid at first and felt like he could handle the trip. However, as the trip intensified, he felt overwhelming guilt. He thought God was judging him and was going to punish him for taking acid when he knew better. He knew his life was hell now because of the drug, and going back to it was like smoking cigarettes after being diagnosed with lung cancer. He was so terrified that God was going to punish him that he started seeing flames around groups of people on the hill and faces were melting (the latter happens when you're tripping so hard that your eyes and mind move so fast that things seem to be melting).

Neil thought he was in hell, so he did the only thing that seemed safe and ran as fast as he could to the 8th district police station (which served that area). He told the cops he was tripping and having a panic attack. They didn't arrest him; they took him to the hospital, and the doctors gave him a shot that calmed him down. He stayed there for a few days, trying to get his mind back to normalcy.

It was a lively story, and we all laughed it off and went back to jamming like before, but Neil had become even more of a born-againer. After a couple times of us jamming, he wasn't sure if he could play in a band with someone like me and my anti-Christ lyrics.

I wasn't sure if my lyrics would be considered anti-Christ, but they were me writing about what I had experienced with the born-againers and how I viewed god. It was a big part of why I wanted to be in a band and write lyrics. My number one enemy or focus was the Christian faith, which I blamed for ruining my life.

Nate tried to calm Neil down and said to ignore what I sing about. It lasted a day or two. Then Neil had a passionate moment telling me how great Jesus is and how god saved him. I believe it turned into a brief shouting match, and then Neil left for good with his guitar and hippie girlfriend. He left the band that just started.

I saw Neil a few times after that, walking around Northeast Philly, but we never jammed again. I think he finally left the Christian life and went back to doing drugs and trying to make songs. His hippie girlfriend broke up with him shortly after he left our band, and she became goth and loved (like a lot of dopey teenagers in 1996) Marilyn Manson. Neil was a genuine, nice person with a heart of gold. Even though I only knew him shortly, I could tell he was good. He radiated positive energy, was honest to a fault, and seemed like he wouldn't hurt a fly.

Neil had an untimely death a few years later, in December 2003. There was an argument over a girl. It led to an altercation with another guy who put Neil in a coma after beating him over the head with a baseball bat several times. He spent some time on life support until being declared brain-dead. His family made the heart-wrenching decision to take him off life support.

As far as I know, the person who killed Neil and his magnetic spirit were never brought to justice. I found out about his death from Nate, who didn't find out about it until a month later. Nate never got to say goodbye to his friend with the biggest heart he knew. I wasn't in the best of mental states in 2003 and couldn't process what happened to good old Neil. Over the years, I have thought about him being a force of good in the world and wished things worked out for him differently with his music and life. He had talent and deserved a lot more out of life. So it goes.

Chapter 76:
I Can't Fucking Curse on PBS

It was just me and Nate in the band again. It was fine since we just started the band and had plenty of time to find other members and play shows. However, Nate showed me his impulsive side for the first time by booking us for the Channel 12 PBS talent show that was happening a few months later.

He didn't ask me, nor did we ever talk about playing shows. We only had four songs and no rhythm section. We were still crafting our mediocre songs. They were not ready to be played live.

I was mad at Nate for booking us for a show on PBS TV without being ready. But I figured he had more faith in our band, and maybe this was supposed to happen, or this show would push us in the right direction.

We had a few months to get ready and sell enough tickets to cover the fee to play the show. It was a bit of a scam. You had to pay to play the showcase. They would give you tickets that they printed out, and you would have to sell them to your fan base (mostly friends). If you couldn't sell enough tickets, you had to pay out of pocket.

It was all about funding PBS, so I guess it wasn't a scam. It was more of a money maker for their programs, and if a band was actually good, they would get studio time and be featured on the showcase when it aired. We started practicing more, just the two of us at first, then we tried to find a bass player to give us a more complete sound.

We had a hard time finding drummers who weren't already in a band. Also, we didn't have a real practice space since we both were poor as fuck and couldn't afford to rent a practice studio.

We decided to go with an acoustic performance for the showcase with just me and Nate or one with a bass player because they were easier to find. We could all practice in Nate's house since the equipment was easy to bring in and out. It was just a couple of speakers that I sang loudly over since we couldn't afford a PA system.

I went along with whoever came in and out of the band since I wasn't a real musician. I was learning as I went (like most things in my life) about being in a band and singing. Nate was the expert, and I trusted his judgment. But he was a maniac and lived moment to moment and made irrational decisions throughout the mediocre existence of our band.

He brought in people we partied with, and he felt a kinship with over music. But these things always fizzled out. Nazi Jim sort of played the bass. He came over and jammed with us on Nate's bedroom couch a couple times, but it didn't stick. I guess he wasn't as good as Nate hoped, or the feel wasn't there, so it was over almost as quick as it started. Then we brought in Nick M., but that only lasted once or twice since he didn't know how to play the bass (like how I didn't know how to sing but was trying). Nick was a fun and energetic guy who would have been fun to be in a band with, but someone decided to move on without him.

We were an unprepared duo, hoping for the best. Then, a bass player who would become one of my favorite people approached me about playing with my band. His band was the first local band I saw and thought were good musicians. They knew what they wanted their band to sound like.

Right after the Tori Amos shows I went to with the girls from the Northeast, I was invited to one of their graduation parties. It was in her backyard on a sunny day in June. Her parents were cool enough to let her friends' bands play (most likely annoying the neighbors). One band was a friend of her dad's, and they played cover songs from shitshow bands like Journey. But the one that really struck a chord (literally) was a band called Strik-9.

Strik-9, or its proper spelling "strychnine," is a pesticide to kill rodents. At some point during the concept or production of acid, it was rumored to be used to bond the LSD to the blotter paper. It may have been true in the '60s but has since become an old wives' tale. The urban legends we heard from other acidheads at parties were that the strychnine is what gave the drug its kick and why you see "out of your mind" things. We couldn't fact-check since the internet was so young and only for those with money, so we all accepted it as facts.

A band named Strik-9 was right in my wheelhouse. I was doing so much acid that I thought everyone was doing it. It was another flaw of mine. Since I was constantly consuming psychedelics, I assumed everyone was in on the world of acid. I thought I was finally catching up to what everyone already knew. It's a constant way of thinking in my sad life. A band named Strik-9 had to be in the know when it came to acid. It turned out they were.

Strik-9 were more experienced acidheads (and musicians) than I could ever imagine to be. I sat at the side of the area where their band was playing, thinking how tight they were. How in tune they were with each other. They were a metal band, and I didn't like metal, but they were so on point playing together. Since I was trying to be in a band, I was impressed with every song. Especially the bass playing of Ken Carbone.

I had seen many local, up-and-coming bands throughout Philly, but none had been as sure of themselves as Strik-9. They were serious about making music. They seemed so real and dedicated to their craft that I blurted out, "You guys are fucking awesome!" without hesitation after one of their songs. I said it so loud that Ken said, "Thank you." I knew he knew that I meant it.

They weren't like any of the music I liked. They were a heavy band like Metallica. The band was just three guys: brothers Mike and Ken Carbone and their drummer Keith (who left the band a few years later). Mike was the lead vocalist, guitarist, and main songwriter.

His voice matched well with their style of music. He looked the part, too. He wore all black (shirt, jeans, and a leather jacket) and had long, brown, unkempt hair down to his mid-back.

Ken was a phenomenal bass player. He knew how to use the bass as an instrument rather than just the bottom or filler for songs. He was also the king of witty lines and clever jokes at any moment. Ken could make fun of something in such a quick way that it was borderline genius. He was as charismatic as could be, down to earth, genuine, and would give you the shirt off his back.

Ken was always in a good mood, even when things were shit. He was always looking for a good time. We were in different friend circles that liked rock music and hung out with people in the Northeast. I brought some mallrats to see Strik-9 play. They didn't get along with them or their friends. It sounds ridiculous that there was a little bad blood between the mall kids and the group that hung out with Strik-9.

When me and Eddie first started hanging out with the mall kids, we thought everyone who liked rock music was on the same side against bullies like the jocks and white rap fans.

It turned out there was a rivalry between one group of rock kids (the mallrats) and another called "The Losers" (named after Beck's song "Loser" b because one guy in the group, Dave Aducci, blurted it out when someone asked if their crew had a name. He said, "I guess we are all like that song "Loser" by Beck, so call us that." And they did. The groups didn't get along over something that happened at their public high school.

When Eddie and I found out kids from the same neighborhood who all liked rock music were fighting, we thought it was ridiculous and laughed it off. We would have loved to find anyone who enjoyed the same music in our neighborhoods. The only fighting came from people trying to rob us. One day, there was supposed to be a huge fight (reminiscent of *The Outsiders*) after school, but only a few people showed up, and the beef fizzled out.

I soon found out that these so-called "losers" were the ones I wish I had known earlier. They were all stand-up guys and girls, more into house parties and being in legit bands than hanging at a mall or hill parties (though some of the losers started doing that as well).

I sort of knew Strik-9's crew from seeing them around the mall and having mall kids tell me to stay away from them. I also saw some of them take the bus from the Northeast all the way to Frankford, where I got off.

Once, I saw Mike, Ken, and Dave Aducci on the bus. I didn't talk to them because I didn't know them yet, so I listened to my music and wondered what they were doing taking the bus all the way down here. As we got off at the last stop in Frankford, I turned to them and asked if they wanted me to stay with them since it was a rough area. I figured they were just kids from the sheltered greater Northeast.

Mike said, "Nah, we're cool." They were fine without me because Ken and Mike grew up on and off in Kensington. No wonder Ken was so witty and always looking for a good time. They lived in the Northeast part of the time with their mom.

Their dad was also funny as shit. When he first met Dave Aducci, he said, "What's your name, Dave A-douchebag?" I wasn't there for that, but it's still hilarious. He had a house around F and Allegheny (five blocks from where I grew up). That day on the bus, they were going home from the greener grasslands of the Northeast, just like me.

Strik-9 was taking a break from playing, and Ken was looking for a band to join. I don't know how he heard I was looking for a bass player for my pipedream band, but it was probably word of mouth. One day that summer, Ken came up to the mall and said he heard I needed a bass player. I was blown away. This guy was a legit bass player and was willing to slum it with the likes of me (not knowing what the fuck I was doing) and Nate (who only half knew what the fuck he was doing). Ken said he was bored since Strik-9 was on a break. He was looking to do something different than metal. Of course, I said yes and thought it was another sign that things were starting to finally go my way.

We went to Nate's house a few times and practiced the three songs we were going to play for the Channel 12 talent show. I told Sarah how exciting it was to be in a band and how I was still nervous about playing live, but being slightly out of step with reality would make it easier to sing on stage for the first time. I really thought this was the start of something good.

The songs weren't hard for Ken to pick up. We had the songs down in no time and would be okay as an acoustic three-piece for the show. In the meantime, we started to sell all the tickets that Channel 12 gave us for the entry fee for the showcase. We hadn't played a show yet, but we had a bunch of people we hung out with, and they were all in on supporting us (which I cherished dearly). I knew they hadn't come to see us play because they liked our songs. They liked us, and they knew this band was important to me. We sold 50-75 tickets and got more than enough for the entry fee. Now, it was more real (and scary).

We practiced every day pretty much all summer and even played for the mall kids on the lawn area on the outskirts of the mall. It was just our regular hangout crowd. We played songs that only a handful of the mall kids paid attention to.

Meanwhile, while Uriah and John H. were getting their band together and the whole world seemed to be into rock music and wanting to be musicians, Jonny M. (of all people) decided he was going to transform overnight into a regular old alt-rocker and picked up the guitar (after two years of Uriah learning to play).

He went from wearing sports gear, like his trademark Patrick Ewing sneakers that had his basketball number on them (33), and his preppy clothing to long hair, Converse sneakers (since that's what you wear if you like alt-rock), and shirts from bands like Bush and Nirvana (though he was five years late with Nirvana). This was a stretch for me to accept. This guy bullied me for years and was the reason I turned to music like Nirvana and Pearl Jam. Now, he was trying to wedge his way into the life that he saw me, Eddie, and Uriah enjoying.

But I was a fucking acidhead hippie and thought the world was changing all around me via alternative rock music and the culture that came with it. So, I told him to come up and play for the mall kids if he felt comfortable doing so. He said he did and was thankful for me letting him hang out and play songs in front of people for the first time. He wasn't half bad (not that I was any good) and played all covers acoustically.

Jonny M. seemed more down to earth now, and I thought he was becoming a decent human. I was wrong, which is a common theme for me. He eventually went back to being the egotistical bully that he was.

This time, he told outrageous stories that no one in their right mind would believe. He was obsessed with Kurt Cobain and Nirvana (three years after Kurt died and Jonny was well into his 20s). He told Eddie he would tell people he met Kurt Cobain in the early '90s, and he autographed a picture for him and wrote, "Don't ever change, Jonny, stay real." Most people listened to his stories in disbelief. The best part was when he told Eddie he really met Kurt Cobain and got his autograph. Eddie was like, "Dude, just told me you were going to lie to people about this story." Jonny, to his con artist credit, denied it and stuck with the fabricated tale. More on Jonny and his rock and roll lifestyle later.

The talent show came faster than we expected. It was on a Saturday in mid-September. I woke up early because I was too nervous to sleep. I wore my favorite pair of jeans with most of my friends' writings on them (and Thom Yorke's), an R.E.M. shirt, a vest, and my trademark newsie hat. Of course, I wore eyeliner and glitter and had a freshly shaven bald head. If Michael Stipe needed a stunt double, here I was.

We had to be at the station's studio around 12 pm. We met all the mall kids at the Frankford station as they got off the bus from the northeast. We took the El down, got registered, and waited for our turn to play the showcase. There were tons of bands. Too many. I don't know how they chose the order, maybe random, or you needed to know someone, but we sat through dozens of bands, with no sign of when we were going on. It didn't help my nervousness and the fear that I would look like a fool when it was our turn to play.

I had Sarah there to calm my nerves as best as she could. My friends and I were hanging outside, killing time, and mingling with the other kids who were in bands or friends of the bands. Nate was making friends inside with other musicians. He was having another moment of flying off the handle and doing something on a whim.

While we were waiting to go on, Nate and Ken were backstage practicing. We were not ready to play a fucking show, and they had to make sure they were in rhythm together. They met another kid (who was there supporting his friends) who played the drums. Nate (as an example of what not to do when you are about to play a show for the first time) asked the kid to play the drums for our showcase set.

I don't know how this meeting went down, but Nate and this drummer somehow found common ground, and the kid convinced Nate he could keep up with him and Ken on the drums. His name was Steve. He was about 16 years old and was into punk rock and ska. He was from a suburb right outside of Northeast Philly.

Steve was an energetic kid who was full of life and authentic innocence. He was positivity in a nutshell. He was so excited about meeting new people and playing music it was addicting. I was on the same wavelength. This kid was a ball of energy who was happy to meet everyone who came down from the mall, especially Nicole M. He developed a crush on her that wasn't mutual, though Nicole was never mean about it and was flattered by his admiration.

Now we had an instant drummer to play our songs. I trusted Nate and thought this was something musicians did. I figured they could just pick up and play with one another at the drop of a hat since they knew their instruments so well. We met Steve, and he joined our band a few hours before we had to play. We went into a corner of the backstage area and "practiced" our songs without amps or a drum set. Nate and Ken played unplugged while Steve drummed in the air or on his knees with drumsticks. We might not have been a punk band, but this was as punk as I could ever get. We had a makeshift band and a makeshift practice session hours before we played in front of people. What could go wrong?

Well, the first thing that went wrong was our band didn't get its slot to play until way after midnight. I don't know who was running the showcase and what the problem was getting things going, but my guess is that they booked too many bands in the hope of more revenue for the station. The bands all had a three-song set, and in most cases, it took longer to load and unload their equipment than play their set. To their credit, the mall kids stayed the entire time we waited to play. They were loyal as could be to their friend's shit band.

I was exhausted when we hit the stage, hoping to get through the set without embarrassing myself too much. We walked on stage, and Nate and Ken plugged their instruments into amps that someone let us use. Steve borrowed another band's drum set since he didn't have his. I learned this is also a thing that happens in the band world. Broke people will ask other bands if they can use their instruments. There is an almost unsaid bond between musicians as far as playing. Most are okay with lending other musicians their equipment when they need it.

I walked onto the stage the size of a high school or college theater stage. I saw hundreds of people sitting in the audience, waiting to hear this idiot sing for the first time in public (or at least try his darndest). I found Sarah in the crowd, and the mall kids were all in the first few rows to cheer us on in support. Sarah seemed happy, and I could tell she fully supported what I wanted the most in the world.

We were going to play our three songs we knew the best: "Soul Trip," "What's With Today, Today?," and "LSD." We didn't even make it through one song.

Nate counted everyone off and then started playing "Soul Trip." The first clue that I was in over my head was I couldn't hear Nate playing. He sounded muffled. I couldn't hear the melody and timing of the song I had sung with him dozens of times. I knew I had to start singing soon, and this was when the panic snuck in. I probably looked like a deer in the headlights.

I remembered something Nazi Jim told me when he briefly played bass for us. I told him I was nervous about singing in front of people (I was in denial and didn't want to hear the obvious truth that I wasn't a good singer and had no musical talent. I couldn't take that blow yet), and he told me that when it comes to original music, no one knows if you're messing up the song or coming in too early or late. He said to act like I know what I'm doing. So, I acted like I knew what I was doing (I didn't know what I was doing).

I tried to sing along with what Nate was playing with my memory of the song. I was off-timing and not singing in key. It was bad and getting worse. It wasn't just me who couldn't hear Nate. Ken and Steve were having problems as well. The sound guy working the show had the mic amplifying Nate's guitar too low and the bass too loud.

All I could hear were Ken and Steve. Since they barely knew the song, they were off time and doing whatever they could to finish the four-minute song without looking dumb). There was a point when I stopped singing because I was lost with where we were at in the song. It turned into a jam session between the three real musicians up there. Ken led with a great bassline that was the highlight of the set. I looked at Nate and saw the same "lost in the woods" look in his eyes I had, so we all huddled together (while they kept playing) and agreed on how bad it was and how we couldn't hear Nate. We decided to just end the song. And that was the first time I sang in front of an audience. It was typical of my life.

Nate yelled at the sound guy to turn up the mic for his amp. I was in a bad mood, and my angst was taking over. It was good for me since I was on a stage and letting out my energy creatively. I started to go on a rant. The word "fuck" (my favorite curse word) flew out of my mouth a few times. A voice from the back where the judges and sound guy were said, "You can't curse. This will be on PBS TV, and you can't curse." In a moment of frustration, I replied, "What, I can't fucking curse?" It led to the voice in the back saying, "That's it, you're done." We were cut off from the sound booth and told to get off the stage.

I cursed some more, and the mall kids got loud and started cursing about what happened. One of the kid's dads yelled at me. He said his kid stayed up all night to see my band, and I got kicked out for cursing. I felt bad for this, but I was in a terrible mood, and I just blew my first show due to a lousy sound guy. My adrenaline was on fire from the nervousness, excitement, and frustration.

This might have killed one's dream of being in a band. It might have made one think about giving up to never feel the embarrassment again. I was still looney and thought this was just a learning process. The only thing that came out of this horror show of a performance was that Steve was still on board with the band. He wanted to play more with us. We exchanged numbers and set up going to his house to play. The miracle here was Steve lived in a suburb that seemed full of rich folk who lived in mansions (they were just big single homes). He had an entire practice area in his furnished basement. He had a drum set, two amps, and a PA for singing.

I don't remember what Steve's parents did. But they made a comfortable living and showered their kids with whatever made them happy. In return, they raised a good kid in Steve, who might have had more money than others but never bragged and would help anyone who needed it. The house he lived in was one of the biggest I had ever been in during my poor-as-fuck life. The basement (where we spent most of our time) was set up as a room you could live in. It was bigger than my current living arrangement altogether.

It had a pool table, carpet, a fridge for sodas, a band set up, a phone, bright lights (which was the opposite of our damp and dark basement in Kensington that we used for storage), and framed posters of bands that Steve and his parents liked. His parents were into rock music from their era ('70s and '80s). Steve's mom loved Aerosmith and Steven Tyler.

His mom was such a huge Steven Tyler fan that once, through a business transaction, she met someone who knew Steven Tyler's agent or friend. Whatever Steve's mom did for this person (maybe something to do with accounting), the person decided to pay her back by talking to Steven Tyler's friend or agent (I can't remember which) and getting Tyler to leave a message on her answering machine. She kept the tape for years and played it for us occasionally.

It was really nice of Tyler to do something like that. I always thought about it when I got tired of hearing the same Aerosmith songs on the radio in the '90s. In the message, Tyler said he heard how big of a fan she was and wanted to say hi and thanks for the support. The pure joy Steve's mom had when she played the tape for us made up for Aerosmith's song "I Don't Want to Miss a Thing," which was played to death a few years later.

We practiced 2-3 times a week and got tighter with our songs. We even started to write some new ones. It felt like a real band was forming. We took the bus to the last stop where Steve lived, then walked ten minutes to his house. This was how dedicated we were to the band.

While playing as a band for a few weeks, Nate got a phone call from PBS. They were sorry we got kicked off the show due to the sound issues and my not knowing the policies on cursing. They said they appreciated our "unique sound" and invited us back to play the next showcase in the middle of October. Apparently, we sold more tickets to the first showcase than anyone else, and Channel 12 was grateful and decided to give us another shot at proving ourselves.

We were ready as a full band to get the songs down for the show. We stuck with the same three songs we knew best and would have played at the last show if we weren't kicked off.

The musicians in the band got tighter. I was still not the best singer, but I was learning timing, and we felt ready for the showcase. My "everything is meant to be" mind thought this was supposed to happen, and this was the band I would "make it" with (haha, Chaz, haha).

On the day of the talent show, we got all the mall kids together again and took the El down. This time, the tickets we got from Channel 12 were free since we made them so much money last time. None of our friends had to pay. Things already looked good for us since we were told we would be one of the earlier bands to play. No waiting until the middle of the night to go on. Nate talked to the sound guy and made sure we would hear each other play and keep the song together.

Everything was coming together this time, and we were ready to prove that the last show wasn't who we were. We could perform better. It seemed nothing would go wrong, but this is my life, and something usually goes wrong. For some goddamn reason, Nate decided right before the show that he didn't want to use whatever guitar he owned. I guess it was a basic-looking guitar, and it wasn't cool enough for a fucking Channel 12 talent show.

In between showcases, Nate and I were hanging out with more musicians than ever, including one of the mall kids named Tim, who lived near the hill party area. Tim had a black guitar that James Hetfield from Metallica would have used. It was almost V-shaped and looked like a heavy metal rock god's guitar. Nate was a sucker for image and looking the part. It was one of the things that drove me crazy about him. He wanted to look like a rockstar instead of trying to be one. I didn't care what guitar he used as long as it sounded good.

He tried to explain that our songs would sound better with this other guitar, so I once again trusted him (the fool I was). When Ken came down for the show (he borrowed his dad's car to load his amp and bass into), he brought Tim's guitar for Nate to use, which led to our second Channel 12 demise.

This time, I didn't get all dolled up to sing. I wore a random pair of jeans and my favorite non-R.E.M. shirt that I bought at a flea market in Port Richmond. It was a parody of the Chevrolet ad from the '80s that read "Chevrolet: The Heartbeat of America." The shirt replaced their slogan (but still in the same font) with "Jesus: The Heartbeat of my Life." It was the perfect mix of irony and cleverness that 18-year-old Chaz was all about. I also wore a pair of jeans with a bunch of writing on them (the only jeans I had) and my trademark tie for a belt. This was my everyday wardrobe, so I just rolled out of bed and went to play this show. I also went to a house party at Ken's the night before and was a bit hungover.

Sarah was so supportive. She believed in me and my efforts. She knew how to calm me down and tell me what I needed to hear in situations like this. I felt we were ready to play this show, and I was hopeful we would be able to play a full set, and I would get the feel of being in a real band.

We came out on stage with something to prove, and we started off right on target. Nate's guitar was clear enough for all of us to hear, and we were in sync when we started "Soul Trip." Everything was working in full force, and the energy from my bandmates kept me focused. I felt every word of the song I wrote about my breaking free of the born-again religion in full force. We got through the first verse and the chorus like pros. Then, in the middle of the song, when Nate played his best effort at a solo, the guitar he borrowed started to falter. There was a problem with the connection from the input to the chord. It was devastating.

I looked at Nate, waiting for his solo to be over to know when it was my time to sing again. I saw panic on his face when he struck the guitar, and no sound came from the amp.

He looked at me and mouthed that the guitar wasn't working. My heart and stomach sank. I thought, "What now?" and "Of course, this would happen to us again." It was going so well before this setback.

We had to end the song, and Nate had to quickly get another guitar. This took so much time that the sound guy said we could only play one more song. So, we played "What's with Today, Today?" It didn't sound half bad. We didn't win the talent show, of course, but at least we played our first-ever song all the way through live.

We also got to meet other bands, like the goth band called The Blood Sucking Vampires. Ken told me their bass player was considered one of the best in the city. Other members of this band would pop up in the Philly area in bars and open mic nights, where Nate and I played as a duo. We also saw them at goth nightclubs that my friends and I went to so we could dance to '80s music in a room cleverly called "The '80s Room."

Our band went back to practicing and writing songs. We had no intention of slowing down, and this is when I did what I taught myself to never do: I let my guard down and thought things were coming together for me. I had a girlfriend and tons of friends, and I was as popular as one could be for not doing anything. I was considered cool or likable by my peers. Meanwhile, my favorite artists were putting out masterpiece albums. It would be the only time I would have confidence or borderline cockiness. Acid and the fact that I was partying or jamming or doing something at all times made me think I was secure and fate was on my side. I was wrong.

Chapter 77:
What do I Have to Do?

Sarah and I were together most days. We got along most of the time, and the relationship was as healthy as it could be for two depressed teenagers who liked to self-loath and cut themselves when they felt the urge.

The guilt from cheating on her with Megan was still in the back of my mind. However, I think I made up for it and then some by giving Sarah all of my attention and not even looking or wanting to look at other girls (besides Laura, of course).

Then, something in May and June drove a wedge between our young love. Sarah started to want to do things without me for no reason. I'm not talking about going to the mall or a hill to drink and do acid. She was doing things like seeing a laser light show for Pink Floyd's *The Wall* in Philly with her friend from school. Sarah's friend also brought boys along, in particular one named Chris. I never found out who Chris was, but it was clear Sarah was cheating on me with him.

I tried to get a straight answer out of her, but she clammed up about why I couldn't go to the things she was doing with her friends. She was usually high on pot, and it was hard to figure out what she was thinking. It went on for weeks. She didn't know what she wanted. We still walked around the mall holding hands and made out at her house, but she was hiding something from me. It wasn't like how I cheated on her with Megan when I was in a stressful situation taking care of a girl I cared about. This was her intentionally seeing someone else while telling me she loved me. It was killing me daily, thinking I was losing her.

After weeks of trying to get the truth from her in May of '96, I was at a breaking point.

We planned on seeing a movie with Amy C. and Severa. Sarah and I were talking in the parking lot facing the street where people came in and out of the mall. Hurtful words were exchanged. I asked if she wanted to break up with me and finally got a straight answer. She said she did want to break up.

It was too much for me to handle. Sarah was my rock, and I couldn't bear to lose her. I felt it would make me completely numb.

So, I panicked and tried to kill myself.

I have always been borderline suicidal. I thought my life didn't matter due to my status in the world. I thought I was the worst, a constant fuck-up, and a loser. I always thought suicide was a backup plan for me. Whenever things got so god-awful in my chaotic, mixed-up, emotional mind, I would have thoughts of electrocuting myself in a tub with a radio, throwing myself into traffic (especially throwing my head under a septa bus wheel and having it crush my head), and my favorite: opening up a car while it was moving to roll to my death.

I rarely acted on these impulses. They were more for relief. The thought of not existing was a comfort. I only tried to kill myself a few times, and two of those times were during this period in 1996.

When Sarah told me the devastating news that she didn't want to be with me, I was overwhelmed (a constant theme in my life). I took off running toward the road. I tried to end my life by throwing myself in front of traffic.

I didn't want to deal with the break-up of the mall king and queen and the muck that would remain after it was over. I was already spent and unsure if I wanted to live any longer.

I decided right there to end it all instead of dealing with the weight of the world crushing me. Not even R.E.M.'s "Everybody Hurts" could have slowed me down (well, maybe if I heard it in a passing car, it would have stopped me).

As I threw my 150-pound body in front of the closest car, Sarah ran behind me, yelling for me to stop. I ignored her. This was it. I was ready to die. I wanted out.

The woman driving slammed on her brakes just in time. Looking back, it probably would have only injured me if she made an impact. Since I didn't get the end of life I wanted, I had a chance to calm down.

Sarah walked me back to the movie theater parking lot. She was crying and more awake and alive than I had ever seen her. The pot in her system must have worn off. She was sorry and promised she didn't want to break up with me. She was doing whatever she could, so I didn't try to kill myself over her. I knew this. I knew I went too far and had to deal with whatever came next. I knew it seemed like I did this stunt to make her not leave me, and I didn't want that at all. If she didn't want me, then I wanted her to leave me rather than stay with me out of pity or fear I might hurt myself.

She told me she loved me a few times, which was always comforting. It made things seem better, like when someone says, "God bless you." when you sneeze. I calmed down for her sake, but the damage had been done. I was bracing for the inevitable. I knew what was coming.

I let her think I was okay and told her I wouldn't do an outrageous stunt like that again. When I came down from the desire to end my life, part of me realized she was just a 16-year-old girl from the Northeast who might be sad inside but doesn't know about a life of misery. She didn't know how it felt to want to end your life because it made sense, and you thought you never had a chance and were fooling yourself, trying to live with people who had it a lot easier than you.

She didn't deserve to have my life and death in her hands. I realized I had to change my outlook on my first long-term girlfriend and be ready for it to end. I went back to the mindset I had after I was head over heels for Jeanne in the summer of '93. I decided to never let myself go through that pain again. I would cut off my love for Sarah and do what I had to do to survive.

I thought maybe Sarah was going through something and would get out of it. Maybe she found out I cheated on her with Megan (from POS) and was getting revenge on me. Or she was trying to balance the relationship with her own cheating. But after that day, I knew our love wasn't the same. I might not have killed myself like I wanted to, but my love died a little. It sucks that it took me trying to kill myself to calm me down and realize I would have to get over Sarah someday. I also learned another lesson that day. In my selfish attempt(s) to kill myself, those who I might use to carry out the deed might have some issues with it.

If I throw myself in front of a car, the person driving the car will have to deal with the fact that their vehicle killed another human being. The woman driving the car that I jumped in front of pulled into the parking lot where Sarah and I were talking and talked to us. She was in her late 30s, or so I thought, attempting to judge an adult on their age. She came off a little harsh but concerned. The reason for these attributes was that she was an off-duty cop.

She sat down and asked me what was going on. I did what every teenager does and tried to pretend everything was okay. I said I wouldn't do anything too crazy anymore. She seemed fine with my assurance and suggested I talk to someone and get help. It was the last thing I wanted to hear. I knew myself, and I knew where my problems started. Even at this young age, people who have had better lives and had it easy enough to go to college and become therapists wouldn't know how to deal with what was happening in my head.

I also didn't have insurance to see someone and wouldn't even know who to see. I wasn't sure my mental problems weren't just god and the devil fucking with me like they fucked with Job in the bible. So, I said I got into a fight with my girlfriend. It seemed to be the relatable thing to say to smooth things over. Then, we all went our separate ways.

It changed my selfish thoughts when it came to my desire to die. I realized that if I did succeed in ending my life that day via the woman's car, she would be traumatized, and that wasn't fair for her. It wasn't her fault my life sucked so much. I never tried to kill myself that way again. However, I would eventually try another way only a few weeks later.

Sarah and I went to the movies and hung out with our friends. We pretended everything was okay. I was getting prepared for the next shoe to fall, which would be Sarah dumping me once she realized I was settled and wouldn't hurt myself over it. In the days that followed, I clung to the one person I trusted, Eddie, and braced myself for the end of Chaz and Sarah and what would likely make me more numb or bitter.

Time to show some courage, Chaz.

Courage, courage, courage.

Epilogue

This concludes the second installment of my interesting (disturbing) life story. I ended this volume at a pivotal moment, as I tried to take my life for the first time. All because I was afraid that another round of negativity was coming, thanks to my girlfriend cheating on me and wanting to leave me. I didn't know if I had the courage to face another letdown and heartbreak.

The next volume, which is nearly completed, will show me picking up the pieces of my life (again). Things get crazier in terms of the people I meet, the adventures I have, the love affairs, and all the acid I put through my brain. Come down the rabbit holes with me, and listen to the holler.

Acknowledgements

I must thank the friends I made through the years who appear in this book. Eddie Mauer, John H., Nate M., Liz D., and Uriah. I also express my gratitude, strong affections, and remorse to the girls with whom I formed bonds and shared love during these tender times. Laura, Megan, Sue and, of course, Sarah Beautyman all have a special place in my heart and memories.

I'm thankful for the music that glued me together. R.E.M. and Tori Amos were the most important to me, but Radiohead was also there for me in my darkest, loneliest moments. I will never forget to immerse my soul in love as much as I can, even when it feels like I can't. This book and series are dedicated to all three artists.

I want to especially thank the editor who reeled me back as much as he could on this book. Alan Ritch made sure I didn't get too carried away with my love of my favorite albums.

Thank you to everyone who took the time to read about my crazy-as-fuck life. I hope that my stories inspire and entertain as much as possible.